Friended at the Front

CULTUREAMERICA

Erika Doss
Philip J. Deloria
Series Editors

Karal Ann Marling
Editor Emerita

FRIENDED AT THE FRONT

Social Media in the American War Zone

Lisa Ellen Silvestri

University Press of Kansas

Published by the University Press of Kansas (Lawrence, Kansas 66045), which
was organized by the Kansas Board of Regents and is operated and funded by
Emporia State University, Fort Hays State University, Kansas State University,
Pittsburg State University, the University of Kansas, and Wichita State University

Library of Congress Cataloging-in-Publication Data
Silvestri, Lisa Ellen.
Friended at the front: social media in the American war zone / Lisa Ellen
Silvestri.
    pages cm — (CultureAmerica)
Includes bibliographical references and index.
ISBN 978-0-7006-2136-1 (cloth: alk. paper)—ISBN 978-0-7006-2163-7 (ebook)
1. United States—Armed Forces—Military life—History—21st century.
2. Soldiers—United States—Correspondence. 3. Deployment (Strategy)—
Social aspects—United States. 4. Social media—Government policy—United
States. 5. United States. Marine Corps—Social life and customs—21st
century—Case studies. 6. Facebook (Electronic resource)—Social aspects—
United States. 7. YouTube (Electronic resource)—Social aspects—United
States. 8. Soldiers—United States—Social life and customs—21st century.
9. Soldiers—Family relationships—United States—History—21st century.
10. War and families—United States—History—21st century. I. Title. II. Title:
Social media in the American war zone.
U766.S58   2015
355.1'294—dc23

                                                2015020375

British Library Cataloguing-in-Publication Data is available.

Printed in the United States of America

10 9 8 7 6 5 4 3 2 1

To My Family

If you want to end war and stuff, you've got to sing loud.
Arlo Guthrie, "Alice's Restaurant Massacree"

Contents

Illustrations

Acknowledgments

This project, like the wars it is concerned with, is a hybrid. It is part field research, part theory, part personal recollection, and part public advocacy. This project, also like its wars, would not have been the same without the presence of a social network—a vibrant tapestry of people, places, organizations, and institutions that I've interacted with over the course of its development. Although the errors are my own, the project would not have been possible without the support, advice, and review of many. I can acknowledge only a few, but I hope the others will recognize their influence and accept my thanks.

I am grateful to the Iowa Army National Guard, the United States Marine Corps, and all the men and women who lent their voice to this project and their service to our country, especially Brent Smith for his encyclopedic knowledge of the Marine Corps and his insistence on my accuracy. Fieldwork is hard work. Human beings are unpredictable. Living texts are messy. Thank you all for your patience.

Thanks to the faculty and students in the Department of Communication Studies at the University of Iowa, especially Isaac West, Jiyeon Kang, Jeff Bennett, Carolyn Colvin, Leslie Baxter. A very special thank you to Caitlin Bruce, Derrais Carter, Ben Morton, and Renu Pariyadath for helping me believe in myself, and to the University of Iowa's Graduate College and Institutional Review Board for believing in this project. Many thanks to the good friends I made in Iowa City, Forksville, and Spokane for sharing laughs, drinks, articles, and encouragement.

Warm thanks to the skillful sets of hands at the University Press of Kansas, especially my editor, Michael Briggs, whose kind words of encouragement always arrived at just the right moment. Thanks as well to my welcoming colleagues at Gonzaga University and the wonderful undergraduate students I've had the pleasure of teaching. They remind me every day why I got into all this in the first place.

Thanks also to Zizi Papacharissi and William Taylor for their generous engagement with my work. I've presented parts of this project at various conferences over the years, such as the National Communication Association; the International Communication Association; the Media, War, and

Conflict Conference; and the South by Southwest Festival. Thank you to everyone who listened and/or provided thoughtful feedback. Parts of this project have also appeared previously, in *Visual Communication Quarterly* 20.2, and in *A Communication Perspective on the Military: Interactions, Messages, and Discourses*, edited by Erin Sahlstein Parcell and Lynne Webb. I feel lucky to be part of such a brilliant community of scholars. I look forward to keeping our conversations going in the years to come.

I also wish to thank my family, to whom this book is dedicated, for their relentless support, especially my parents, Peter and Linda, who have never doubted me and continue to be my greatest supporters and investors; and my brother, Jason, who has always demonstrated a genuine interest in my work, pushing me to do more and be better. And finally, I am grateful for the love and support of two handsome distractions, my cat, Stewie, and my sweetheart, Peter William.

Military Abbreviations

ANA   Afghan National Army

CIC   Commander in chief

COP   Combat outpost

DOD   Department of Defense

DTM   Directive-type memorandum

FOB   Forward operating base

FRO   Family readiness officer

IED   Improvised explosive device

ISAF   International Security Assistance Force

MOS   Military occupational specialty

MRAP   Mine-resistant ambush protected vehicle

NCO   Noncommissioned officer

NJP   Nonjudicial punishment

OEF   Operation Enduring Freedom, the Afghanistan front in the War on Terror

OIF   Operation Iraqi Freedom, the Iraq front in the War on Terror

OPSEC   Operational security

PAO   Public affairs officer

PFC   Private first class

POG   Person other than grunt

SJA   Staff judge advocate

UCMJ   Uniform Code of Military Justice

USO   United Service Organization

INTRODUCTION
New Faces of War

To cheer me up before his deployment to Helmand Province in Afghanistan, my brother said with an uneasy chuckle, "I guess I better get a Facebook account, huh?" Like most things my big brother says to me, this was sarcastic. He was referring to my research about the way US troops use social media, but also to his own prideful defiance against participating in contemporary social network culture. During his last deployment, to East Hit, Iraq, in 2005, Facebook was just starting out; it wasn't even public yet.

During that deployment, my brother and I communicated primarily through traditional postal mail.[1] This time, however, in 2014, I didn't expect to send or receive any handwritten letters, because most US troops have access to Facebook and other social network platforms from the field. Even my brother, a traditional media stalwart, recognized that if he wanted to stay in touch, he better log on. Social media are now part of a service member's deployment kit.

When I formally began working on this book in 2010 I wasn't aware of the extent to which deployed personnel interacted with social media; my initial research interests centered on advancements in digital photography. I was taken aback by my brother's enormous photographic archive capturing his Iraq deployment, which he saved on his laptop's hard drive. The extent of his digital documentary efforts stood in stark contrast to my father's handful of black-and-white photos depicting his thirteen-month tour of duty in Vietnam. Around the same time as my brother's return from Iraq in 2006, and on the heels of the infamous digital photos at Abu Ghraib, both popular and academic sources began paying closer attention to US troops' snapshots of war.[2] Like those authors, I found myself compelled by service members' propensity to document war, and I continued to assume that digital photography would be the crux of my research. I even framed a lot of my early interviews with military personnel around the subject of digital photography. But the service members I interviewed did not want to talk about advancements in digital photography, or at least they wanted to talk about them only in relationship to social media. In the words of a lance corporal I interviewed at Okinawa, "It's Facebook today, ma'am. Facebook is everything."[3] Until then I never considered the significance of Facebook at the front. I didn't even have a personal Facebook account. I hadn't realized

Figure 1. Marines using field internet lounge. Defense Department photo.

how much the communication landscape had changed in terms of social media and internet access since my brother's 2005–2006 deployment.[4]

Since 2006, internet access has become much more widely available to US troops on deployment. Today, although some of the most remote outposts in the mountains of Afghanistan do not have access to running water, many of them do have access to "internet cafés," or as some service members refer to them, "lounges" (see figure 1). They are portable satellite units where US troops can share a set of computers with satellite feeds to communicate back home. Military officials provide the units, which come equipped with a router, up to eight laptops, and phones, to provide service personnel with free internet access and phone calls home.[5]

US troops in Iraq and Afghanistan gained internet access via cable modem and satellite feed around the same time Facebook emerged as a public sensation. As a result, the majority of our fighting forces adopted the platform as their chief mode of communication with loved ones back home. In fact, during our interviews, many service members described experiences with "pre-Facebook" and "post-Facebook" deployments as qualitatively different, referring to them as two distinct types of deployment.[6] For example, an Iowa Army National Guard soldier described the difference between his first 2006 pre-Facebook deployment and his most recent 2010 post-Facebook deployment as follows:

It's definitely a change from the first [deployment] 'til now. There's a lot more connection, I mean, it's—you can even as a unit—AKO can be a real pain. AKO is our military e-mail. And unfortunately to say, it's much easier to get a hold of a deployed soldier on Facebook than it is on AKO. As sad as it sounds it's the truth. That's been a big deal.

The soldier's comment references improvements in terms of efficiency. But speed and access are not the only ways technological advancements impact communication. The soldier initially makes an ontological distinction, sensing a definite "change" between deployments resulting from "a lot more connection." But what exactly constitutes connection? Is it speed or access? Is it related to what you disclose or how often you make contact? Digital media scholar Clay Shirky argues, "We are living in the middle of the largest increase in expressive capability in the history of the human race."[7] Radical changes in our ability to communicate with one another change society at the most fundamental level—changing the very nature of "connection" or what it means to be connected. Shirky uses a beehive metaphor to illustrate the ways in which new communication technologies like Facebook transform (and are transformed by) social relations, via processes that lead to new and revised social routines, rituals, and communicative habits. He writes, "The tools that a society uses to create and maintain itself are as central to human life as a hive is to bee life. Though the hive is not part of any individual bee, it is part of the colony, both shaped by and shaping the lives of its inhabitants."[8] My perspective toward communication technologies is similar. Rather than focusing on the technologies themselves, I am more interested in how people interact with those technologies. The goal is to understand how new modes of expression influence processes of human living.

From this perspective, new media do not simply replace old media. E-mail is not a handwritten letter electrified.[9] Instead, new communication technologies create *new* forms of interactions and *new* kinds of relations of power between participants, giving rise to entirely *new* social functions, subject positions, and conceptions of individual agency. In other words, new technologies are new in the sense that "they do new things. They give us new powers. They create new consequences for us as human beings. They bend minds. They transform institutions. They liberate. They oppress."[10] New technological advancements are not merely aids to human activity; they are powerful forces that reshape both the form and quality of human relationships.[11] In his theory of technological politics, Langdon Winner uses the example of introducing a robot into an industrial workplace. Not only does the robot increase productivity, it also radically changes the process of production, redefining what "work" means in that setting.[12] Mapping Winner's example onto troops in a war zone, the introduction of social media to a theater of war changes not only the process of communicating with the home front but also what it means to be "at war" on a more fundamental level. In other words, if robots change what it's like to be at work, social media changes what it's like to be at war. Working from this assumption, several questions arise: How do instantaneous, domesticated (as opposed to professional) communication technologies redefine what it means to be at war for troops in Iraq and Afghanistan? How does the war experience change when a warrior's social network is portable? And in what ways has war transformed from the mythic account of a lonely soldier suffering through months of desperate isolation?

To answer these questions, I propose using the concept of technological agency, which draws from Winner's philosophy of technology. Like Winner, I want to move beyond a vocabulary of "use" to imagine technology as a form of life. My point is not that technical systems have independent, fully formed agency, but rather, to quote the title of Winner's famous essay, that artifacts have politics.[13] A technology's politics derive from the series of choices embedded in it; the ramifications of those choices far outlive the original design's intent. Today constant connection and instantaneous contact are so embedded in the technological structure they have become standardized values that inform how, when, why, where, and to whom we communicate.

Technological Agency

Broadly speaking, the idea of agency supposes that factors beyond our control enable and constrain our capacity to act in the world. These can be things like environments, institutions, cultural norms, traditions, and so on. Added to those factors are technological opportunities and constraints. It's important to distinguish technological agency from technological determinism, the idea that technology directly affects human behavior. Instead, technical structures represent one piece within a web of various influences. Michel de Certeau uses the example of a person walking in a cityscape to show how technical structures or other imposed systems do not necessarily determine human behavior. Individuals are creative. They do not always take the prescribed route. They hop over hedges, duck down alleyways, and cut through parks. To use de Certeau's language, individuals deploy "tactics" within environments "strategized" by government agencies, urban planners, and city developers.[14] De Certeau's conceptualization of strategies and tactics is not only useful in thinking about troops using social media in a war zone; it is also fitting because of its invocation of military vocabulary. However, I want to add more dimension and complexity to the relationship between individual agents and the powers that be. Agency is more complicated than street-level tactics and institutional strategies. So in order to more fully conceptualize agency's complex relational dynamics, I borrow from Lundberg and Gunn's discussion of the Ouija board as a way to imagine the varying power circuitries at play.[15] The mysterious movement of a planchette on a Ouija board derives from a confluence of factors—the participants, their histories, their expectations, their physical interactions with each other, the planchette, and the board, as well as the board's communicative possibilities (letters of the alphabet, numbers 0–9, and the words "yes" and "no"). In other words, the origin of agency is in neither the technology (the board) nor the individual agents (the players), but rather, it emerges in the lived moment through a collision of influences—personal, cultural, technological, political, and social. In this spirit, my interest is with the way US troops *interface* with social media. Who are they talking to? How, when, where, why, how often, and about what? How do their uses of social media differ from earlier forms of communication like pen-and-paper letter writing? These types of questions shift the domain of study from individual agents or socio-technical structures to *practices*, making it easier to recognize that individuals' power to act—their ability to respond, or their "response ability"—is compromised, dynamic, and in relation to a variety of factors including audience, history, tradition, and so on.

As an orienting framework, technological agency neither reduces technologies to what humans designed them to do nor claims agency for the technology itself. To be sure, there are values built into technologies, but they do not determine the uses of those technologies. They do, however, constrain those uses. One Marine described Facebook as "the nucleus of communication." His point was that Facebook represented a multifaceted communication platform. Just as a nucleus is the core of an atom made of composite parts (protons, neutrons, and electrons), to him, the value of Facebook was the summation of its different features—chatting, posting, messaging, and so on. Over the course of my research, I found that each communication feature correlates to different imagined audiences, with different purposes, goals, and effects. Supposing that human behavior changes to suit new technologies' forms and processes, the very act of using Facebook generates patterns of activities and expectations that soon become second nature.

This book focuses on those activities as a way to understand the various opportunities and constraints associated with storytelling the self in liquid times. What are some of the implications instantaneous and direct communication across fronts can have on a service member's mental and emotional processes and sense making? The personnel featured in this book are telling both a story about the war and a story about themselves and who they are becoming. They also perform that story, using it to feel their way through the current situation. A major influence on their story-telling power is how internet access and the prevalence of social media in Iraq and Afghanistan enable US troops to import civilian norms of casual conversation into a war zone. The central features of social media communication—immediacy, constant contact, and networked audiences—impact existing frames of reference for war. Participation in social media culture facilitates a constant tacking back and forth between war and home, ultimately collapsing important practical and ideological distinctions between the two. Each chapter focuses on specific, ground-level discursive practices such as real-time chatting, posting photos, and making memes, in order to understand how they change what war looks like in this millennium. The idea is that paying attention to concrete utterances reveals the imagined contexts in which service members are operating. And the dominant context for social media communication, even from a war zone, appears to be everyday life in the United States.

Social Media at War

From the perspective of US military personnel in Iraq or Afghanistan, social media platforms allow their social networks to become portable for the first time in the history of modern warfare. This marks a revolutionary change from how we once imagined combat deployment. It used to be the case that deployment to a war zone excused a warrior for being out of touch, unreachable, or generally ignorant to American pop culture. For example, one of my father's favorite Vietnam anecdotes was that when he left for his deployment, the Beatles were singing "I Want to Hold Your Hand," and when he came home they were singing "Hey Jude." Today, by contrast, not only are US troops able to stay up-to-date with civilian culture, but they can also *participate* in our conversations, effectively engaging in a firefight one minute and uploading a hilarious meme video in the next.

Beyond the context of war, the widespread use of personal computers, internet accessibility, and the proliferation of social network sites pose fundamental challenges to the maintenance of dualities between work and leisure. When communication takes place over nonphysical networks, it complicates distinctions between work and home as well as the social roles that go along with them. Applying these ideas to US troops in a theater of war significantly raises the stakes on these types of dilemmas. The service members I spoke with, for example, expressed concern for "the nightmare reader," an imagined other who could potentially misinterpret their messages or use their messages against them. According to my interviews, US troops often imagine the nightmare reader as both their mothers and the enemy combatant. This point speaks to the collapsed nature of communication contexts on social media and the increasingly porous boundaries between war and everyday life.

Questions about audience provide a useful starting point to parse the complexities surrounding social media at war. Paying attention to audience brings into focus the multiple dimensions through which professional war fighters simultaneously communicate their personal deployment experiences to public and private audiences. And further, examining these processes reveals how new and revised communication habits shape what it means to be "at war" for both the troops and their social network members.

Another factor shaping what it means to be at war in this millennium has been the nature of these wars in particular. The United States has been engaged in a multifronted global war on terrorism that has lasted over a decade. In May 2014, President Barack Obama announced that US forces would withdraw from Afghanistan by the end of 2016.[16] He said, "Our military will draw down to a normal embassy presence in Kabul, with a security assistance component, just as we've done in Iraq."[17] According to this projection, around ten thousand troops will remain in Afghanistan. Yet the president's statement did not anticipate reengaging over three thousand more troops in Iraq just a few months later in September. All this is to say that the nonlinear nature of the current security environment has left policy makers scratching their heads. Linear front lines have given way to circular perimeters or mobile patrols. The divisions between front and rear and the associated dangers of each are less distinguishable in places such as Mosul and Fallujah than during the Battle of the Bulge, for example. During an interview, I casually asked a Marine how it's even possible to identify potential threats in such a complicated environment. He looked at me, paused a moment, then said matter-of-factly, "The bad guys wear sneakers."

As powerful and as telling as that Marine's comment may be, it's even more unsettling that it is a genuine derivative of the administration's policy. The second Bush administration conceptualized something called the "Greater Middle East," which ostensibly stretches from North Africa through the Khyber Pass, subsuming (and ignoring) the distinctiveness of South Asia.[18] The assumption, which sounds embarrassingly similar to Edward Said's notion of Orientalism, is that managing a US military campaign in one Muslim country must be the same as doing it in another.

An additional factor muddying the boundaries of these wars is that new communication technologies have made it so that the war front and the home front are just a mouse click away. In fact, the meaning of a "front" has changed dramatically in the last ten years. And so it goes with the meaning of "friendship." Social media platforms like Facebook have made it so that new "friends" are just a mouse click away as well. The relatively rapid semiotic evolution of "friend" and "front" occurred concurrently and in conjunction with one another.

The two stories told in this book, then, are of social media as they are practiced by "boots on the ground" and how these fraught, messy, and undefined social media serve as a metonym for the war itself. As a case in point, the summer of 2014 found Facebook awash with home videos of people dumping buckets of ice water over their heads in support of the ALS Foundation, an organization dedicated to curing Lou Gehrig's disease. "The Ice Bucket Challenge," as it came to be known, operated on a dare. Functioning like a remediation of chain mail, participants were to pour ice water over their heads and "publicly" nominate three individuals (via social media) to do the same within twenty-four hours. Not surprisingly, since troops and home-front civilians can share the same digital space, Ice Bucket Challenge videos made in Afghanistan began circulating online.

While my brother was at Camp Leatherneck he received e-mails from command warning troops about participating in this online "charity meme." His unit's regional command legal advisor wrote, "If anyone is thinking of doing the 'Ice Bucket Challenge' or any similar fundraising scheme here in Afghanistan, you need to talk with SJA first to make sure you don't run afoul of the ethics rules." Another e-mail, this time from the assistant general counsel on ethics, warned, "Participation . . . must be carefully vetted with an eye to the applicable authorities."[19] The difficulty associated with anticipating and prohibiting participation in these types of digital activities and the lack of clarity regarding expectations for appropriate participation show how policy makers, even in 2014, are still trying to negotiate a comprehensive strategy for social media policy. It seems that in the current security environment, both terror and social media represent relatively unclear but decidedly present dangers.

Updating War's Status

Americans have experienced continuous war for the past 250 years. In my lifetime, which encompasses the last three decades, the United States has had boots on the ground in at least eight military engagements: Operation Urgent Fury in Grenada, Operation Just Cause in Panama, Operation Desert Storm in Iraq, Operation Restore Hope in Somalia, Operation Joint Endeavor in Bosnia, Operation Enduring Freedom in Afghanistan, Operation Iraqi Freedom in Iraq, and Operation Odyssey Dawn in Libya. We are still involved in three of those military engagements. These types of war are political conflicts that use military force.

But we have also endured an ongoing *cold* war, a state of political tension and economic competition between the United States and the former Soviet Union. And what is more, the contemporary American war culture extends to domestic issues as we wage simultaneous wars on poverty, cancer, drugs, terror, and the middle class.[20] Recently I have even heard of a "Republican war on science" and a "Liberal war on Christmas."[21] It seems that we have stretched the meaning of "war" to include conventional definitions—an organized armed conflict between political groups—as well as "softer" definitions—a deliberate act meant to transform existing conditions in cultural, political, social, and even medical domains.

Consistent metaphorical application of "war" to matters social, cultural, and medical, and not necessarily to military conflict, changes its dominant discursive meaning.[22] Broadening a term's conceptual base can be productive, but what happens when the concept of war is stretched beyond its literal meaning as the ultimate transgression, a political last resort, a brutal and ugly enterprise causing catastrophic loss and immense human tragedy? What happens when war is normalized to the point where it is considered a *good* thing to go to war? The war on drugs, or poverty, imagines war to be a serious commitment toward accomplishing a specific objective. War becomes a strategy to eradicate an undesirable target, whether communism or Christmas. A war on cancer implies resolute dedication to overcoming an obstacle. In this sense, waging war is a positive problem-solving method. The pervasiveness of "war" in American culture has given it something of an "everyday" quality.

This book argues that social media's habitual prevalence contributes to our collective attention fatigue and has helped create an abundance of war-as-mundane and an absence of war-as-extraordinary. There is something ideological at stake in the loss of war's distinction. My goal is to reiterate war as extraordinary, that is, to keep war out of the ordinary.

Studying War

Growing up, I found war to be a compelling and mysterious drama. My grandfather, father, and brother are all combat veterans. In my eyes, the three of them were reluctant heroes, members of a burden-laden boys' club that I could never be a part of. I wanted to understand the culture they shared. I knew I could never access it by studying war in its mythic sense, or as it existed in the mass media. Homer's epic poems, Hollywood's blockbuster films, Ken Burns's famous documentaries, or Dan Rather's news reports couldn't tell me anything about what the men in my family experienced, even if they could get me close. Instead, I knew that if I wanted to understand how boots on the ground experienced war, I would need to access their daily practices. Short of embedding in Afghanistan myself (a path I nearly took with the help of the International Security Assistance Force [ISAF] in 2010), studying war's contemporary communication culture meant plumbing the symbolic boundaries between two cultures—combat culture and social media culture.

Cultures are made up of ideas realized and materialized in practice. The best way to access "culture" is to pay attention to the recursive practices constituting it. As critical cultural scholar Lawrence Grossberg eloquently describes, it's about appreciating "the texture of life as it is lived."[23] Following Grossberg, I take a methodological perspective that represents the growing symbiosis between rhetorical studies and critical cultural studies. These camps tend to adopt a performance lens as an outlook and a method with the common goal of apprehending culture through the perspectives of those who live or have lived it. It involves understanding symbolic, aesthetic, affective, and political realms in light of social fields of meaning. The focus is on concrete, specific instances of expression to address larger, theoretical questions about culture, power, and what it means to be human. An emphasis on practice causes these perspectives to adopt a multisited approach to participant observation. Because I am interested in *digital* lifeworlds, I had to broaden my outlook on community beyond the traditional anthropological view to include both geographically contained communities as well as those constituted by the circulation of discourse in a variety of mediated forms. Just like any speech community, membership in an online social network community is performative, relying on members' ability to call up intelligible discourses.[24] In other words, I pay attention to the way troops perform their identities online to gauge which community they are speaking to. Social media communication is not merely about producing texts but also about participating in a common space, community, and conversation. From this perspective, Facebook is significant only insofar as it is currently the most popular social media platform and host to a plethora of different conversations and communities.[25]

Context becomes important when studying new and revised social routines, rituals, and communicative habits, because people tend to establish meaning locally. As a site of study, however, the internet makes siphoning an individual context nearly impossible. The cacophony of voices and discourses swirling through the inherently hybrid space of the net emphasizes the constructed nature of text and context. As anthropologist Vered Amit points out, "In a world of infinite interconnections and overlapping contexts," a domain of study "has to be laboriously constructed, pulled apart from all the other possibilities of contextualization."[26] The process of contextualization begins with the types of questions being asked and oftentimes continues throughout the project as initial questions are answered, thrown out, added to, or refined. For example, although the book you are holding examines how US Marines interact with social media, and to what extent those interactions impact their deployment experiences, I did not begin with that line of inquiry. It took several missteps, false starts, happy accidents, and moments of genuine epiphany to finally arrive at that orientation. For over three years I continued to ask questions and assemble fragments, digging, building, and slowly molding the contours of context. Ultimately I settled on the intersection of two primary contexts—war and Facebook.

Through direct interviews and online participation, I examine how US troops interact with social media during their deployments in Iraq and Afghanistan. In the spring of 2010, I began conducting on-base interviews with service members who had recently returned from deployment to learn about their communication norms, habits, and rituals while at war. After an initial set of interviews with the Iowa Army National Guard, I decided to focus exclusively on the US Marines because, of all the branches, it is the unit most frequently deployed to combat environments. Also, our collective imagination holds the Marine Corps to be the most rigid and inflexible institution. For these reasons, I felt the Marine Corps would serve as a useful point of juxtaposition against which to study social media culture. Added to that is the fact that my brother, a US Navy doctor, deploys with Marines, so I also have a personal investment with the Corps.

In 2011 I conducted a set of ten semistructured interviews with US Marines on base in Okinawa, Japan. After one year to digest all that I had learned, I had many new thoughts, ideas, and clarifying questions, so I conducted another set of interviews with US Marines at Camp Pendleton in California, where I also had the opportunity to observe an educational initiative on social media use. The social media class is a new, mandatory safety course meant to stave off "negligent behavior." During the particular session I attended, there were around three hundred Marines present, roughly an entire battalion.[27] I recognize that my sample size cannot possibly reflect the entirety of the Corps, or the diversity of deployment experience. Nonetheless, I offer some of the more compelling patterns and themes I noticed over the course of my research. Early on, for example, I recognized a trend that helped me define the parameters of my study.

Older personnel who experienced multiple deployments (spanning 1997 to 2012) tended to flag the years 2007 to 2009 as a critical threshold of change in combat's communication culture. Evidently, this was the point where internet access became more widely available in the field. This time frame also coincides with the 2008 introduction of Facebook's real-time chat feature.[28] And according to a 2012 US Marine Corps demographics report, two-thirds of the Marines currently deployed are twenty-five years old and under, meaning that most Marines were not eligible to serve until 2006 or after.[29] Taking all these factors into account, I focused my research on social media use among Marines deployed between 2008 and 2012, because those years mark a critical flashpoint for the use of real-time social media software in Iraq and Afghanistan.

Conducting in-person interviews on active bases offered two key benefits to my research.[30] First, as I alluded to above, the information I gleaned from the interviews helped me establish a lay of the land by identifying recurrent topics, themes, and ways of speaking about particular subjects. Second, in-person interviews on active bases allowed me to get a sense, in a very real and embodied way, for the military as an institution and as a culture. Appreciating any culture requires close attention to repeatable habits and practices shared by a group. I want to avoid the impression that I offer my sample group as representative of military culture, yet for the sake of readability I often use inclusive labels like "service members," "deployed personnel," or "US troops" as comparative signposts to distinguish this generation of warrior from previous generations.

Paying attention to recurring practices illuminates a culture's "politics of doxa"—the backdrop of shared values and beliefs, or the vaguely held notion of common sense that motivates behavior.[31] Often, the best way to access a group's shared practices is to observe them operating locally in their respective social fields. For example, after each interview on base in Okinawa, a designated lieutenant Marine "escort" accompanied me to the next location. We entered barracks and office buildings bustling with junior Marines in camouflage uniforms who immediately stopped what they were doing to snap to attention and salute the lieutenant every time we entered a room. This performance denotes respect for rank. During the interviews, the escort waited outside a closed door. At the forty-five-minute mark he knocked on the door to indicate that we should begin wrapping up our conversation. The length and privacy afforded during these interviews allowed junior Marines to be more open about their experiences. Being on bases in Okinawa, Japan, and Camp Pendleton, California, helped me better appreciate the military's cultural milieu. Yet military culture represented only one aspect of the critical juncture I was examining—the other was social media culture.

Accessing service members' participation in social media culture required online fieldwork. I followed the Facebook pages of nine Marines over the course of their deployments, closely reading their wall posts, video posts, photo posts, and all the accompanying sidebar commentary, making field notes and taking screen grabs.[32] These methods drew my attention to circulation patterns and processes of text production. When I first began online observations, I didn't know what I was looking for; I simply took it all in. But as I began to transcribe my interviews from Okinawa and eventually Pendleton, some of the Facebook activities I was observing (i.e., time stamps and photo genres) began to take on relevance. Throughout the interpretive process, interview conversations illuminated online observations and vice versa. Their interdependence is a genuine reflection of how my methodology unfolded.

Carefully listening to interview responses and paying close attention to Facebook activities allowed me to explore instances of agency in action, the moments where individual utterances vibrate against institutional, social, and technological structures. For example, questions guiding my exploration included: What challenges do military personnel face as they negotiate institutional and cultural expectations for social media use? How do they communicate their deployment experiences, if at all, with social network members? What discourses do they draw from in order to sustain conversations across multiple publics and collective audiences? When, why, how, and to whom are particular utterances intelligible?

My research practices pull from a variety of techniques, tools, and methods to understand a mix of practices, representations, structures, rhetorics, and technologies. In the words of qualitative internet researcher Christine Hine, "The key to insight is immersion, not necessarily through being in a particular field site, but by engaging in relevant practices wherever they might be found."[33] I believe that within the limitations conferred by context, this bricolage methodology was the best way to access some of the details of digitally mediated social behavior across fronts. I hope the reader will agree.

What Lies Ahead

The scope of this book moves from broad to narrow, beginning with an overview of military guidelines for social media engagement (chapter 1), moving to an examination of particular social media practices (chapters 2 through 4), and concluding with a discussion of how those practices reflect and refract broader cultural narratives about war. I organized the chapters structurally around conventional understandings of public and private communication. Chapter 2, for example, looks at letters and personal messages, what we commonly consider to be private modes of communication. By contrast, chapter 4 examines YouTube videos, a decidedly more public form of communication. Bridging the gap is chapter 3, which takes a historically private medium, a personal photo album, and considers its digital descendent: the Facebook photo album. Taken together these chapters aim to trace evolving ideas and attitudes about what it means to be "at war," for both the service members and their social networks.

The first chapter introduces readers to military culture by examining the US Marine Corps Social Media Guidance document. A close reading of the institutional guidelines allows for a deeper appreciation of military culture in its explicitly governed form; that is, the document represents military culture inscribed. This chapter outlines some of the contradictory cultural commitments faced by Marines when they log onto Facebook from the field. For example, hierarchical structures and broadcast models no longer resonate with contemporary society. The age of the mobile network introduces a fundamentally different communication structure with an entirely new production model. Whereas other digital technologies like texting and instant messaging contribute to social interaction, they mostly continue to operate on a familiar one-to-one, interpersonal level of communication.[34] By contrast, social media platforms are a less orderly cacophony of voices enabling users to connect with, articulate, and make visible existing or extended social networks.[35]

The "network" function is an important distinction in social media compared with "new" or "digital" media.[36] Social media offer individuals nearly limitless possibilities on the net: Persons can share, collaborate, follow, and correspond with minimal material restriction—save for their personal privacy preferences or security concerns.[37] In this way, social media are slightly more useful for individuals over organizations, businesses, or governments, because larger institutions are often subject to multiple preferences and stricter security concerns. Though they integrate seamlessly with businesses and organizations, social media offer the greatest number of possibilities to *individual* users. However, as I demonstrate in chapter 1, increased opportunities are balanced by increased responsibilities. Easier publication of photos, videos, pranks, gaffs, and faux pas has increased the average individual's media literacy and general awareness of being observed. As sociologist Zygmunt Bauman writes in *Liquid Modernity*, "Individuals to an increasing extent are made responsible for their lives."[38] New forms of literacy, revised definitions of privacy, elaborate strategies for identity management, and enhanced self-reflexivity and social responsibility are some of the ways social media have impacted individuals in everyday life.

To be sure, the present moment operates by a new set of values and ideas about what it means to communicate in an era of globally connected, perpetual contact. Some communication researchers have begun to examine the emergent relational practices and "mobile maintenance expectations" unique to this era.[39] Digital media scholars Jeffrey Hall and Nancy Baym argue, for example, that "while being able to contact others is one of the most liked qualities . . . being continuously available for others' contact is also one of its disliked qualities."[40] Hall and Baym describe a tension between the ability to stay in touch through technology and feeling *entrapped* by technology.[41] My work raises the stakes on emergent social pressures by examining how they operate among US troops in the context of war.

Historically, troops in a war zone were exempt from home-front relational commitments. In previous American conflicts a lack of communication with the home front kept war fighters focused on their immediate well-being, the health and safety of their comrades, and the goal of the mission. My father's tour in Vietnam, for example, caused him to miss an entire Beatles album—a point he acknowledged with a shoulder shrug. His attention was unapologetically one-dimensional. His focus was on the mission and the safety of himself and the guys next to him. He wasn't worried about Facebook posts or YouTube clips. The Beatles were just white noise. By contrast, the Marines in this study describe an increased connection across fronts and, with it, a compulsion to remind the home front of their connectedness through mundane exchanges via social media.

The second chapter focuses on social interactivity across fronts, the sense of constant connection and immediate contact afforded by social media in Iraq and Afghanistan. The chapter draws out the culture clash described in chapter 1 by comparing Facebook communication to war's former dominant mode of communication, the handwritten letter. This comparison highlights the ways in which communicative norms, values, and expectations have evolved in recent history. Prevailing communication attitudes about "keeping up" and staying connected promote a particular type of communication, a more phatic or ritualistic style.[42] The quantity, frequency, and immediacy of social network messages create a previously unmatched feeling of closeness or "digital intimacy" between war and home fronts. Although civilians also value "connected presence," its ubiquity in daily life causes it to go relatively unnoticed at home.[43] For deployed service members, however, Facebook presents the impression of casual civilian conversation, a form of communication previously excluded from the war zone. One of the major issues I introduce in chapter 2 and develop further through examples in subsequent chapters is that the dominantly operating values of social media—constant contact and immediacy—promote a fixation on the "what" of right now, but *not* the "what" of a war zone.

Today war has a new representational form. Just as television defined Vietnam and the First Gulf War, the internet is defining what we know, see, and remember about Iraq and Afghanistan. And these wars have been mediated more than any other conflict in history.[44] Chapters 3 and 4 examine the way user-generated content, in the form of photos and videos, alters what "war" looks like in this millennium. In previous American conflicts, professional war reporters and photographers were the sole arbiters of war's image. Therefore, much of the existing literature on war's representation evaluates professionally produced texts for their persuasive force or epistemological contribution to civilian, public audiences.[45] But today service members document and disseminate their deployment experiences themselves.

A handful of communication scholars has begun paying attention to the role that "warrior-produced" footage plays in the broader cultural narrative of war.[46] Some argue that videos shot by service members offer more authentic, "raw," and "unfiltered views" since they appear to "lack prescribed framings and official narratives."[47] This view celebrates warrior-produced imagery for contributing a necessary dissonance, which serves to "restructure the balance of storytelling power."[48] However, these arguments assume that the horror of war is synonymous with the reality of war. From this perspective, an authentic experience of war hinges on exposure to violence and bloodshed. As I found in my interviews, even boots on the ground use this representational logic to evaluate their wartime experiences. And sometimes in an effort to legitimize their deployments, they end up perpetuating many of its visual tropes.

Chapters 3 and 4 explore some of the ways US troops directly involved in Iraq and Afghanistan mediate their experiences to each other and their broader social networks and how their meaning-making activities speak to and are spoken through broader, discursive formations of "war."[49] Rather than focusing on the *product* of war mediation, these chapters consider their interactions on social media to be localized, discursive *practices*, or sites of struggle for how military personnel make sense of their wartime experiences. Chapters 3 and 4 emphasize the fact that these activities are not only about producing texts but also about participating in a common space and community.

Chapter 3, for example, looks at US Marines' digital photo album–making practices. The chapter argues that Facebook's social, cultural, and aesthetic logics shape war's visuality on the web. As US troops in a war zone filter their deployment experiences through the collegiate conventions associated with Facebook's visual culture, a visual discourse emerges that shows a more domesticated, socially inflected, and distinctively youthful representation of the wars in Iraq and Afghanistan. At issue is the fact that when troops render their wartime activities suitable for social media, it impacts how they perceive and remember their deployments, and subsequently how their social networks make meaning of their wartime deployments as well.

Chapter 4 considers how troops engage the values of the home front through the creation and dissemination of YouTube videos. On the whole, the videos mark an attempt to convey a voice to a collective civilian audience. Like the Facebook messages in chapter 2, warrior-produced videos, especially ones that participate in popular internet memes, reflect copresence with rather than absence from the home front. Chapter 4 suggests that, as home-front attention to the Global War on Terrorism continues to wane, service members commandeer popular culture conversations to maintain relevance within the existing attention economy. As my brother said, in preparation for war, "I guess I better get a Facebook account, huh?" The tacit rule is that if you want to keep up, you better play the game.

A major theme throughout the book is the nagging question about representation's role in understanding. If knowledge of war hinges on its representation, then what do these messages and images contribute? The book concludes with a consideration of how the new communication environment is changing what it means to go to war and what it means to be at war in this millennium. Examining the social media habits of personnel on deployment is one way to illustrate war's evolving realities and might reveal something larger about our collective attitudes toward war. The bottom line is that the narrative for war is changing. War looks and feels a lot different than it used to. Social media contribute to a feeling of routine in an already perpetual war. Today war consists of both firefights and friend requests.

CHAPTER 1

Incongruities across Social Media and Military Cultures

For Marine Corps sergeant Gary Stein, fifteen words on Facebook cost him a nine-year military career. His Facebook post said that he would not follow certain orders issued by the president and included an image of the president's face superimposed on a poster for *Jackass: The Movie*. Stein made those comments to a Facebook group called the Armed Forces Tea Party, which he founded in 2010 as a platform to criticize President Barack Obama's health care plans. When he created the Tea Party website in 2010, his superiors at Camp Pendleton cautioned him about posting political opinions online, citing a possible violation of the Uniform Code of Military Justice (UCMJ). Two years later, when he posted the *Jackass* image, the Marine Corps reduced his rank, docked his pay, and eventually discharged him less than honorably without benefits. Stein tried to appeal the decision, but a federal judge of the US District Court for Southern California, Marilyn Huff, denied his request, reportedly telling one of Stein's attorneys, "You understand it's a pretty sensitive comment that he made. He can't do that."[1] Yet, at the time, it was not entirely clear what Stein, or other service members like him, could or could not do online.

The internet poses a new set of questions concerning the degree of service members' digital freedoms, especially the boundaries distinguishing their professional public lives from their personal private lives. In the case of former Marine sergeant Gary Stein, military officials circumvented the murky waters of online personhood by indicting him on charges that he breached service custom and violated Department of Defense (DOD) directive 1344, which states that service members cannot speak out against leaders currently in office.[2] Military service custom dictates respect for rank. Although personnel do not necessarily have to respect the person holding the rank, they must respect the rank they hold. This includes the commander in chief (CIC) of the armed forces, the president of the United States. Sergeant Stein violated that code, so the military dismissed him. Yet Stein's case also signifies an emergent and rather incongruous cultural conjuncture between the military's top-down, professional chain of command and the impossibly fragmented social space of the internet. As such, Stein's Facebook activities presented military officials with a chance to meaningfully address increasingly complicated boundaries between a service member's professional identity and personal life in the Web 2.0 era. The legal proceedings, however, did not fully address this issue, thereby neglecting to establish a solid precedent for future social media cases.

Stein's case and others like it raise important questions about managing our lifeworlds, both online and off-line. The widespread use of personal computers, internet accessibility, and the proliferation of social network sites (even in Iraq and Afghanistan) pose fundamental challenges to the maintenance of dualities between our public/professional and private/personal selves.

Some communication scholars advocate seeing *private and public as a continuum* rather than as a dichotomy. Distinctions between public and private messages used to be so clear that we could distinguish between them by the type of medium used. Words written in a postmarked letter and addressed to a specific recipient were unequivocally private. But "tagging" someone in a Facebook post is a little more complicated. The message's production style changes from one-to-one to a relative one-to-many. It's not quite private because the message can be shared with hundreds of "friends," but the nature of the closed network keeps it from being entirely public as well.[3] "No content is ever either private or public, but potentially both, depending on who you are asking," argues digital media scholar Malin Sveningsson Elm.[4] Teenagers, for example, have developed a new definition of privacy. According to Sonia Livingstone's in-depth interviews with teenagers about their social media habits, they display personal information that previous generations would have regarded as private (age, politics, income, religion, sexual preference, etc.). This is not to say they are wholly unconcerned with matters of privacy; they just view it differently. Unlike previous generations, the teenager's definition of privacy is not tied to the disclosure of certain *types* of information but rather to having *control* over who knows what about them.[5] A concern for military officials is that social media can present an impression of control that is not necessarily in line with the level of security the institution seeks to maintain.

Personal social media use by members of the armed forces, specifically US Marines, clashes with military culture in at least three primary ways. First, the military historically bases its freedom of expression policies on relatively uncomplicated notions of publicity and privacy, which hinge on the idea of an intended audience. Social media, of course, disrupt those formerly tidy distinctions with multilayered, semipublic, semiprivate, networked audiences. Second, the military is organized as a top-down hierarchy based on age, rank, and expertise. By contrast, social media are organized laterally as a network and present opportunity for multivocal participation. And finally, military culture actively seeks to diminish or eradicate a sense of self, whereas social media culture celebrates individual ego to the point that some call it narcissistic.[6] The incongruities between military and social media culture present an opportunity to consider how individual social actors, in this case, US Marines, negotiate a network of pressures, expectations, traditions, conventions, and norms each time they operate online.

All communication technologies and cultures, to some extent, prescribe uses and behavior. And oftentimes their respective social codes overlap. When service members interact on social media, they invoke a collision of cultures.[7] The culture of perpetual contact ushered in by social media technologies collides with an institution and, in the case of war, a context quintessentially associated with a lack of contact. It is important to examine the Marine Corps Social Media Guidance document because it represents a conscious effort to erect the confines in which Marines interact on social media. Moreover the context of military communication makes the case even more provocative and worthy of study because until recently the military focused almost exclusively on functional modes of communication—connecting planes to the ground, coordinating strikes and ambushes, and reporting needs to medics. But now social media use among military personnel (even in a theater of war) introduces a new and previously overlooked social dimension to information sharing that is forcing the DOD to reconsider existing strategies to manage access, uses, and content creation.[8] The guidelines for behavior in the Marine Corps Social Media Guidance document are rather ambiguous, yet the consequences for misuse are serious. As a result, the policy shoulders individual Marines with the pressure and responsibility of self-monitoring and self-branding—activities that require a tremendous amount of time and emotional labor.

Because of the complex circumstances surrounding social media use in the military, the policy should be studied from historical, social, and cultural perspectives. Toward this end, my reading highlights the role of human agency in the creation and implementation of social media policy. An agential view holds that individuals are born into confines over which they have little control but that they are free to act within those confines.[9] Studying the Marine Corps Social Media Guidance document from this perspective lends insight to the animating forces among institutions like the military and individual social actors like Marines as they attempt to manage contradictory cultural commitments. Or to put it differently, in what ways do military culture and institutional policies inform Marines' storytelling power?

Historically Speaking: Free Speech in the Armed Forces

The policy that indicted former Marine sergeant Stein has been in effect since the Civil War. Restraints on free speech in the armed services derive from a need for rigid and thorough subordination to superior authorities, especially during times of crisis. According to legal scholar Detlev Vagts, "The armed forces are intimately allied with war and crisis, and war and crisis are closely tied to that clear and present danger to the national interest that calls forth and justifies restrictions on free speech." Vagts goes on to point out, "A sad paradox requires that the serviceman sacrifice some of the liberties which he is called upon to protect."[10] The regulatory code limiting service members' free speech is the UCMJ, a congressionally enacted code that establishes the basic machinery of the military criminal system.

The US Supreme Court grants the military wide latitude to restrict service members' freedom of speech in matters pertaining to national security and military effectiveness. Thus, although the freedom of speech guarantee applies *in theory* to the military, in practice, command has the authority to narrowly construe its protections. Stein's lawyers and the American Civil Liberties Union (ACLU), for example, tried to argue that the First Amendment protected his views. "The military may be different from the civilian world," said San Diego ACLU legal director David Loy, "but it's not exempt from the First Amendment. Sgt. Stein didn't say anything for which the Marine Corps has any right to punish him." Loy went on to argue, "He did not threaten order or discipline or take positions that anyone would attribute to the Corps."[11] Yet the Supreme Court upheld the military's position and dismissed Stein less than honorably from the Marine Corps.

Historically courts tend to rule in favor of the military in cases such as Stein's because of the condition of crisis.[12] In 1972, the military punished a service member for publishing an on-base underground newspaper that protested military involvement in Vietnam. The court upheld the punishment, stating, "The military was well within its authority to punish a single serviceman for publishing his criticism of the armed forces because such words could lead to larger dissent within the troops." Similarly in 1980, the Supreme Court favored the military again when a service member distributed petitions on base. The ruling stated that a service member's freedom of speech "yields somewhat to meet certain overriding demands of discipline and duty."[13] Historically speaking, there are three statutory provisions explicitly regulating military expression.

For the most part, the three statutory provisions refer to in-person, or face-to-face, communication contexts. The first forbids "provoking words or gestures," essentially interchanges between military personnel likely to cause an immediate breach of peace (i.e., drunken obscenities).[14] The second also applies to face-to-face insults and contempt, penalizing "any person . . . who behaves with disrespect towards his superior officer." According to Vagts, the *Manual for Courts-Martial* directed a restrictive administration of this clause, declaring that "it should not be used so as to hold one accountable for things said or done in 'purely private conversation.'"[15] The third provision prohibits contemptuous words against the president, vice president, Congress, secretary of defense, governor, or legislature of any state or territory. Although precedent for the third provision imagines circulation beyond an interpersonal encounter, it still assumes the utterance of such contemptuous remarks to be in the physical presence of others.

On its face, these rules are not entirely objectionable. In fact, they make sense within an institution and culture predicated on rank and file. However, the potential contexts for prohibited speech and behavior continue to expand with technological development. Mobile, internet, and social network communication makes it difficult to identify a "purely private conversation," as many conversations occur beyond our physical contexts.

The wording of most military regulations is directed at "public" rather than "private" pronouncements. Delineations between the two are not explicit in the provisions. Instead their application appears to rely on a theoretical distinction between speech directed only at family and friends and speech that may have a wide and harmful impact. Simply put, the qualifications center on questions of dissemination and audience. In his sweeping analysis of military free speech, Vagts argues, "A gathering of more than a few individuals would be considered 'public,' particularly if they were not exclusively military personnel and more particularly if news correspondents were present."[16] A reference to news correspondents suggests a concern over dissemination. Yet the majority of UCMJ articles cited during Stein's trial (articles 82, 88, 117, the general punitive article 134, and DOD directive 1344.10) do not explicitly address questions of publicity, circulation, audience, or dissemination. Rather, they *imply* these concerns by referencing particular types of media, namely, broadcast. For example, the DOD directive that ultimately convicted Stein includes a provision prohibiting his participation "in any radio, television, or other program or group discussion as an advocate for or against a partisan political party, candidate, or cause."[17] In other words, instead of addressing how social media complicates audience, dissemination, and visibility, Stein's case ultimately centered on the quality of his activities themselves and whether or not they were "political" in nature.

Stein's case is a productive entry point to discuss social media in the military because it presents (even in its lack) a framework for how the institution legally and culturally envisions appropriate and inappropriate social media activity. Prior to Stein, there was little legal precedent in military free speech cases regarding social media, especially as it applies to directive 1344. The most recent revision occurred in 2008, prompted by the popularity of online blogging. Although social media services experienced widespread success long before 2008, military regulation and legal precedent often lag behind technological advancement. As a result, military justice compared Stein's Facebook activities to provisions regarding participation in public rallies, the dissemination of printed materials, or an appearance on television or radio.

Prior to services like YouTube and Facebook, blogging was the internet activity that prompted the DOD to revise regulation. Early on during the conflicts in Iraq and Afghanistan, senior levels within the DOD were unaware of milblogging (military blogging), and it was therefore loosely regulated. As it continued to grow in popularity, rules became tighter as the military began to understand the potential negative consequences milblogs could have on operational security (OPSEC) and public image.[18] In August 2006, the DOD issued an "Information Security/Website Alert" directing, "Personal blogs . . . may not contain information on military activities that is not available to the general public. Such information includes comments on daily military activities and operations, unit morale, results of operations, status of equipment, and other information that may be beneficial to adversaries."[19] According to the alert, commanders must consider service members' First Amendment right to free speech and weigh OPSEC concerns prior to establishing milblog regulations and guidelines. As I mentioned, although the US Supreme Court has given wide latitude to the military to determine the limits of its members' right to speak out, the Court has not completely removed that right. If commanders decide to limit a service member's right to free speech, they must ensure it is done in the context of operational security.

A problem arises, however, with implementation and enforcement. The idea that every blog entry should be cleared with chain of command prior to its posting is impractical. If this policy were literally enforced, it would cause a backlog in entries that would render milblogging's unique qualities worthless (namely direct, instantaneous, ground-level access to the front). The same holds true for social media regulation. In addition to direct, instant access to the front, social media allow communication across a network of people. The very nature of social media's unique affordances is what makes it so difficult to regulate. Unlike blogging, which is more amenable to an analogy with broadcast media, social media's networked audience structure and linking function demand a redefinition of publicity and privacy and the regulations concerning each type of speech act.

Marine Corps Social Media Guidance

The service branches, particularly the Marine Corps, have struggled over how to manage service members' online behavior.[20] The military's early response was to retreat from social media altogether. In 2009 the DOD instated a blanket ban on social network sites from government networks and computers, which governed all branches from 2009 to 2010. The Marine Corps order justifying the ban stated, "These Internet sites in general are a proven haven for malicious actors and content and are particularly high risk due to information exposure, user-generated content and targeting by adversaries."[21] The language of the order imagines the internet as a space of overwhelming threat, danger, and risk. Because of this, many Marines and sailors were surprised when the Marine Corps, arguably the strictest of the branches, lifted the ban in 2010 after the DOD issued a department-wide directive-type memorandum (DTM), or temporary ordinance, allowing access to social network sites and other Web 2.0 platforms.[22] DTMs usually last only 180 days, but the DOD reinstated the social media DTM three more times until the release of an official forty-nine-page policy in September 2012.[23]

Between 2010 and 2012, the time of Sergeant Stein's Facebook indiscretion, the only departmental guidance was the two-page DTM superficially outlining the rules and responsibilities for social media use under Pentagon jurisdiction. During an interview in 2011, a Marine recalled his astonishment when he initially heard about the DTM allowing access to social media. He said, "My jaw dropped when we were deployed and then we got this message saying that Facebook was allowed at work. I was amazed because to be honest with you most of the time I can't even plug in my camera after taking pictures of a Marine reenlisting to post that photo on e-mail, but I can go on Facebook and update status." The Marine mentions his inability to "plug in," referencing a 2010 ban on removable media following Private First Class Bradley Manning's WikiLeak. Beyond digital media hardware and software, online social network services introduce an even more expansive (and unpredictable) dimension to information sharing.

Personal social media use poses a threat to institutions like the DOD, bent on regulation, security, command, and control. In an interview, a staff judge advocate (SJA) spoke about the incongruities between networked communication culture and the values of military society. In civilian terms, an SJA is a trained attorney who acts as general counsel for the unit. The SJA said that a perceived "loss of control" makes command very uncomfortable. Moreover, military society presumes a right to access its members' private lives. The SJA explains:

We belong in a society that is the military society that prides itself on knowing what's going on in everyone's life. And we tend to think that we have or should have more access to what's going on in your private life than most other people. And so sometimes social media represents to somebody who's in charge a loss of control over their people, right? So if I can communicate with my . . . whomever in a . . . and I'll use the word "clandestine," but in a nonobserved means, that makes people uncomfortable.

The SJA consciously uses the term "clandestine," which suggests intentional secrecy. Although social media platforms represent a more private means of communication (as opposed to blogs, for example), they are not necessarily secretive. Imagining social media as *clandestine*, however, will certainly make those in charge feel less comfortable. The Marine Corps Social Media Guidance document reflects one strategy to alleviate discomfort.

Following the logic set forth by Sergeant Stein's court case, the guidance document imagines online behavior as analogous to personal public engagement. However, many communication scholars are quick to point out that the internet and the public sphere are not exact translations. Rather the internet, especially social network sites like Facebook, generates unique complications for public-private distinctions.[24] In fact, digital media scholar Zizi Papacharissi imagines publicity and privacy on a spectrum, contending that social networks more closely align with our conceptions of the private sphere rather than the public sphere (interacting with "friends" from the comfort of home, for instance).[25] Although her performative distinctions between publicity and privacy are useful and I am inclined to agree that the way we communicate on social network sites is more similar to the way we communicate in private settings, her discussion keeps the binary in place. This is the binary that Marines find so confusing. To an individual Marine, Facebook *feels* private. Yet the Marine Corps guidance document describes it as public. This is why internet scholar Mark Poster rejects the Habermasian sphere metaphor altogether, arguing instead for a new, more fitting frame of reference. "The internet," writes Poster, "shouldn't be viewed as a new form of public sphere. The challenge is to understand how the networked future might be different from what we have known."[26] All this is to say that our language, and therefore our thought processes, and subsequently our legal treatments, lags behind technological advancement.

Without an accurate vocabulary to describe online communication contexts, it is difficult for institutions like the military to specify, classify, and police appropriate and inappropriate behavior. A lack of clarity leads the DOD to imagine social media to be so unwieldy and unpredictable that the target for control becomes the individual social media participants themselves—making categorical demands for Marines to become a particular type of social media user.

Making categorical demands on personhood is not exactly new to military culture. In fact, it is central to membership. Military philosopher and ethicist Nancy Sherman points out that the practice of referring to yourself by your last name, instead of "I," breeds unity, homogeneity, and loyalty to the Marine Corps.[27] The ego-less subjectivity that military culture strives for runs counter to the individual identity required for social media participation. Nonetheless, the DOD's social media policy attempts to graft military identity onto social media use.

Punishment for misuse is disparate—dependent on the service branch, location, and chain of command. Different commanders can issue differing orders, with unique prohibitions. In his critique of the DOD's internet policy, military judge Joshua Kastenberg argues, "If every military base, post, encampment, or station has its own separate set of rules, those particular rules have to be visible and understood by the persons falling within the jurisdictional reach of those specific rules."[28] Kastenberg's criticism finds saliency with social media policy as well. Like the internet policy that came before it, expectations for social media use are not very clear. And in spite of the variance by which it can be enforced, the Marine Corps Social Media Guidance acts as a catchall document for Marine Corps bases worldwide. Therefore, the policy's force derives primarily from a respect for military culture and a fear of breaching service custom rather than a clear understanding of the policy's prohibitions. Sanctions become visible only where some sort of designated transgression actually occurs or is perceived as likely to occur. This is the trouble with the social media DTM, or really any anticipatory and prescriptive policy measure. It is nearly impossible to predict transgression. The only recourse is to place limits on the range of options available in a given circumstance or type of circumstance.

The Marine Corps Social Media Guidance document consists of two sections: an "overview" and a list of "guidelines" (see figure 2). The title, "Social Media Guidance for Unofficial Posts," is indeed nebulous, but it carries a very definite constitutive force. The unthreatening label, "guidance," does not effectively communicate the very real material consequences faced by Marines who do not abide by its provisions.

The text's language and tone are at once urgent and uncertain, a reflection of the attitude surrounding social media in the military at large. The style and format of the document are also striking. Yellow highlighting and

Social Media Guidance for Unofficial Posts

ONLINE SOCIAL MEDIA GUIDANCE
For
UNOFFICIAL INTERNET POSTS

1. Overview

a. This guidance is provided for Marines who, in their personal capacity, desire to make unofficial posts online, regarding Marine Corps-related topics. (The term "Marines" on this guidance refers to active-duty and reserve Marines and sailors).

"Unofficial Internet posts," referred to below, are considered any content about the Marine Corps or related to the Marine Corps that are posted on any Internet site by Marines in an unofficial and personal capacity. Content includes, but is not limited to, personal comments, photographs, video, and graphics. Internet sites include social networking sites, blogs, forums, photo and video-sharing sites, and other sites to include sites not owned, operated or controlled by the Marine Corps or Department of Defense.

b. Unofficial Internet posts are not initiated by any part of the Marine Corps or reviewed within any official Marine Corps approval process. By contrast, official Internet posts involve content released in an official capacity by public affairs Marines, Marine Corps Community Services marketing directors, or commanders designated as releasing authorities. Policy for Family Readiness Officers will be provided in separate guidance.

c. In accordance with these guidelines, Marines are encouraged to responsibly engage in unofficial Internet posts about the Marine Corps and Marine Corps-related topics. The Marine Corps performs a valuable service around the world every day and Marines are often in the best position to share the Marine Corps' story with the domestic and foreign publics.

2. Guidelines

a. Marines are **personally responsible** for all content they publish on social networking sites, blogs, or other websites. In addition to ensuring Marine Corps content is accurate and appropriate, Marines also must be thoughtful about the non-Marine related content they post, since the lines between a Marine's personal and professional life often blur in the online space. Marines **must be acutely aware that they lose control over content they post on the Internet** and that many social media sites have policies that give these sites ownership of all content and information posted or stored on those systems. Thus Marines should **use their best judgment at all times and keep in mind how the content of their posts will reflect upon themselves, their unit, and the Marine Corps.**

b. As with other forms of communication, Marines are responsible for adhering to Federal law, Marine Corps regulations and governing policies when making unofficial Internet posts. Marines must abide by certain restrictions and policy to ensure good order and discipline. Federal law, regulations and policies that directly impact a Marine's conduct mandate personal standards of conduct, operational security, information assurance, release of personally identifiable information, ethics regulations, and the release of information to the public. **A Marine who violates Federal law, regulations or policies through inappropriate personal online activity is subject to disciplinary action under the Uniform Code of Military Justice (UCMJ).** See the references listed below for more details.

Figure 2. "Social Media Guidance for Unofficial Posts"

boldface font appear sporadically throughout, directing the readers' attention to key points, forcing them to read in a specific way. The highlighted and/or bolded items (shown in gray scale in figure 2) appear to emphasize key aspects of legal culpability—you are responsible for your actions and must comply with already agreed on conduct for other forms of speech. In other words, speech is speech whether online or in other forums, and you are always guided by the UCMJ, not another mode of law. That is, you can't claim constitutional guarantees to free speech because your message is online. You are always a Marine regardless of where your message originated.

The overview section includes three alphabetized bullet points and provides five distinct definitions. The first definition listed in the overview refers to the primary agents, "Marines," as "active-duty and reserve Marines and sailors." The rest of the text continues to refer to the agents in the third person as "Marines" as opposed to alternative subjectivities such as "users" or even the second-person pronoun, "you." According to sociologist Anthony Giddens, language has the power to position people within social relations conferred by specific social identities.[29] As one might expect, a

"Marine" carries a lot of baggage containing heavy expectations (and consequences) for interaction. Using the label "Marine" reinforces unity and homogeneity. It aligns with corporate ideology, which promotes streamlined missions, identities, and messages.

In fact, the metaphor of a corporation surfaced several times throughout the course of my interviews, especially and perhaps not surprisingly from public affairs officers (PAOs). One PAO told me, "When I was in Afghanistan we used social media; it was just one more avenue to push out our products, whether they were photos or stories or a combination of the two." Indeed, the military has been very progressive in its adoption of social media to streamline its messages. According to the Marine Corps' corporate ideology, the identity of a Marine has been smoothed and polished to such an extent that it is almost flat and cartoonish. To borrow the PAO's term, the Marine identity has become a "product." Consequently, when the guidance document invokes the label "Marine," it establishes an implicit set of expectations tied to the Corps' corporate identity.

As "products," individual Marines are part of the Marine Corps brand. As such, they are expected to engage in "brand monitoring," an activity that social media scholar Alice Marwick describes as "a form of labor that can be both emotional and taxing." Personal brand monitoring is a form of "internalized surveillance" that requires "continually imagining oneself through the eyes of others."[30] It is not unlike General Charles Krulak's conceptualization of the "strategic corporal," which described a need for more professional development and critical decision making at the lower ranks following from the growing complexities of modern battlefields.[31]

Facebook's linking function within a networked audience causes self-branding to become an exercise in context management. As Marwick explains, users must constantly monitor friends' activities "to make sure that nothing they did in a social context showed up in more professional contexts."[32] In this way, Web 2.0 technologies ask people to apply advertising and marketing strategies to the way they view themselves and others.[33] The emphasis on self-regulation, however, doesn't mean institutions like the military will leave Marines to their own devices.

The language of the Marine Corps' policy reminds Marines that they are always potentially fulfilling a professional role or duty to the Corps, even in their personal unofficial internet posting. The text reads, "The Marine Corps performs a valuable service around the world every day and Marines are often in the best position to share the Marine Corps' story with the domestic and foreign publics." The document states that Marines should discuss Marine Corps issues related only to their professional expertise, personal experiences, or personal knowledge. Furthermore, it asks them to "professionally and respectfully correct errors and misrepresenta-tions." In other words, not only should Marines abstain from inappropriate online behavior, but also they should actively promote a positive image for the Corps (all the while policing others). Simply put, the text positions a Marine as a twenty-four-hour employee of one of the wealthiest and far-reaching businesses in the United States. So in the context of social media communication, is it possible for Marines to communicate as individuals, or are they always speaking as members of the Corps?

The document defines "unofficial Internet posts" as user-generated con-tent "posted on any Internet site by Marines in an unofficial and personal capacity." By contrast "official Internet posts" refer to "content released in an official capacity" by "designated releasing authorities." The guidance broadly defines internet sites as "social networking sites, blogs, forums, photo and video-sharing sites, and other sites" not operated, owned, or controlled by the DOD. Given the expanse of the internet, "other sites" represents an immeasurable category. Research indicates that more than two-thirds of internet sites accessed from DOD computers are for per-sonal, nonofficial purposes—dating service sites, resort and vacation sites, car purchasing sites, electronic stock and commercial trading sites, sports sites, and "streaming video" sites.[34] Because of the DOD's vague language, the social media rules include these "other sites" should something upset-ting happen involving a service member.

Following the definitions established in the overview, the rest of the document similarly defines the Marine as simultaneously public and pri-vate—an unofficial PR agent for the Corps. This can lead to confusion over the boundaries between "personal" and "professional," a discrepancy the document admits is not altogether clear. The first bullet point in the guide-lines section reads, "The lines between a Marine's personal and profes-sional life often blur in the online space." According to another bullet point in boldface font, a Marine's opinions are his own; they do not reflect the sentiment of the Marine Corps: "Marines should make clear that they are speaking for themselves and not on behalf of the Marine Corps." This sen-timent complicates previous proclamations that a Marine is never wholly separate from the Corps. Adding to the confusion is the next point, which likens internet activities to other forms of "personal public engagement." As I mentioned, prior military court cases suggest the distinction between public and private pronouncements hinges on audience. If, as Vagts ex-plained, "a gathering of more than a few individuals" is considered public by military law and "speech directed only at family and friends" is consid-ered private, one can see how the network structure of social media, which allows for an individual to disseminate messages simultaneously to both types of audiences, would complicate previous notions of public and private communication.[35]

Marines' Perspectives on Social Media Guidance

Through the interview process, I had the opportunity to ask a PAO some clarifying questions about the definition of personal public engagement. She began by referencing the 2012 presidential election, which was in full swing at the time of our interview. She said Marines were allowed to "like" Mitt Romney or Barack Obama's Facebook page, but they were not allowed to comment on it. I asked her to describe the difference between "liking" and "commenting." She said "liking" enables Marines to have an opinion, but they cannot act on their opinion. Our conversation went as follows:

> PAO: I would say that commenting on it or suggesting it would be more of soliciting it, but then, I know you could argue that "liking" it is soliciting for it too. But I, they, I mean, according to the guidance we've been given, you can "like" their page, but that's it because I guess liking it gives you your opinion. You know, you are able to say, "Yeah I have an opinion," however they can't act upon it.
>
> SILVESTRI: Does "liking" Mitt Romney imply that you dislike President Obama? He is your CIC.
>
> PAO: Yeah. Yep. There's a gray line always between, you know, how things are dictated and how people decide what you mean by your actions online. But according to the guidance that we've been given by the Marine Corps we are allowed to "like" the page.

The inference here is that the Marine Corps conceptualizes "liking" as a personal (private) disposition whereas "acting," "commenting," and "posting" are synonymous and represent public activities. Beyond these implicit conceptual distinctions, the classification for what kind of behavior is acceptable is still imprecise and under constant negotiation.

One of the reasons it is difficult to anticipate problematic social media activities is because they occur within a digital culture that shifts daily. Participants, content, forms, and norms change regularly.[36] Nonetheless, military officials create guidelines such as the Marine Corps Social Media Guidance document to operate as a form of insurance. Instituting a list of rules or "guidelines" is a way for the DOD and the Marine Corps to offload risk onto the shoulders of individual personnel. "Avoid offensive and inappropriate behavior"; "don't click links unless the source can be trusted"; "do not disguise, impersonate, or otherwise misrepresent identity or affiliation with the Marine Corps"; "don't give classified information"; and "don't use copyright material without permission." It is safe to assume that most social media members today recognize there are risks associated with posting content online. And the most adept participants on social media resemble entrepreneurs of the self—hypervigilant self-monitors, editors, and promoters concerned with cultivating a personal brand (while protecting the Marine Corps brand) through participation in online community.

As I mentioned, personal brand monitoring is a time-consuming and emotionally taxing activity. The linking function of most social network sites ostensibly extends a Marine's realm of accountability beyond his own Facebook page to include the Facebook pages of his entire social network. In other words, if a Facebook friend posts something damaging to the mission or against service custom on a Marine's Facebook page, the Marine is responsible for that commentary. He must monitor and edit his own page carefully. Additionally, if a Marine's Facebook friend posts something damaging on his or her *own* page, the Marine can be held responsible for that content as well. In other words, if the average Facebook user has 130 friends, then that user has approximately ten thousand friends of friends, and more than a million friends of friends of friends.[37] According to this logic, the liabilities for a single Marine are exorbitant. During our interview the PAO explained the rationale behind the Marine Corps' philosophy: "We don't really have a legal hold over the family members, so we really have to have the Marines hold their families accountable. . . . You have to make sure your families know this and this and this." Her eyes and her smile widened as she said with a chuckle, "So, yeah, there's no pressure for the Marine!" Simply put, a Marine's responsibility extends beyond his own behavior to include the potential actions of his entire social network. Marwick's research on self-monitoring describes its negative emotional effect: anxiety, information overload, lack of time, and hurt feelings due to audience comments and interactions. She describes a theme among her interview data: "Constantly monitoring one's actions and maintaining a 'dual gaze' was often exhausting and time consuming. Keeping up with the sheer amount of work that self-branding requires means neglecting other aspects of life."[38] My research found similar recurring themes associated with deficits in time, emotion, and attention that I will explore in the chapters to follow.

A Risk Society Approach to Social Media

The urgent yet noncommittal tone of the Marine Corps Social Media Guidance document reflects an impending need to act in the face of profound uncertainty. Sociologist Ulrich Beck describes this to be the active impulse in a "risk society."[39] Risk societies are predominantly future oriented, with an eye toward managing future risks instead of solving present

problems. In the case of former Marine sergeant Stein, the DOD did not
seize the opportunity to prevent future risk. Command ignored complicated questions about networked audiences and online and off-line identities, opting instead for a swift resolution by indicting Stein on tried-and-
true codes of military justice. Risk assessment, however, is most crucial in
circumstances where emergent practices mark a threshold between a familiar past and an uncertain, problematic future.

If the primary goal in a risk society is to prevent nightmare scenarios
from occurring, profiling risk is essential to preparing for the future.[40] The
trouble is that risk assessment amid the contemporary media climate is
difficult. Change occurs very quickly, the boundaries between public and
private are blurry, audiences are networked, and any personal photograph
represents a potential Abu Ghraib. These factors produce a new set of challenges and anxieties for institutions like the DOD, which previously functioned by using systemic strategies to achieve clearly defined objectives.
With the rise of amorphous dangers like the internet (or global terrorism),
linear thinking is impossible. Social network sites represent both spatial
and temporal anomalies, a "new riskiness to risk."[41]

To alleviate the discomfort associated with risk, the Marine Corps follows an insurance model. It is important to note, however, that insurance
models do not eradicate risk; they simply redistribute it. As Vagts argues,
"The primary purpose of such regulations should be to inform and crys-
tallize custom rather than serve as a basis for punitive action."[42] But the
prediction of potential risk is always inherently imperfect, leaving a rather
ambiguous set of "guidelines" that do little to prevent undesirable behavior.
Instead, delineating guidelines and creating policy documents are insurance measures, which allow the DOD to offload risk onto the shoulders of
independent actors.

It is impossible to control future action, so the next best thing is to bur-
den the agent with constraint. During our interview, the SJA described
social media policies as inherently "prophylactic in nature and somewhat
reactionary in nature." He went on to say, "You know we are living the
fallout of Gary Stein, right? And we don't want to repeat that. And so we
are trying to save ourselves from ourselves, if you will." Self-preservation is
the priority. The "prophylactic" does little to stop undesirable behavior but
rather acts as a face-saving device, demonstrating that the proper measures
are being taken to protect "ourselves from ourselves, if you will." This new
strategy reflects a preventive logic, stemming from Giddens's observation
that today nations "mostly no longer have enemies, but instead face risks
and dangers."[43] The problem, according to security and defense policy ana-
lyst Mikkel Vedby Rasmussen, is that a strategy of risk management "does

not translate well" to amorphous, undefined, and prospective security is-sues.[44] Therefore, although the idea of profiling threat is not exactly new to the DOD, these types of risks introduce new challenges because they have been around for only the last half-century.

The military has a long history of governing behavior and caring about its reputation. Therefore it's no surprise that the DOD created a set of guidelines in response to online behavior that was harmful to the institution's public image. In so doing, command extended its regulatory reach to include "unofficial" social media use by individual personnel from their personal computers. Not many other institutions have documents like this. The military, however, is a distinct culture with deeply rooted customs, values, and expectations for behavior. During our interview, the SJA tried to explain the notion of "service custom," a cultural performance and system of knowledge that evidently operates tacitly among personnel.

> SJA: If I don't necessarily tell you, give you an order to do something or not to do something . . . let's say, for example, over a span of time Marines are known for doing a certain thing, okay? And you violate that or you aren't in compliance with that, I could make an argument that you are not acting within service custom, and that potentially could lead to both administrative and punitive treatment. Okay? . . . Um, and it's . . . I'll give you a silly example, but we talk about not chewing gum in uniform, right? . . . Um, as a service custom, because it's not an activity befitting the stature of the Marines and the uniform they wear. I'll give that to you as an . . .
> SILVESTRI: Is that real?
> SJA: [*Smiling*] Yes. There are people who believe that to be real.
> SILVESTRI: So how are service custom and misconduct related?
> SJA: If I don't adhere to custom, I could be considered having committed misconduct. Service custom is one way—a violation of service conduct is one way of committing misconduct, if you will.

The socializing power of service custom is so strong that most Marines assume there are rules about social media without ever having to read them. If there are guidelines about when you can chew gum, there are probably guidelines about what you can post online. The difference, however, is that the off-line rules are extremely specific. You can't chew gum in uniform. You can't walk and talk on a cell phone, but you can stand still and talk on a cell phone. You can put your hands in your pockets only if it's cold outside or you need to retrieve something. Your haircut must be faded evenly above your natural hairline using a zero-to-three setting with no more than three inches on top. Your mustache must be one-eighth of an inch above your top lip and cannot extend beyond the corners of your mouth. Your shoes must be laced left over right, and so on.[45] By contrast, the expectations for social media use are vague.

The elusive nature of such expectations does not necessarily make them less influential in limiting the activities of most Marines. In fact, Vagts argues the contrary: "A man who feels that a certain way of expressing himself is frowned upon by superiors, or may be deemed contrary to the 'customs of the service,' or may provoke a bad efficiency rating, is more likely to abstain from both the conduct directly disapproved and conduct resembling it than a man concerned only with avoiding a clearly defined criminal enactment."[46] Even though social media guidance is relatively nebulous and its interpretation and implementation varies depending on command and service station, it maintains a palpable chilling effect. During an interview with a corporal who drove armored trucks in Afghanistan, he explained that his self-censorship practices are more or less intuitive.

> MARINE: They don't want pictures of the basic stuff that you wouldn't normally take a picture of anyways, but like, if you saw anybody that died, you don't take pictures of that; that's just something you don't do.
> SILVESTRI: Did they tell you that?
> MARINE: They didn't tell us that I don't think, but I think that's just . . . or maybe? I thought somebody briefed us on that . . .

In the context of some of the other interviews, it is evident that the personnel like the service member above are aware of a general set of expectations. Many use the phrase "common sense" to describe their perception of military social media policy. It is unclear in the interview excerpt above, however, which code the Marine is privileging. Is it military code not to take a photo of a dead body or is it a moral code applicable to social media culture more broadly? The most accurate answer is probably both. Without a clear understanding of the boundaries delineating a Marine social media user from a regular social media user, many Marines default to naming OPSEC as the primary concern. A sergeant who deployed as a combat engineer once to Iraq and once to Afghanistan said, "As long as it wasn't secret or . . . uh, any kind of . . . uh, sensitive information everything was okay. . . . Personal stuff is fine. Personal stuff they haven't cracked down on." But in fact, depending on a commander's interpretation, "personal stuff" is within the military's jurisdiction.

Confusion over this point arises from nebulous policy, superficial briefs, and a general lack of attention on the part of personnel. In reference to the Facebook debacle involving former Marine sergeant Stein, the SJA said, "I would speculate that as these things happen . . . they are contained in regulations and policies that your junior service members don't know about, they don't pay attention to, so they run afoul of them in some respect." For those service members who actually take the time to read it, the unthreatening title of the document, "Social Media Guidance for Unofficial Posts," does not effectively communicate the very real material consequences faced by Marines who do not abide by its stipulations, such as a dock in pay, loss of rank, and so on.

Undoubtedly the document's open-endedness is to leave room for adaptation amid the ever-changing techno-cultural landscape. The practical implication of its ambiguity, however, holds individual Marines responsible for negotiating contradictory cultural ideologies. On the one hand, social media culture is built on an architecture of democratic participation. Social network sites value disclosure, friendship, and individual expression.[47] But on the other hand, the military adheres to a vertical hierarchy, valuing security, rank, and collectivism. Marines—and presumably members of other service branches—experience this critical juncture every time they log on to Facebook. It is not an uncommon experience for users outside of the military, but the military offers a pointed example because it is an institution well known for strict behavioral control.

Practical Implications and Lived Practices

In addition to complicating notions of publicity and privacy, social media also present a challenge to military culture by inverting the hierarchy of expertise and disrupting fraternization customs. Social media unsettle the institution's calcified hierarchies based on age, rank, and skill level because command must rely on younger, low-ranking personnel to inform and educate them about the rapidly changing media environment. Unlike civilian companies such as Google that can instantaneously make a twenty-year-old employee the lead technology officer, the military does not accept lateral transfers or rapid promotions. It takes twenty years to produce a colonel or first sergeant, regardless of their talent. This is one systemic reason for the time lag between organization and technology.

Similarly to the milblogging activities that came before, many higher-ups were unaware of the pervasiveness of social media among personnel, especially in the field. One PAO told me, "As with most corporations, the senior leadership of the Marines and of all the military services are older than the young troops and not as technically savvy." Therefore, when older, higher-ranking personnel address the potential dangers associated with social media use, some of the younger Marines find the lectures to be condescending. In some cases, it can breed resentment. As a Marine at Camp Pendleton tells it:

> MARINE: We were given a few briefs in Afghanistan about the policy on social media networking this or that.
> SILVESTRI: You receive the briefs in country?
> MARINE: Yes. You sit down in a chair, and several Marines, like the whole room is full of Marines, and there's a guy with a shiny collar sittin' up there preaching to you, "Don't do this, don't do that." But most of us Marines already know because it's common sense.

His description of a "shiny collar" at the head of a room "preaching" suggests that he does not identify with or relate to that person. In fact, he goes on to refer to "most of us Marines," further alluding to an "us" versus "them" dichotomy. The "shiny collar" is, of course, a Marine, but he is an officer. He is not an infantryman like "us." This individual-level distinction exists on a larger scale as well—between institutionalized military communication and combat/field communication. The infantrymen, or grunts, are quick to tell me they find social media briefs to be frustrating and redundant. A second Marine at Camp Pendleton described his experience with social media briefings:

> MARINE: We like, we get it jammed down our throats . . . every time, like, "Don't take pictures of nothing you're not supposed to take pictures of. Definitely don't put it on Facebook."
> SILVESTRI: Can you describe what the instruction process is like?
> MARINE: Death by Power Point.
> SILVESTRI: [*Smiling*] That's a phrase I've heard several Marines use to describe it.
> MARINE: [*Laughs*] Yeah. You're sittin' there all day . . . well not all day but it feels like it, just sittin' there zoning out on a screen . . . the thing's run by people with a lot more rank on their collar than that [gestures at the chevron on his uniform].

His comment about rank reflects a theme among my interview data. New impositions with regard to social media exacerbate existing acrimony among ranks. Lower-ranking personnel, who spend a disproportionately larger amount of time in the field (and on social media platforms), perceive admonishments from "shiny collars" about social media use to be paternalistic and condescending. The Marine I quoted above went on to say, "We never get handed a booklet, but it's more like higher-ups saying, 'Don't do this,' and we're like, 'Okay, won't do it.'" Evidently, the form and content of in-country briefs are similar to the safety stand-down I witnessed at Camp Pendleton.

The overall aim is to instill anxiety over social media by suggesting the enemy will assemble fragments of information mined from personal web pages. The Marine who described his in-country brief recounted an anecdote about an army soldier in Afghanistan who posted photos to his Facebook page that depicted features of his forward operating base (FOB) with descriptive captions detailing information about how many men could fit in the living quarters, and so on. The Marine said the base was attacked "because someone got a hold of that." He went on to say, "They showed us Power Point slides of the pictures he took, the pictures the man had posted, comments, captions, and everything." The "shiny collar" likely used this story to relay the possible dangers associated with social media in the field. Similarly to the indirect voice of the guidance document, this brief used a story as an indirect means to produce a direct effect. The anecdote about the soldier's misstep essentially communicated to a group of Marines who were sitting on a base in Afghanistan that if they aren't careful with their Facebook pages, they too could be attacked. It's a Web 2.0 revival of the old World War II adage "loose lips sink ships."

Festering resentment among lower-ranking personnel can lead to a sense of righteous arrogance, at worst, and the belief that they will never get caught, at least. Because the method of control is so disjointed, many Marines perceive the policy to be less threatening. In one interview a service member told me that he was fairly confident command would never be able to monitor the media that personnel produce. He said:

It's hard to control [media misuse] unless you have proof of it and stuff. And so they didn't, you know, I mean we had, when we left, our computers were subject to be searched, but it never happened. We had too many coming out of theater to manually go through everybody's stuff, but they do have systems where they can run programs through your computer to pull all of this information if they have suspicious thoughts . . . but the numbers are too great; it would take forever to do that.

The military lacks the authoritative follow-through to monitor all the unofficial communication that occurs between "fronts" in contemporary warfare. On a forum hosted by Joi Ito, director of the MIT Media Lab, a poster called "PFC Zaku" lambasted the possibility of banning personal media in Iraq:

> A ban, on digital media? What kind of farce is this? We get packages from Amazon.com, I own a laptop, have two digital cameras and a camcorder. The [military] will not raid my supply and steal my digital camera. And they won't be taking my pin drive either. And they can't ban us from mostly anything. And that's the saddest part. "Fixing" the chain of command will do nothing. We're human beings, we're men trained to do what most people wouldn't think of doing. Believe me, we'll find a way to work around it.[48]

Private First Class Zaku's comment about the chain of command is likely in response to the Pentagon's issuing a set of "directives to commanders in the field to strictly monitor the use of consumer wireless technology."[49] But as Private First Class Zaku points out, containment is a "farce," akin to conquering an infinite game of Whack-a-Mole. For Private First Class Zaku, sources of constraint provide opportunities for radical innovation. As he says, "We'll find a way around it." Some of the personnel I interviewed shared Private First Class Zaku's sentiment.

Perhaps Brigadier General Mark Kimmitt, deputy director for coalition military operations in Iraq, put it best when he said: "You can't put the genie back in the bottle. Soldiers have cameras in the battlefield. They have telephones in the battlefield. They have access to the Internet cafes on the base. At a certain point you just have to trust them to do the right thing."[50] On its face General Kimmitt's sentiment is contradictory. He describes the new media environment as an unstoppable threat. The "genie" is out of the bottle. But in the next breath he references "trust."

For Giddens, trust is required in the modern world since we know so little about the systems with which we have to deal. Giddens defines trust as "the vesting of confidence in persons or in abstract systems, made on the basis of a 'leap of faith,' which brackets ignorance or lack of information."[51] From Kimmitt's commentary, it sounds like he is placing his faith in the personnel more than in the abstract system. For him, the system is inherently threatening, and future actions are unpredictable, so all that is left to do is try to preemptively regulate the person and hope for the best.

Another way social media challenge existing military cultural norms is by dislodging existing fraternization customs. Typically the military's chain of command does not allow inter-rank friendship as directed by UCMJ article 134. But on Facebook, personnel of every rank can be "friends." This posed a problem for one Marine I interviewed whose comrade tagged him in an "unbecoming" photo on Facebook. The photo depicted a young Marine from his unit riding a cactus in nothing but a flak jacket. Although the Marine I interviewed did not face punishment, several Marines from his unit were "NJP'd" (nonjudicially punished). A higher-up and "friend" of the cactus-riding Marine discovered the photo on Facebook and brought it up the chain of command. The Marine relating the story to me remarked, "It's more stupid than anything. It's kinda like—it's a bad look—a guy on deployment with a flak on—naked—riding a cactus." He smiled and shook his head. "So you are friends with higher-ups on Facebook?" I asked. "Yes," he nodded. "Does that influence what you post on Facebook?" "Not really," he shrugged. "I just keep them under a certain status on there. I don't let them see everything." This Marine's response was relatively typical.

There is a vague recognition that posting photos like the cactus cowboy is "stupid" or promotes "a bad look," but because Facebook's technological infrastructure presents an impression of control (and thereby a sense of privacy), some personnel do not believe they have to be as vigilant with their posts. In an essay exploring the various notions of privacy on the net, Malin Sveningsson Elm explains, "Even if [users] are aware of the publicness of the arena, they may forget about it when involved in interactions. It can sometimes be that even if a certain internet medium admittedly is public, it doesn't feel public to its users."[52] Through the course of my interviews I heard a number of stories recounting privacy-setting oversight—everything from a benign embarrassment over a photo of a Marine holding tumbleweed over his genitalia, to more serious instances of helicopters targeted because an army soldier posted a photo of their landing without disabling his geolocation app.[53]

It would be unfair and inaccurate, however, to suggest that these instances represent the norm or that service members are largely ignorant about social media privacy concerns. Rather, as the Marine indicated above, he develops specific privacy designations. "I don't let them see everything." Most of the Marines I interviewed were extremely technologically savvy. As I mentioned, many of them are in their early twenties, born in the age of the internet as fluent "digital natives."[54] Yet some of them, even the young and confident, do not want to risk expulsion, so they adopt alternative methods of communication like instant messaging or restrict wall activity to the most benign content possible. These moves reflect an emergent "idiom of practice." In the following chapters, I pay particular attention to such "idioms of practice," those unspoken rules of social media engagement, as a way to back map a broader "media ideology."[55]

Establishing idioms of practice is a collective enterprise. Diverse groups with their own unique values, goals, and circumstances will generate distinctive idioms of practice.[56] Such is the case among military officials and boots on the ground. At the institutional level, military officials share horror stories about social media use gone wrong. For them, the internet is a threatening space where the most appropriate uses would resemble carefully monitored public relations management. Since boots on the ground fall within this institutional culture, they absorb this view. But they are also part of a more exclusive combat culture, where they adapt institutional expectations to meet their unique needs and interests in the field.

Without a doubt, Facebook is the most popular mode of communication from the front. In the words of a young lance corporal, "Facebook is pretty huge." In spite of efforts by commanders to regulate Facebook, personnel cannot find a substitute for its ease and accessibility. A sergeant who deployed to combat on four separate occasions between 2005 and 2010 said:

> I think most of the Marines probably spent close to 90 percent of their time on Facebook doing online chat with family members and friends back home, updating statuses or whatever just cause you know, I mean, if you have something happen to you or have something happen to a friend you have to write about it and let everyone else know what's going on. So I mean it was used quite a bit. Check e-mails. That and Amazon.com. I bought a lot of stuff from Amazon.com.

The sergeant's reference to online chatting reflects what I argue to be an emergent "guerilla tactic" on the part of deployed personnel. According to the social media rhetoric emanating from Quantico, the DOD, and public affairs officers, the chief anxiety appears to be user-generated content in the form of wall posts, photographs, and videos. In response, personnel manage this concern by replacing content creation with real-time "chatting."

Marines describe Facebook's instant message feature as less public, less traceable, and less permanent. Although the accuracy of those claims is debatable, the perception is real. In the words of one Marine, "I prefer chatting. It's more like a conversation." The conversational component to Facebook's instant message feature is something I will explore in the next chapter. For now, the trend to note is a move away from posting content— the one-to-many feature on Facebook—and a move toward a more familiar one-to-one style of communication.

In addition to real-time chatting, the most common way Marines cope with the cultural impasse they confront when they log on to Facebook is by self-censoring their wall activity. Ambiguity over behavioral expectations becomes a threat because it is unclear what counts as negligent and who has the authority to declare it as such. After all, this is a culture where Marines can receive NJP for arriving to an appointment five minutes early instead of fifteen minutes early. In the words of an infantry sergeant, "In the Marine Corps, if you arrive five minutes early, you are already ten minutes late." One count of NJP could mean a Marine never gets promoted. Three could get him kicked out. So who could blame Marines for erring on the side of caution when the guidance is so unclear and the punishment is so erratic and individualized?

When I arrived at Camp Pendleton for my interviews, the public affairs office was still buzzing about a Marine sergeant who, one month before, had written a Facebook post lamenting his frustration with pregnant colleagues. Among other belittling remarks, he described them as "dumb fat pregnant bitches." The public affairs office responded quickly to the negative press, demanding the sergeant issue a public apology and incur several counts of NJP.

This Marine's NJP included the loss of two martial arts belts and a transfer to a different company. His commanding officer debated demoting his rank or kicking him out of the Corps, but the SJA advised against it, forcing the Marine instead to publicly apologize, write a contrition letter to the pregnant women in his office along with their parents, and personally relate his story in front of his comrades during a new series of social media education classes at Camp Pendleton. During my visit, I had the opportunity to attend one of these social media classes, now part of a mandatory educational component, along with other "safety stand-downs" on sexual harassment and alcohol abuse. Personnel stationed at Camp Pendleton must fulfill these classes annually, an achievement verified by a Marine's signature on an attendance sheet. The class I observed was conducted by a PAO who stood on an auditorium stage in front of a battalion of Marines. The class lasted approximately fifteen minutes, a third of which was devoted to a YouTube video called "Social Media Revolution 2012." Although rudimentary and imperfect, the social media class suggests a move toward developing social media literacy among military personnel. To my knowledge, and at the time, Camp Pendleton's social media class was the only one of its kind across all the Marine Corps bases worldwide. As it stands, however, and because of vacillating expectations for a constantly shifting medium, the educational aspect leaves much to be desired.

Punishment seems to be the most effective way to inform Marines about the DOD's stance on social media. The policy critique highlights the fact that responsibility for internet posting falls on the shoulders of individual Marines. Although most of the Marines I interviewed could not remember reading the actual policy, many of them could recount a story about someone who got in trouble for inappropriate social media use. As I mentioned earlier, disciplinary action is disjointed and inconsistent, entirely dependent on bases, branches, and commanders. The only way to get a sense for NJP rationale is to live in the culture. NJP is an observable instance of ideology in practice. My interview with an SJA at Camp Pendleton illustrated the arbitrariness of punitive practices.

> SJA: It's not like when I take off my uniform and go home at the end of the day . . . again . . . the military has a very unique criminal jurisdiction, and it has its own criminal code that governs us. That regulates us *all . . . the . . . time.*
>
> SILVESTRI: What's criminal though? Is a Marine saying he doesn't like working with pregnant women a crime?
>
> SJA: No. In that particular case, and I know what you're talking about, that's not considered a crime. I don't know. He did it from his own private computer so it shouldn't have been considered misconduct. . . .
>
> SILVESTRI: So what is it? He suffered material consequences, right? He lost a couple of belts, he was moved to a different company. . . . Like what is this?
>
> SJA: Yeah. What is that? Okay, well, again, that is a . . . if I can try to explain it because it is not easily apparent. . . . That's not, um, . . . those consequences aren't criminal in nature, right? So he was never, ever, ever in my mind, going to be subject to going to jail or being fined money. However in any sort of organization that prides itself on leadership and adherence to order, his is an example of "I've lost faith in your ability to lead your Marines." . . . So the things that you see . . . um, you know, the loss of say the martial arts belts that you refer to . . . um, there's a tie-in with attaining a black belt with moral character. We've tried to tie the two together. Okay, so whether you believe in that sort of process or not, that was a reflection of, okay, you've kinda taken yourself down a few pegs on the moral ladder, if you will, by saying such stuff.

The actual process of implementing punishment is perhaps even more confusing than the document's vague references to "disciplinary action," which agents are "potentially subject to." For the Marine sergeant at Pendleton who spoke disrespectfully about his pregnant colleagues on Facebook, his punishment derived primarily from his personal character (the loss of martial arts belts represent a demotion in morality) rather than his unprofessional conduct.

Even beyond the context of social media, the trend toward overlapping personal and professional behavior is growing. In a historical account of American military command from World War II to the present, Pulitzer Prize–winning journalist Thomas Ricks argues that higher-ups are no longer relieved for occupational incompetence. Instead, he argues, they are fired for embarrassing the institution through personal peccadilloes, the most common of which he refers to as "zipper problems," or having sex with a subordinate.[57] The point is that focus in the military has shifted onto *personal* rather than *professional* behavior. Ricks argues that during World War II there were consequences for your work on the battlefield. Either a campaign was successful and you were rewarded for it, or it wasn't and you were relieved of duty. But today military officials are not being fired for mediocre professional performances but rather unsavory personal ones, specifically the personal behavior that brings public shame to the institution.

Employees in other large-scale organizations are facing similar dualities and incongruous commitments. For example, in 2002, Sherron Watkins, who was selected as one of *Time Magazine*'s "People of the Year" for being a major "whistle-blower" in the Enron scandal, had actually written only an internal (private) e-mail message to Enron CEO Kenneth Lay warning him about misstatements in financial reports.[58] Watkins's internal whistle-blowing demonstrates how complicated the definitions of public and private have become. Ten years later, with the rise of social networking sites like Facebook, the situation is even more complex.

The widespread use of personal computers, internet accessibility, and the proliferation of social network sites pose fundamental challenges to the maintenance of boundaries between work and leisure. In her study on workplace social networking, Stefana Broadbent found that employees with restricted access found other ways to stay connected. She writes, "Once the walls of the workplace have been breached, and employees become used to the idea that being at work should not be at the expense of key forms of connectivity, such as with their close family, they will devise a solution to ensure communication."[59] So implementing restrictions is not necessarily the answer. Yet it seems to be a direction in which we are moving.

Likewise with punishing "misconduct." In December 2013, the Kansas Board of Regents introduced a social media policy that allows Kansas state universities to fire employees for "improper" social media use, including posts that are "contrary to the best interests of the university."[60] Rules and regulations of the sort illustrated by Kansas and the Marine Corps (via the DOD) should be understood as forms of organizational control over our attention and an attempt to preserve the boundaries between social spheres. But as the Marine Corps demonstrates, preventive social media policies are nearly impossible to get right. So how should policy makers proceed? Will they slice up our lifeworld into fragments of context-specific rules and regulations? Texting-while-driving legislation is one such example.

Indeed, the proliferation of mobile social media has complicated the borders of context. When Marines log on to Facebook from a theater of war, they confront contradictory cultural commitments. I highlighted three incongruities in particular—convolution over professional and personal identities, social media's lateral organization as opposed to the military's top-down hierarchy, and social media's ego-centered style of communication, which is at odds with the ego-less ideal of military "brotherhood."

Because social media are so new, and we are still negotiating appropriate uses, policy is almost forced into a reactionary role. Gatekeepers such as the FCC control profanity over the airwaves, but today regular people have access to public platforms. How do we make them behave? And should we? The context of military communication, especially during a period of global conflict, constructively raises the stakes on these types of dilemmas. When the "employees" in question can include service members in a zone of combat, they cannot afford an attention deficit on their mission focus. Does this mean the DOD needs to create policies about "tweeting while droning," or "Facebooking while fighting a war"?

CHAPTER 2
From Posting Mail to Posting Status

Lance Corporal Sutton sat across from me with his legs crossed at the ankle. I remember feeling a little exposed without a table between us. I wondered if he felt the same way. My audio recorder rested on my right knee. His camouflage "cover" (military hat) rested on his. Less than a month before our interview, Lance Corporal Sutton had returned to Pendleton from Afghanistan, where he drove armored trucks for the Marine Corps. His 3531 MOS (military occupational specialty) designated him as a motor vehicle operator. When I asked him about his interactions with Facebook during deployment, he said:

> At first I thought it was kinda cool because you know you're . . . you kinda get homesick right away, and you wanna talk to your family and friends and stuff. But like after a month went by, I kinda got tired of it because your head kinda . . . you have one foot over there and one foot here. You just wanna focus on things that are going on over there. So I kinda stepped away from it a little bit. And then I was constantly busy like. . . . I left the wire a lot.[1] I just wanted to be more focused. People would actually get mad at me 'cause I wouldn't be on as much.
> SILVESTRI: Okay. So who would get mad at you?
> SUTTON: Uh, family, friends. And then . . . uh, at the time, I had a girlfriend, you know, of three years. But we ended up breaking up when I was over there, and that was one of the reasons why . . . is, 'cause talking and things like that.

Lance Corporal Sutton shifted in his chair. His eyes were down. As he spoke, I could hear a lump forming in his throat. I didn't press him on the breakup. It was hard to tell whether he considered talking or *not* talking to be the reason for his relationship's end. In either case, the level of connectivity and access between fronts was an issue. And as painful as it was, Lance Corporal Sutton's story was not unique among the interviews. It did, however, capture an emerging dichotomy with regard to social media at the front.

As I mentioned previously, battlefields are not commonly associated with a sense of connectedness to the home front. In fact, the front lines of battle are famous for their *inaccessibility* in this regard. Yet today, US troops are not only connected to the home front, but they also feel a level of obligation to remain in constant contact.[2] In many cases, the copresence afforded by social media is a source of stress for the contemporary war fighter. Lance Corporal Sutton described a pressure to "be on" and maintain a dual footing "over here" and "over there." His description of how this impacted his relationships alludes to a contemporary (re)negotiation of what it means to "keep in touch," especially during wartime. Lance Corporal Sutton's girlfriend assumed that since it is *possible* to be on Facebook, he *should* be on Facebook. This appears to be a moral dilemma unique to the new mobile media age.

The constant connection afforded by new communication technology produces a "tethering" effect. Technology sociologist Sherry Turkle describes the twenty-first-century "tethered soul" as a "a new state of the self, itself," whereby our new online intimacies create a world in which it makes sense for Lance Corporal Sutton to say things like he wasn't "on as much." Turkle argues that phrases like this suggest "a new placement of the subject, wired into society through technology."[3] Communication researchers argue that the communication environment of constant connectivity results in obsessions over work.[4] As Turkle describes, "There is much talk of new efficiencies; we can work from anywhere and all the time."[5] US troops in a war zone represent a unique demographic to study using Turkle's "tethering" thesis because their relationship to work and home is an *inverse*. Unlike the rest of us, their professional lives are fixed in a physical location for an extended period of time. Although they can have downtime, troops on deployment are technically clocked in for months on end. This is opposite stateside drone pilots who clock in and clock out of war's theater every day. For troops deployed to war, their tether is not grounded in a sense of a private life as Turkle and many other organizational communication scholars describe. Instead, they are anchored in a work environment but mentally and emotionally tethered to their private lives back home.

Tethered service members experience brief, frequent, and mediated interactions with the home front, which are not necessarily interruptions from work but are certainly representative of a new attention economy.[6] Today's troops must negotiate an environment where communication technologies are ubiquitous, presenting simultaneous, multiple, and ever-present calls on their attention.[7] Ten minutes further into Lance Corporal Sutton's interview, he described his experience as an attention deficit. His decision to quit Facebook came from his desire to focus on the mission and his safe return: "I didn't want to worry about problems in Afghanistan and worry about problems at home. I just wanted to focus on being there, being safe, and coming back. That was the biggest thing for me." Lance Corporal

Sutton's decision to log off represents one way of managing this distraction. After all, as the famous World War I song suggests, war is supposed to be "over there."

Lance Corporal Sutton's zero-sum response was uncommon in my interviews. Most Marines figured out a way to make do. They all, however, recognized the double-edged sword presented by Facebook at the front. On the one hand, ease and accessibility make it an appealing option for service members and their families. On top of that, the institutional PR machine I discussed in the previous chapter encourages personnel to update and monitor their Facebook pages regularly. But, on the other hand, the social expectations of family members and friends back home make it difficult to focus on the deployment's mission.[8]

Using Facebook in a theater of war is particularly fascinating, in part, because of the inherent irony. The platform's motto involves "improving how the world communicates."[9] But war does not represent an improvement in communication. Rather, it represents the ultimate transgression—communication through force. And on a more personal level, Facebook's relational principle of *connection* is not one we commonly associate with a war zone. In previous American conflicts, when a service member deployed to a war zone, he was virtually inaccessible to his civilian social network. This is no longer the case. In the contemporary combat environment, the culture of perpetual contact ushered in by social media technologies like Facebook collides with a situation quintessentially associated with a lack of contact.

For troops on deployment, Facebook offers a feeling of casual, everyday civilian conversation, a form of communication previously excluded from the war zone. Replicating this form requires constant access, and immediate direct contact, causing these communication ideals to be the most highly prized in contemporary combat's communication culture. According to interviews, service members imagine Facebook chatting to be a remediation of talking. In Lance Corporal Sutton's commentary, for example, he said Facebook was "cool" because "you wanna *talk* to your family." This is an important observation not accounted for in policy discussions and indicates an alternative media ideology at work among troops on deployment. Whereas policy makers imagine Facebook communication to be a form of publicized digital writing, akin to a billboard on a college campus, the troops imagine Facebook chat to be a mediated form of talking.

New Modes of Wartime Communication

The two most prominent features of the new communication environment, constant connectivity and immediacy, shape what the troops value and how they use social media on the battlefield. These are the characteristics of communication that enable deployed service members to obtain a sense of copresence, rather than absence, with their social networks. Although civilians also value these communication ideals, their ubiquity allows them to go relatively unnoticed in daily life.

Constant connectivity represents the tethering effect theorized by Turkle—the idea that we are "always on" and "plugged in." Immediacy is the quality of bringing one into direct and instant involvement with something or someone.[10] The best way to illuminate these qualities and other aspects of technological agency associated with the Facebook era is through a comparison with older media. Comparing Facebook communication with the handwritten letter, for example, illustrates the evolution of our collective beliefs about what it means to communicate. This comparison lends itself to a more detailed discussion about emergent forms of interpersonal address and new types of audiences for personal messages from the front.

The handwritten letter is a useful point of comparison because, until recently, it was the medium most closely associated with communication from a war zone. Facebook is the other point of comparison because, according to interview responses, Facebook is the primary method of communication today. As one Marine told me, "I found it the best method to stay in contact; the best way to stay in contact with everybody. I was in contact with people I worked with; I didn't use e-mail, I used Facebook." As technology changes, so do our means of communication and, consequently, our communicative norms and values.

Warriors have been writing pen-and-paper letters to their loved ones for centuries. But today, writing letters is an endangered practice. As one service member said, "The only letters I wrote were to this first grade [class]. . . . Otherwise it was all e-mails, you know, or send a card on special occasions and stuff." Another said, "I still think it's cool to get a letter. If someone takes the time to sit down and write a letter as opposed to a quick e-mail or text, I think it's cool that they're willing to take that time to do that." The idea that it has become "cool," in the novel sense of the word, to receive a letter while at war demonstrates just how dramatic the recent shift in communication norms, habits, and values is for US troops and their loved ones.

Describing handwritten letters in terms of novelty and romance was a theme among my interviews. A gunnery sergeant who served fifteen years in the Corps (his first deployment was in 1997, and his most recent was in 2010) described letter writing as pointless. He said, "There was no point. To be honest, there was no real . . . well, I wrote a couple of letters just so my wife . . . she was like, 'Are you gonna write normal?'" The gunnery sergeant smiled, raised his eyes to the ceiling, and shook his head. According to my interviews, most handwritten letters were to romantic partners (mostly wives and girlfriends), grandparents, or the occasional elementary school class. The lack of letter writing surprised me since our cultural imagination holds war as the prototypical context for handwritten letters with its own well-known subgenre, the "Dear John Letter," a phrase coined by American troops during World War II to describe the breakup letter. But today letter writing is relatively uncommon on the battlefield. Lance Corporal Sutton's "Dear John" arrived via Facebook chat.

As I noted in the introduction, the internet became widely accessible in Iraq and Afghanistan around the same time Facebook became a public sensation. According to my research, most warriors opted to use Facebook instead of e-mail. As one twenty-year-old Marine said, "I only e-mailed one person one time, and that was like a high school football coach." Thus, around 2007 the history of combat communication transitioned almost directly from old-fashioned postal mail to Facebook communication. While at Camp Pendleton, for example, I spoke to a nineteen-year-old lance corporal who had just returned from his first deployment to Afghanistan a few months before our interview. He enlisted in 2010.

SILVESTRI: Did you write any snail mail letters?
MARINE: I don't even know what that is.
SILVESTRI: Like old-fashioned letters. They're called "snail" because snails are slow.
MARINE: Ooh, I got it.
SILVESTRI: [*Laughs*] So did you send any?
MARINE: Um. No.

I do not suggest that this young man's inexperience with traditional mail represents the experiences of all our current service members. But the conversation was illuminating with regard to generational norms nonetheless. According to a 2012 demographics update released by the US Marine Corps, roughly two-thirds of Marines are twenty-five years old and under.[11] This means they were born in 1987 or after. They were in elementary school when the wars began. And most notably to my interests, they grew up as fluent natives in the digital age. This is the generation shaping war's communicative culture today.

Beyond its efficiency as a multimodal communications platform, Facebook is also an archive of relationships.[12] Some personnel said they did not send e-mails simply because they did not have contact information for all their friends and family. In addition to displaying an entire network of "friends" complete with profile pictures, Facebook allows its members to compose a personal message with minimal contact information. Facebook members need only to know the first name of the recipient before a drop-down menu appears containing the recipient's full name and e-mail address. In other words, Facebook remediates the address book. Now warriors have a larger pool of possible recipients, and, as I discuss later, they will often communicate with whomever is available. This new communication habit broadens potential audiences for personal messages from war. By contrast, handwritten letters force writers to choose recipients from a smaller pool of available addresses. As a result, letter writers typically send their messages to intimate kin.

Indeed, even beyond the context of war, humans are amid a critical threshold of change in the way we communicate. One place to witness this change is the structure of the internet, which has shifted dramatically from a concentration on content to a concentration on people. Less than ten years ago we primarily interacted with content on the net—webpages, games, and so on. By contrast, most internet use today centers on interaction with people—customer reviews, social networking platforms, and dating sites. According to a 2011 list of the most accessed websites, Facebook, YouTube, Bloggers, Wikipedia, and Twitter were among the top ten.[13] Each of these sites center around *people* and sharing personal content, whether it is writing online diaries, sharing audio-visual content, cocreating knowledge, or staying in contact. The restructuring of the web around people marks a subtle yet certain aggregation toward our current climate of temporally and spatially boundless communication with other human beings.

At the start of my research, I assumed the context of war would have more of an influence on the ways in which Marines make sense of their communication habits. I thought they would make more unprompted parallels between their deployments and those of earlier generations of war fighters. But through our conversations it seems that today's warriors carry their media ideologies over from the home front, modify them according to institutional regulation, and then adopt particular practices that enable them to maintain the communication norms, values, and customs primarily associated with civilian life. This finding is at odds with Paul Adams, who argues that a person's environment will ultimately impact their attitude. Although environment does have an impact for Marines in Iraq and Afghanistan, they ultimately strive to maintain their predeployment communication habits and attitudes. As the former global head of brand design at Facebook, Adams places heavy stock in people's attitudes. He admits that it is very difficult to change people's attitudes; it is much easier to invoke behavioral change first and attitudinal change will follow. Simply put, from this perspective, behaviors become habits and habits become attitudes.

That is why Adams recommends changing people's environments in order to change their attitudes. He writes, "Environment stimulates specific behaviors so it's much easier to try something new in a new environment."[14] My research indicates, however, that even though personnel experience a drastic environmental change when they go to a theater of war, their behaviors, or the idioms of practice they develop in the field, ensure that their attitudes about communication can remain the same as they were before they left.

New Idioms of Practice

The turn toward Facebook in lieu of letter writing signifies a relatively new idiom of practice for contemporary war fighters. People create idioms of practice by interacting with others and implicitly or explicitly defining the norms of using particular media.[15] It is easiest to identify a set of idioms of practice by being confronted with practices that fall outside of the norm. Using Facebook to compose a "Dear John" message is such an example. Subtler still are the unspoken rules, or normative idioms of practice, that guide the way personnel differentiate among Facebook's communication features (post, chat, message, etc.). Deployed troops attach ideas about what constitutes acceptable content, audience, and subject matter to each feature. Different groups naturally create their own idioms of practice. Sometimes people do not realize that they have formed idioms of practice until they encounter someone who has different practices. An illuminating disjuncture, for example, would be the idea that people do not write handwritten letters to someone they live with. A handwritten letter signals separation. Given the contemporary premium on constant connection and immediacy, this could be another reason US troops do not write letters, because they value a sense of copresence. Handwritten letters denote absence.

Mobile and internet communication technology has become so pervasive that many Marines today appear to take their access to the home front for granted. Like the Marine who didn't understand the reference to "snail mail," I caught another Marine off guard with a question about traditional postal mail. What is more, he seemed genuinely taken aback by his own response. Our conversation went as follows:

SILVESTRI: Did you send any snail mail while you were over there?
MARINE: Um, I did not. I . . . I'm trying to think. You caught me off guard with that question. But I don't think I sent . . . uh, I don't think I sent any snail mail the entire time I was there. . . . Like I said I had fairly good access to internet, so I didn't send any mail. Yeah. Very

much different from a deployment would be in the Korean War or World War II or something like that.

The Marine's amazement, reflected in this exchange, resonates with Winner's observation that human relationships to technologies can sometimes seem too obvious to merit serious reflection.[16] Recurring patterns of everyday activity tend to become taken-for-granted processes wherein we are unaware of a pattern taking shape until we notice a discontinuity. In this case, the discontinuity occurred when I asked about snail mail. I was taking a historical view, positioning this young man's deployment experience among previous generations of warriors. He did not consider his communication practices along this trajectory, an oversight that is not uncommon. As Winner argues, "Vast transformations in the structure of our common world have been undertaken with little attention to what those alterations mean."[17] It is worthwhile dwelling on the discontinuity of the war letter in order to reflect on some of the significant changes to the ways US troops communicate from the theater and what those changes mean for combat's communication culture.

Like the sentiment expressed by the Marine above, I was equally surprised to find how infrequently letters were posted from Iraq and Afghanistan. In my mind, which I can only assume is an iteration of the broader cultural mindset, letters from the front marked a staple subgenre of the handwritten letter.[18] Yet the Marine referenced two wars over sixty years past in response to a question about handwritten letters. Electronic messaging has become so prevalent we often forget how short its history really is, especially in the context of war. Gulf War service members and even many post-9/11 service members (until a few short years ago, and even now depending on where they're deployed) could communicate with the home front only via snail mail.

The Marine's comment about the Korean War and World War II point to a sense of nostalgia I perceived in many of my interviews. The nostalgia seems to center on an image of conventional warfare where nation-state fought nation-state, artillery pieces squared off against one another, and enemies wore uniforms. The nostalgia for this form of war fighting includes the communication culture that went along with it, which primarily meant handwritten letters.

Mainstream media texts like *Saving Private Ryan*, *The Thin Red Line*, and *Platoon* romanticize letters home from war. In these films, recipients cherish letters from the front for their tangibility. They become immediate keepsakes. As mementos they are alive with the author's bodily actions. The letter represents a tangible connection, evidence of a relationship spanning time and space: the physical paper, its folds, its familiar smell, that it was touched by a loved one, and each word written by his hand.[19] He scribbled one word out and wrote a different one in the margin; he misspelled another and forgot to cross the second "T." He licked the envelope and carried it in his pocket for a day, maybe two. In addition to the letter's materiality, the form and content of the message are usually considered to be more personal and detailed. This is in part because pen-and-paper letter writing is commonly thought of as more time consuming than its digital counterparts; not nearly as haphazardly written or encumbered by technological constraints such as word count restrictions.[20]

Indeed, a medium's structural attributes inform characteristics of communication. To continue with examples of written text, what is say-able in a sticky note, an e-mail, or a textbook depends, in part, on the medium's inherent opportunities and constraints. These can include an amalgamation of factors, ranging from concrete practical concerns (literacy, space, etc.) to more intangible influences (audience expectations and social conventions). It's important to guard against becoming so charmed by new media technologies that we miss a full consideration of influences like sociocultural context and perceived audiences and authors, as well as tradition.

Characteristics of Handwritten Letters and Facebook Communication

Letter writing has ritualistic qualities associated with its materiality, its composition, and its delivery and reception.[21] Similar to how we imagine prison mail operating, for troops on deployment, mail calls are also emotionally charged and highly sensory events. Receiving a letter can be a high point of the week.[22] Recipients get to touch and see the letter and hear their name called to collect it. They oftentimes keep, preserve, display, share, and reread letters as physical affirmations of interacting with the "outside" world.[23]

Indeed, e-mail has changed many material aspects of letter writing in addition to the way it has changed the content and form of correspondences.[24] But it would be an oversight to focus on materiality and ignore the generic conventions associated with form and content introduced by electronic messaging. For example, e-mails are more likely to resemble stream-of-consciousness ramblings than a letter's thoughtful content.[25] Social media are thought to promote an even more phatic and potentially impersonal style than e-mail, favoring narcissism, superficiality, and disclosure.[26] Social media encourage a particular form of self-expression, asking users to differentiate themselves and act as individuals. Sociologists Lee Raine and Barry Wellman refer to this phenomenon as "networked individualism," a new communication "operating system" that hinges on three primary characteristics—the individual is the autonomous center, people are interacting with multiple others, and people are engaging in several tasks simultaneously.[27]

The introduction of social media to the battlefield, then, is a particularly compelling context since messages home from war, until a few short years ago, were imagined to be a deeply personal affair. Not only that, they represent a relatively calcified genre, a subgenre of epistolary marked by temporal and spatial references, themes of separation, loneliness, and fears that death or misdirected mail will interfere with the relationship between addressor and addressee. In her sweeping analysis of over two hundred letters, spanning approximately 140 years of American warfare—the Civil War, World War I, World War II, Korea, the Cold War, Vietnam, the Persian Gulf, Somalia, and Bosnia—communication scholar Christine Knopf argues, "Correspondences from afar typically employ descriptions and narrations, designed to illuminate distant realities . . . reflect[ing] the remoteness in experiences, not only locations, between the lives they are living and the lives of those to whom they are writing, not to mention the lives they left behind."[28] The correspondences taking place on Facebook, however, do not reflect remoteness or absence but rather emphasize commonalities and copresence between troops and their social networks.

Knopf's research convincingly illustrates just how important activities associated with letter writing were to the life of a warrior. However, in the wars of today, letter writing is less common, mostly associated with, and motivated by, a sense of novelty and romance rather than a desire for functional communication and human interaction. The novelty associated with pen-and-paper letter writing suggests a fundamental shift in what it means to communicate. The ubiquity by which we interact with electronic communication technologies encourages a prioritization of constant connectivity and immediacy. The incessant speed and volume of messaging today changes the nature of communication altogether. What this means for the personnel I interviewed is that letter writing no longer fits with what they define or value as communication. They write a letter to their wife because it is romantic, and they saw it in a Tom Hanks movie. But for today's service member, letter writing is not communicating. In this culture, communication means having direct contact with others electronically and being able to respond to them immediately.

The new has meaning only in relation to the old. To make better sense of how the communication culture of combat has changed, I revisit some of my brother's letters to demonstrate the long-standing rhetorical conventions associated with handwritten letters from the front. His letters were written in 2006 during the Iraq War, whereas Knopf's analysis ends with the Bosnian conflict in the 1990s. Yet my brother's letters maintain the rhetorical forms described by Knopf in her study. Confirming the conventions associated with handwritten war letters provides a useful backdrop against which to appreciate the new forms of communication emerging from Iraq and Afghanistan today, where social media are the most prominent modes of contact.

By examining some of the socio-technical aspects of Facebook relative to the handwritten letter, it is easier to see how the emergent communicative values of constant connectivity and immediacy shape what it means to communicate from a war zone today. As guiding communication values, constant connection and immediacy promote a particular style of self-centered phatic or "chit-chatty" communication that is not necessarily conducive to the battlefield, where separation from family and close friends and a commitment to the people around you are largely considered to be essential to successful combat operations.

My brother wrote me eleven letters over the course of his Iraq deployment. He was in and around the city of Hit in Al-Anbar Province between November 2005 and April 2006. Social media had not yet become mainstream, so we communicated via snail mail. When he had the opportunity, he called my parents' house by satellite phone. One time he called when my mother was at the grocery store. She gasped when she heard his voice on the answering machine. Then she cried. Since my brother's deployment to Iraq, a lot has changed. For one thing, no one writes letters anymore.

The Role of the Recipient/Addressee

In letter writing there are distinct interpersonal roles, most prominently that of sender and receiver.[29] "At the heart of a genuinely communicative event is some awareness on the part of each participant of the needs and perspective of the other person, in other words, an understanding of audience."[30] For example, nearly all my brother's letters begin with a reference to the act of letter writing and/or my receipt of the letter. In addition, his opening remarks usually establish some semblance of an interpersonal exchange by drawing on conventions of spoken discourse by referencing something in the moment. Talking about the weather is a common form for such an exchange. This is not to say that social media lacks an understanding of audience, but relative to the handwritten letter, social media audiences are more complex. They are often not as singular and easily controlled as the audience for a handwritten letter. As such, the constitution of an interpersonal exchange on social media takes a different form than it would in a letter.

Following the conventions identified by Knopf, in the examples below, my brother begins his letters with a temporally situated greeting that successfully figures into our existing interpersonal relationship.[31] At the same time, however, he alludes to his temporal and spatial remoteness by referencing his uncertainty over the timeliness of the letter's receipt.[32] According to Knopf, most letters position the deployed service member in a particular place, time, and emotional state, letting the reader know where the sender was physically and mentally at the time the letter was composed.

[November 30, 2005] If this letter finds you before the GRE, then happy Bday and good luck! If it finds you after, then happy belated Bday and I'm sure you did fine.

[January 3, 2006] Happy New Year! Not much going on here. We've occupied an old school-house in East Hit. Built a nice deck with a fire-pit in the center. No activity insurgent-wise yet. We are planning a big offensive though to sweep from Hit up North to the town of Baghdadi. I'll be on the East side of the Euphrates, which is safer I think.

As a social practice, handwritten letters are conducive to establishing an interpersonal exchange because they follow a one-to-one sender-receiver model of communication. Presumably the sender has an established relationship with the receiver and can draw on that in the letter's construction. By contrast, social media have a more nebulous audience. Even when the sender constructs a message with a singular recipient in mind, the medium allows for easy copying and forwarding. Many Marines flagged their wives or mothers as the "communication hub," indicating that messages sent to them would spread to the rest of the social network. One post from a service member's Facebook page, where his wife used the wall post feature to effectively write a status update on his behalf, reads: "Just wanted to let everyone know that [Bob] wanted me to tell you all HI for him and let you all know he is doing well" (see figure 3).

Given the broader, more indistinct audience for social media messages, there is less of a tendency to establish an interpersonal exchange on an individual level like my brother did by acknowledging my birthday and graduate school entrance exam. Since the audience for a wall post is relatively anonymous, in the sense that it is more general than a letter recipient, the construction of an interpersonal exchange takes a new form. Even when a user creates a wall post with a specific recipient in mind, the network structure does not always promise a direct delivery. For example, during an interview at Camp Pendleton, a Marine recounted a story about a Mother's

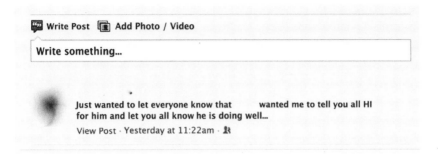

Figure 3. Wife's message to the social network

Day message that went to audience members beyond his mother. He said, "I posted a . . . I took a photo of . . . we made a sign that said like, 'Happy Mother's Day from Kabul,' and I posted a photo of it thinking my mom would see it, and I had like everyone I know on Facebook comment on it. I tagged my mom in it, but then everyone saw it." Although it is safe to assume he is aware, at least on some level, of Facebook's quasi-broadcast structure, he was nonetheless surprised that other network members beyond his mother would engage with the message. Most of the time when we communicate via social media, we do not know who our audience is. Yet activities such as "liking" or "commenting" offer evidence of an audience.

The Mother's Day scenario provokes questions regarding audience, medium, privacy, and forms of address. Who is this message for? Is it for his mother or for his social network? Why would he use a near-broadcast medium to deliver a tailored message? Although he "tagged" his mother in the photo to call her attention to the message, the act of "posting" made it available to everyone in his social network. What is more, during the interview, he said, "*We* made a sign," presumably speaking about his comrades who also wanted to send a Mother's Day message from Kabul. As a medium, Facebook does not typically compel collective senders unless they are part of a corporation or group page. In general, Facebook participants cannot post on behalf of other people. That is why most people categorize Facebook's primary message structure as one-to-many. It is usually clear who the sender is, but the potential recipients, as this Marine found out, are numerous.

Although networked audiences are not as singular or specific as a letter recipient, since they can consist of hundreds of "friends," service members (and their loved ones) use Facebook as a direct mode of communication between two parties. In so doing, they create a sense of intimacy, albeit a digital intimacy. And like the Mother's Day example, Facebook allows participants to publicize affection. In another instance, a Marine changed his profile photograph to send an anniversary message to his wife. Using a profile photograph to communicate a specific message to a particular audience is compelling. The profile photo is the first photograph visible on a Facebook page. Regardless of friendship status or privacy settings, the profile photo is generally visible to anyone. Practically speaking, the profile image represents *you*.[33] In this particular instance, the profile photograph depicts a warrior in desert camouflage fatigues standing in front of a sand-colored wall (see figure 4). He holds a yellow legal pad, which reads in all capitals: "HAPPY 4 YEAR ANNIVERSARY [wife's first name]. I LOVE YOU." His straight face combined with the head-on angle and placard beneath are reminiscent of a criminal's mug shot. It also resembles a ransom photo or the Wile E. Coyote's plea for help from viewers at home. What these types of images have in common is that they communicate the subject's immediate context and they do not communicate much else. Upon log-in, Facebook asks members to update their status through a series of rotating

Figure 4. Happy Anniversary

prompts: "What's on your mind?" "How are you feeling?" "What's going on?" Answers to these questions reflect an individualized immediacy.

In this case, it is relatively clear that the Marine is deployed and he wants his audience, particularly his wife, to know "what is on his mind." This Marine elects to change his profile photo instead of updating his status, a move that can be read as a more potent declaration of his affection since it is accessible to more than just his "friends" list and is inherently linked to his online identity. According to time stamps, his wife responded within hours by posting a photo of their son to her husband's Facebook wall. Presumably their son saw his father's profile photo and tried to replicate his facial hair with a magic marker. The photo's caption reads: "Look at my mustache, Daddy!!!! It's just like yours, lol."

Response Time
Unlike my brother's letters, the Facebook posts never referenced a concern over the timeliness of the message. The wife's receipt and response occurred almost instantaneously. She responded by posting to her husband's wall rather than by changing her profile photograph. This is likely because he would receive a notification about a new wall post, whereas if she were to respond in kind by changing her profile picture, he would not receive a message to draw his attention to the change. We can see the value of immediacy operating here. A rapid response appears to trump message content. The wife's wall post did not directly respond to the anniversary message; instead it was a new conversational thread about their son and his father's mustache. Facebook's emphasis on the new and the immediate through prompts like "What's on your mind?" encourages users to present their current "status" as "I'm happy," "I'm tired," "I'm listening to the Cure," and so on.[34]

Overvaluing immediacy causes us to confuse *responding* with *reacting*. The former requires thinking and thinking takes time. Reactions are knee-jerk flinches. Warriors are trained to have finely tuned, context-dependent reactions. Responses require an opportunity to think. Constant contact and immediacy, two prevailing values attached to the new communication age, do not necessarily encourage deep thought. This is not to say, however, that Facebook cannot be or is not used for deep thinking. In fact, toward the end of this chapter I describe the way Marines use the Facebook walls of fallen comrades for grief and reflection.

Use of Photos
The use of photos with minimal writing is another noteworthy feature of these new forms of interpersonal exchange. Scholars who study computer-

mediated communication and interpersonal relationships often describe
what they call "cue systems."[35] Holding face-to-face as the ideal, all other
forms of interpersonal exchange operate at a cue deficit. For example, a
written text lacks audial and visual cues. A phone call contains audial cues
but lacks visual cues. A Skype session would contain both audial and visual
cues. Using this logic, we can imagine a photo post on Facebook participating in this cue economy. The age-old adage "a picture is worth a thousand
words" comes to mind. Perhaps that is why these photographs are posted
with so few words. The written text accompanying these photos, however,
serves a similar purpose to the temporally dependent greetings included in
my brother's letters. Just as my brother wrote "Happy Birthday" or "Happy
New Year" to cultivate a semblance of interpersonal exchange, these Facebook posts similarly rely on such rhetorical devices. "Happy Mother's
Day," "Happy Anniversary," and "Look at my mustache, Daddy!!!!" figure
into preexisting interpersonal relationships.

Privacy

Perhaps the most influential distinction between the handwritten letter and
Facebook posts is the level of privacy. Prior to the internet, we imagined
media operating in two ways. One form was broadcast media such as radio
and television, designed to publicize messages for a general audience. The
second form, communications media such as telegrams, phone calls, and
postal mail, was meant to facilitate two-way conversations. The distinction between these two types of media, which is to say between one-to-
many and one-to-one tools, used to be so clear that we could distinguish
between a personal and impersonal message just by the type of medium
used. Today, however, social media's network structure complicates ideas
about audience, privacy, and forms of address. When a warrior posts "I
miss you" on his Facebook wall, the message's production style is a relative
one-to-many. Whereas when he writes "I miss you" in a postmarked letter
addressed to his wife, the message is an uncomplicated one-to-one.

For the most part, social media users are aware of "the network effect"
and how to use their privacy settings.[36] The trouble is that Facebook presents an impression of privacy despite its relative publicness. This point
leads to a phenomenon Susan Barnes calls the "privacy paradox," an apparent discrepancy between privacy concerns and actual privacy settings.[37]
A contributor to the privacy paradox can be the sense of control associated
with electronic communication. For example, one Marine perceived the
handwritten letter to be too fixed of a medium relative to Facebook messaging. He said, "I personally like Facebook because I can actually, if I don't
intend to say that, I just backspace. . . . I can also delete the things that I

post. I can't do that if I sent a letter out. I can't say, 'Oh no, I didn't mean that.'" This commentary reveals his assumptions about internet communication. He considers his posts to be a "living document" as opposed to a fixed letter. A letter requires commitment toward saying something.

New communication technologies complicate matters of conviction. On the one hand, immediacy encourages reaction rather than response. Presumably, committing to a thoughtful response is easier than committing a knee-jerk reaction. But on the other hand, constant digital contact demands intense self-monitoring of our identities as they are represented in images and texts circulating on the web. As psychologist Robert Williams argues, "Because I am not physically present, I am thus reduced to my documented interests and behavior."[38] So it would be reasonable to assume that people have committed to their online self-representations, even if they feel effervescent.

This Marine's perception of control was especially surprising since he had just, moments before our interview, attended Camp Pendleton's social media class. What is even more surprising is that he was not alone in his perception of control. Another Marine at Pendleton said, "I rarely post things I don't want the world to see. I use the chat function instead." Here we can see an emergent idiom of practice designating appropriate uses for "posts" and for "chats." The idea that "the world" is watching contributes to a phenomenon Alice Marwick and danah boyd refer to as "context collapse." Marwick and boyd describe "context collapse" as the flattening of multiple audiences into one such that communication in networked environments operates by the lowest common denominator. They argue, "Context collapse creates an audience that is often imagined as its most sensitive members: parents, partners, and bosses."[39] Instead of a general public, social network members imagine what Marwick and boyd call the "nightmare reader," someone who would not read messages favorably and would likely become offended. Or in the case of war, the ultimate "nightmare reader" would be an enemy combatant who could "assemble fragments" of information to launch a lethal attack. As a result, according to Marwick and boyd, social network members engage in a level of self-censorship to render messages safe for the "nightmare reader." What this means for military personnel who try to represent their war experiences on Facebook is that their representations need to be intelligible and acceptable to the most sensitive, unforgiving readers, which can include their grandmothers as well as their commanding officers. They also have to avoid any references to their "work" in case an enemy is watching. So in terms of technological agency, the concept of a nightmare reader haunts decisions about content from the beginning. As I mentioned in chapter 1, real-time chatting becomes an outlet to avoid this phantom because it is a one-to-one form of communication. You know your interlocutor. Writing for an individual letter recipient with whom you have an intimate relationship versus writing for a social network that could include your "nightmare reader" will undoubtedly inform what you write about.

New Audiences and Contexts

While observing Facebook pages of personnel on deployment, I was struck first by the *frequency* of their posts and then by their *banality*. As I mentioned, Facebook's emphasis on newness and immediacy temporally situates participants in the moment so they write about their immediate environment, including their immediate thoughts. But concerns over OPSEC and the threat of the nightmare reader constrain what information they can post. In this way, personnel stationed in a war zone occupy a unique double bind. Facebook's socio-technical structure encourages them to write about "what's on their mind," but institutional and cultural constraints inhibit what is and is not say-able on the web. As one Marine explained, "[I'm] not much of a poster, saying, 'Hey, today I went to this.' Obviously OPSEC is out there so you can't just really post all these things on Facebook. You can't really say 'Hey, I'm going to downtown Herat today' or yesterday because anyone can access Facebook." The idea that "anyone can access Facebook" is a notion driven home by briefs like the ones described in the previous chapter. But when warriors have such frequent and dynamic access to the home front and cannot communicate about major events, there is little left to talk about. What they end up discussing, then, is relatively mundane.

In one case, a Marine told his social network about his new hobby in Afghanistan—"Insanity"—a sixty-day extreme home workout DVD.[40] The time stamp records the post at 11:22 a.m. US central time. That means it was around the same time in the evening in Afghanistan when this Marine announced he was participating in his "new favorite night time activity . . . in Afghanistan." Beyond my initial surprise that he had the time and/or energy to embark on an intensive workout program, not to mention post a "status" that he was doing so, I was struck by how much his post reflected Facebook's shallow and narcissistic cultural repertoire, despite his being "in Afghanistan."[41]

By contrast, if I were to guess what was on my brother's mind from the letters he wrote, I would say mostly combat operations (interspersed with occasional lamentations over a bad breakup). His writing was very detailed, often including specific date, time, and location stamps. On a practical level, the exclusion of date/time stamps on Facebook could be because they are auto-recorded beneath each post. My brother's letters were in line with Knopf's research, which found that handwritten letters from the front make regular and frequent reference to time and place in very concrete and exact terms. Letter writers note days and times of events to precisely reconstruct chronology. They specifically note place through the use of mileage, changes in distance, and map-based reference points. Three different letters home from my brother illustrate this:

[November 30, 2005] Currently the plan is to offload in Kuwait City on your Bday and fly to Al Asad via C-130 and convoy to the town of Hit from there where we will setup base. So if you hear Al Asad, Hit, Baghdad or Western Al Anbar Province in the news, that will be us.

[January 26, 2006] We just finished a 10 day 40 mile sweep of the East Euphrates River Valley. We found a ton of explosives hidden randomly in the desert.

[January 27, 2006] So we have 2 more small operations left, operation Thresher, which I will not be a part of, is a 48 hr. sweep of some of the areas we missed during the KOA Canyon. Immediately after that from 1–6 Feb is another sweep, this time South. We retrograde back to Al Asad between the 13–15 Feb and to Kuwait between the 20–23 so I'll probably be back on ship sometime around 23 Feb. Then we have a stop in Djibouti Africa (I don't know the dates) and supposedly 2 port calls (I don't know the specifics yet).

These excerpts are markedly different from the electronic communication of today. The inclusive pronouns "we" and "us" position my brother among his unit. His attention is focused on his men and the missions ahead. This point is significant. According to Glenn Gray in *The Warriors: Reflections on Men in Battle*, there is a critical difference between friendship and comradeship. He writes, "The essential difference between comradeship and friendship consists, it seems to me, in a heightened awareness of the self in friendship and in the suppression of self-awareness in comradeship."[42] This distinction is why there are so few individual relationships in war. As war correspondent Chris Hedges observes, in war "there are not the demands on us that there are in friendships."[43] Yet "friendship," albeit digitized and in some cases perfunctory, is central to Facebook. And it is the individualized, ego-centered relationship that Gray and Hedges imagine to be antithetical to camaraderie—the type of social support most suitable to the context of war. Beyond the camaraderie (as opposed to friendship) reflected in my brother's letters, it is also evident that he takes a longer-range view of his deployment relative to the transient commentary exchanged on Facebook. Although the narratives in his letters are often temporally situated in the moment of letter writing, the content reflects a broader perspective on combat operations in Iraq. He is not focused on his immediate environment or momentary musings.

This is in contrast to Facebook's emphasis on the now. A Marine in Okinawa said that knowing he had instant and constant access to Facebook shifted his focus from the bigger picture to the immediate. He said, "When you know you have more access to it, you can just explain something right there and then." He compared his Facebook interactions to what he would write in letters. He said:

> When you write letters you only talk about the big stuff that happens and then when you are like actually talking through Facebook, you're on it all the time, you can actually say you know what's on your mind then, what's happening then. But when you're writing letters. . . . Like I actually wrote letters out there. I never sent them, but I talked about big stuff. . . . Just bigger things. Not small details.

The "small details" this Marine references contribute to an ambient sense of intimacy. Digital technology researcher Marc Davis calls it an "aggregate phenomenon," where the banality of the message contributes to feelings of closeness and intimacy. He argues, "No message is the single-most important message. It's sort of like when you're sitting with someone and you look over and they smile at you. You're sitting here reading the paper, and you're doing your side-by-side thing, and you just sort of let people know you're aware of them."[44] Personnel post messages to their Facebook wall that say things like "Just finished *The Hunger Games*," or they might click "like" under a network member's Facebook status that reads, "sale on my favorite chips at the grocery store." These types of messages differentiate users from one another. They reflect Raine and Wellman's "networked individualism" and provide a stark contrast to my brother's use of inclusive pronouns in his letters. Moreover, relative to longer and possibly more reflective content in a letter, this level of communication might seem trite. However, the quantity, frequency, and immediacy of social network messages create a feeling of closeness and intimacy different from other forms of communication.

The Emergence of a New Communication Culture at War

Warriors today are tethered to the home front. They can participate in their domestic lives from their FOBs. Recall Lance Corporal Sutton, who described having "one foot over there and one foot here." Digital ethnographer Stefana Broadbent argues that new media technologies enable people to "rekindle the sense of intimacy" created by "sharing a space with someone you care for."[45] Broadbent was mostly talking about Skype, but Facebook enables a similar sense of copresence. The only thing is, Facebook is built on an architecture of active participation. Having a presence on Facebook requires that a person post many pictures, have active discussions with friends, and share personal interests and information.

The desire to maintain a presence on Facebook can be quite demanding. A senior enlisted noncommissioned officer (NCO) admitted that he was happiest and felt most secure when he was leading a small patrol base five kilometers away from the company base where they did not have access to the internet. He said, "As bad as it may sound, there are a lot of issues that arise when young guys have unlimited communication access to their loved ones. Being in an extremely kinetic area I needed the Marines to remain focused on their mission and not left wondering what their young, newly married wife may be doing." In spite of the dangers associated with a lack of focus, the compulsion to keep up with friends and family remains. For example, the gunnery sergeant I mentioned previously who served fifteen years in the Marine Corps and whose first deployment was in 1997 described the way he used Facebook during his most recent deployment in 2010: "We used it honestly to keep up. You read your family's posts, you read your friend's posts. . . . Kinda update status . . . and you know, pictures, you see your whole family. . . . You know whatever stuff they were doing that week; I got to see it. Maybe a week later, but at least I was in the current, not six months behind like before." The desire to "keep up" or "stay current" was a recurring theme in the interview data. One young man went so far as to say that he couldn't imagine his deployment without the ability to stay in touch with friends and family. He said:

> Um, yeah, it'd . . . I don't know how that deployment would have been without Facebook. I think it might have been worse. You know, not knowing what's going on back home. My sister got pregnant again, my nieces are growing up, my brother just graduated high school. . . . I didn't know my little brother graduated high school. And I see graduation pictures. And I was like, "Oh my God, congratulations!" I Facebooked him before I talked to him.

One could imagine that "not knowing what's going on back home" was always an anxiety for deployed service personnel. But now, social media access from the battlefield provides a tempting opportunity to find out and keep up. But beyond the opportunity, an underlying sense of obligation goads their interaction with the home front. Recall Lance Corporal Sutton's heartache over his girlfriend leaving him for what he felt was a logical decision to quit Facebook. He felt too removed and distracted from his missions. The NCO I mentioned previously diagnosed this sort of condition as a need for "immediate gratification." He said, "E-mails and instant messaging are examples of our society's dependence on immediate gratification. If you are communicating daily, chances are not a whole lot of things are new in your loved ones' life back home, and you damn sure don't want to tell them what's really going on where you are."

Even if there is nothing new to communicate, the emotional capital derived from participation, or the dependence on immediate gratification compels troops to continue Facebooking from the front. Turkle concludes a similar diagnosis when she says that our current communication technology's emphasis on the new leads to an obsession over immediate affective exchanges. I message you, you chat with me. If you do not, I become anxious. Why aren't you e-mailing me back right now? This anxiety is exacerbated when a loved one is in a war zone. Civilian counterparts often assume the troops have constant connection, but, in reality, ease of internet access depends on their military occupational specialty (MOS). And even when they can access the web regularly, it is an imposition to expect that they will or even should, a dilemma that caused Lance Corporal Sutton a great deal of heartache.

Much of the pressure to stay in constant contact derives from the communication culture that many of today's young personnel grew up in. In her theorization of the "tethered adolescent," Turkle describes how the introduction of the cell phone helped to cultivate our cultural expectations for immediate feedback. She explains, "Kids get cell phones from their parents. In return they are expected to answer their parents' calls."[46] These early learned habits establish the conditions for our current state of constant connectivity. It should not be a surprise, then, that service members and their social networks operate according to the same set of expectations. On the one hand, Marines are tethered to their domestic lives and feel compelled to stay in constant contact. They also derive a sense of emotional capital from doing so. It feels good to connect with your social network. On the other hand, they also feel obligated to update their statuses, responding to a social network that feels entitled to such notifications.

The context of war emphasizes how egregious our demands have become. One Marine told me that he got in "big trouble" with his wife after he lost contact with her following a serious accident in Afghanistan. An eighteen-wheeler struck his Humvee, throwing him from the vehicle, knocking him unconscious, and causing serious injuries. As he tells it, "I wasn't able to contact her for the better part of a week while in the hospital, and when I finally did, she was more a wreck from wondering why I hadn't mentioned anything than from me actually being injured." This Marine's wife was operating by a new set of communication norms ushered in by social media. For the most part, because it is possible, we have come to expect frequent and regular "status updates" from everyone in our social network, including deployed service members. Our taken-for-granted sense of entitlement becomes more noticeable in the context of war, which used to be a case where lack of contact was not only accepted but also to be expected.

By contrast, today's warriors are not excluded from participating in the broader communication culture. During my online observation, two Marines wrote posts to reassure their family and friends of their safety after word got out of an attack near where they were stationed (see figure 5). A major concern for public affairs officers, vocalized during interviews, is that sensitive information such as deaths or injuries can pass to families and friends via Facebook before the military has the opportunity to inform them according to procedure.

A sense of obligation to the home front can inhibit a warrior's ability to stay focused on his mission. In her piece "The Democratisation of Intimacy," Broadbent argues that until recently, places like the battlefield were settings in which people were removed for long periods of time from their closest ties, family or friends. Going to war "meant leaving behind the family and its concerns," and "going on a mission meant limiting contacts to

Figure 5. Safe and doing well

a few letters."[47] According to Broadbent, the geographical distance of the battlefield was not the only reason for this isolation; the social expectations were just as binding.

Service members on deployment were expected to leave behind the personal world and embrace the professional one, focusing squarely on the tasks to be accomplished and the companions at hand. According to Broadbent, the strict separation between home and workplace meant that when entering the work arena, the "personal" self must be shed. The individual was expected to concentrate uniquely on the professional environment, and all distractions coming from the private sphere of life could hinder or jeopardize the job to be accomplished. Focus, dedication, and commitment guaranteed not only the positive outcome of the job but also the safety of the other team members and the atmosphere of the group. Today, however, warriors exist in a liminal state straddling private and professional spheres and trying to steady their balance with "one foot over there and one foot here." Operating within a culture of communication that values constant connectivity and immediate, direct contact only exacerbates feelings of in-between-ness.

Chatting across Fronts

Most of the personnel I spoke with told me that the most beneficial feature of Facebook is the speed. One Marine said, "You can tell if somebody's on and you wanna tell them something really quick. Just the speed of it." The ease, access, and immediacy of new communication tools create a feeling of connection and digital intimacy for personnel on deployment in Iraq and Afghanistan. The difference is, *whom* you connect with matters less. In a handwritten letter, senders must *choose* their recipients from a finite pool. Facebook multiplies opportunities to talk to "somebody" or "someone" about "something." As the Marine went on to say, "Just to be able see if they're on you know even though most the time they weren't because of the time difference but you'd always have that small hope that someone was on and you could talk to 'em even if it was just for five minutes." If your addressee is not planned, the conversation is also not planned. As a result, the form and content of social media messages often reflect unfocused, idle chitchat.

Being able to "tell them something really quick" results in a new rhetorical form that has less to do with the depth of disclosure and more to do with the frequency of contact. Broadbent compares the temporal shift ushered in by new communication technologies like Skype to older forms of communication like the telephone. She says the landline typically involved a narration of past events whereas Skype conversations focused on the present—what was happening in the moment. In my interviews, I noticed that Facebook's chat function emphasized the immediacy of the moment whereas the longer messages, whether they were writing longer messages or not, were perceived to involve more reflection of past events. In *Media, Modernity and Technology: The Geography of the New*, David Morely argues that the difference relates to the technologies' mobility. He writes, "The first question in many mobile-phone conversations is often 'Where are you?' (just as the answer, so often is 'I'm on the train/stuck in traffic, I'll be a bit late')."[48] I would take Broadbent and Morely's arguments a step further to account for changes brought on by social media like Facebook, where the emphasis is on *what* rather than *where* or even *how*. One reason *what* supersedes *where* is because we often assume mobility today. The advent of geolocation software saves us from even having to ask. Especially when we are talking to an active-duty service member, we can assume mobility. And even if someone were to ask a service member to state *where* he or she is located, the ideology put forward by the military that I described in the last chapter prohibits the service member from doing so. Not to mention the fact that the military designates family readiness officers (FROs) to instruct family members not to ask for or disclose location information. Moreover, the fleeting, stream-of-consciousness style of communication associated with social media platforms like Facebook reflects an emergent cultural curiosity in *what* interlocutors are doing (as with Facebook's prompt, "What's on your mind?") rather than *how* they are doing or *where* they're located.

Communication today, especially that which occurs via social network sites, is less about communicating ideas and more about establishing an affective connection. The nature of the communication is *phatic*. That is, its primary function is to perform socially, as opposed to convey information. The establishment of an affective connection through phatic expression requires an immediate audience who can respond. The need for instantaneous feedback leads many of the personnel I interviewed to describe Facebook's chat feature as the most popular, beneficial, and frequently used.

Facebook introduced the chat feature in April 2008. Before chat, Facebook assumed a relative broadcast model. The chat feature can stand in as a signpost for the new era, which occurred around 2008, when communication (across fronts and elsewhere) became more direct and immediate. During the week of the launch, the lead engineer of "Facebook Chat" described the new feature as follows: "The Wall and Inbox have been the primary ways to communicate, but when more immediacy is necessary— for example when making plans for lunch in half an hour or arguing over a foul call in the NCAA tournament—they might not be enough. Chat aims to fill this gap."[49]

Many Marines described the difference between posting and chatting by referencing the different audiences and discussion topics associated with each. They preferred to "chat" with friends. As one Marine said, "Instant chat I used with good friends, and it was about unimportant things like you know finding out what they did over the weekend." Another told me that he instant messaged with friends because "friends are more 'What's goin' on now? What's goin' on now?' Family is more like, 'How are you doing?'" He went on to say, "Instant messages [are] more now, not all week. More like, 'Yeah, it's really hot out here' or 'Yeah, it's really cold.'" The perception that chatting is preferable for friends because they are more interested in "what's goin' on" or your experiences rather than your well-being suggests associations between a particular form of communication and the quality of the relationship. If the Library of Congress were to save contemporary service members' Facebook chats as archives representative of a twenty-first-century deployment, the substance of the messages would be a tapestry of banal moment-to-moment commentary about the weather.

Although the Facebook engineer may have intended for chat to be used for instrumental purposes—making plans or argumentation—an engineer's intent does not dictate idioms of practice. A technology's politics derive from the series of choices embedded in them and the ramifications of those choices, which far outlive the original design's intent. In addition to the utilities intended by the designer, Marines describe using Facebook chat for phatic purposes as well.

Facebook chat, in the lifeworld of deployed service members, acts as a communication tether to the home front. I asked a Marine who deployed twice (summer 2010 and winter 2011) with combat logistics battalions what he talked about on Facebook and whether he spoke about his deployment experiences.

MARINE: We didn't really talk about the war experience much. Just how's the weather. Small talk, pretty much. I don't know. It's hard to explain.
SILVESTRI: Well, can you try?
MARINE: [*Laughs and shakes his head*]

Although there may not be much substance to the conversations, there is still a desire to remain in contact. This could very well be the sensation that this Marine found "hard to explain." Communication scholars argue that an emerging dependence on immediate affective exchanges developed out of our new communication environment's idealization of rapid-fire messages. New technology brings us to the point where we are used to sharing thoughts and feelings instantaneously. According to Turkle, the speed at which our electronic networks can connect us to others augurs a new relationship to emotion: "Emotional life can move from 'I have a feeling, I want to call a friend,' to 'I want to feel something, I need to make a call.'"[50] In either case, it comes at the expense of cultivating the ability to be alone and to decipher and manage one's emotions.

A growing cultural need for constant and immediate connection is fascinating because it is not necessarily a need to feel connected to someone in particular. It is not a need to feel connected to your mom or your sister or your best friend from high school. *It is a need to feel a sense of connection, period.* Knowing that someone is out there in your network matters. You never have to be alone with your thoughts. A Marine who deployed to Helmand Province in 2012, one of the deadliest areas in Afghanistan, told me he "lived on Facebook" during his deployment. When he could, he would structure his day in order to create opportunities to chat with family and friends back in the States. As he explained it, "I woke up in the morning, I woke up relatively early so I could get on Facebook to talk to my family for a little while before they went to sleep . . . and then I'd come back during chow, and some people I know would be up at that time, and we'd have a small conversation, and then I'd again talk to my family again before I went to bed at night." Chatting with someone in real time cuts through any sense of seclusion.

Even older, experienced Marines familiar with the hardships of deployment describe a sense of relief when they log on to Facebook. A sergeant who earned a 2011 medal of valor during his deployment in Afghanistan said, "I get on there and you know view—I've got an older brother and a younger brother, so I get on there and see what they're doing. It just gets my mind out of the . . . um, off that combat environment for a minute. It just lets me take that deep breath and relax for a minute and just remember the good times." Unlike the escape we may experience from watching a movie or playing a video game, instant messaging offers feedback, an immediate affective exchange.

This sense of continuous connection with a few important people is particularly strong because it is happening in environments where individuals are isolated, even if temporarily, from their core social group. And isolation for warriors can be even more exaggerated since it can happen beyond the social and geographical levels to include the emotional and ideological realms as well. Through my interviews and personal experiences living with veterans, I have come to understand war as an experience that is both "solitary and shared all at the same time." As a Marine sergeant explained during our interview in Okinawa, "The only people that can [understand] are the brothers that [you] served with, but it's their own hell. We share the experience, but we internalized the feelings, scars, and memories associated with it." This feeling of isolation can exacerbate the need for contact. In fact, some Marines told me that when the United States was sleeping, they would Facebook chat each other: "Like . . . uh, me and like my roommate would be messing around and messaging like, 'Ha ha ha, you're gay,' you know . . . like a little chat would pop up real quick, 'Ha ha, you're next to me,' 'Oh hey, how's it goin'?'" At its most basic, this type of phatic exchange tests the line of communication. Is it open? Is this person available to me? Even if you do not necessarily have anything to say, there is something comforting about knowing the line is open. You are not alone.

At issue is Turkle's concern that new media interaction is "less risky" and enables the "illusion of companionship without the demands of friendship." She writes, "We communicate with instant messages, 'check-in' cell calls and emoticons. All of these are meant to quickly communicate a state. They are not intended to open a dialogue about complexity of feeling. . . . When interchanges are reduced to the shorthand of emoticon emotions, questions such as 'Who am I?' and 'Who are you?' are reformatted for the small screen and flattened out in the process."[51] For deployed troops who know they are experiencing the same things but don't talk about them, all that is left to say is "Hey, how's it goin'?" or the masculine ritualistic insult, "You're gay." Each seems to fulfill a social utility similar to the familiar sleepover question, "Are you awake?" When you are alone in the dark, in a strange place, it is comforting to know someone else is conscious.

There seems to be a growing discontent with solitude today, as people confuse the state of being alone with feelings of loneliness. Although it may feel comforting to avoid solitude, according to Turkle, the inability to be alone with one's thoughts inhibits the development of autonomy. As she describes, "There used to be a moment in the life of an urban child, usually between the ages of 12 and 14, when there was a first time to navigate the city alone. It was a rite of passage that communicated, 'You are on your own and responsible. If you feel frightened, you have to experience these feelings.'"[52] Turkle argues that the tethering enabled by mobile communication technology buffers discomfort and can impact a children's sense of self; they do not perceive themselves as self-sufficient. Demographically speaking, Turkle's "tethered adolescents" represent this generation of war fighters. In previous conflicts, links with home were sporadic at best. Those who could not handle separation, focused attention, and team solidarity were sanctioned as weak and unreliable slackers, bad team members, or even traitors.[53] But the tethered warriors of today do not need to handle separation because they can remain in constant contact with their social networks.

SILVESTRI: How often did you send and receive messages via Facebook while you were away?

MARINE: Um, I'd have four or five different people like popped up sending messages, and I'd be talking to all of them at once. A lot.

SILVESTRI: Did you access Facebook every day?

MARINE: Every day that I could. Yeah.

SILVESTRI: What was that like?

MARINE: The day that I didn't it was nice 'cause I'd come back and have seventeen notifications, and I'd be like, "Woohoo, people love me!"

The first thing that struck me about this conversation is the fact that he could be chatting with four or five people at once. With his attention split across five Facebook chats, it is safe to assume that the depth of conversation was at a minimum. But what I found most striking was the way he attached his sense of self-worth to how many notifications he received. For him "love" means "people want to talk to me." And therein lies Turkle's main concern—that we are producing a generation of people who experience solitude as loneliness. If "love" is equated with "notifications," it can be a devastating blow to your emotional psyche when your inbox is empty.

While a Marine stationed at Camp Pendleton was telling me about his appreciation for Facebook's chat function, he mentioned a new form of online presencing that helped him determine whether or not he was being "ignored" in Afghanistan. He said, "If the person you want to talk to is online you can message them right away. They get it. Now Facebook has it to where you can tell when that person has opened your message and read it. So that's really beneficial because if someone doesn't respond, you know they're ignoring you."[54] If "love" is being contacted, what does it mean to be "ignored"? What does it mean when someone "has opened your message and read it," but chosen not to respond? In a communication economy built around immediate affective exchange, this can be quite an insult. People have come to expect immediate feedback in order to feel valued. This is an emergent form of emotional dependence.

Social Media's Impact on Mental Processing and Sense Making

The propensity for contact with others moves us away from opportunities for stillness and self-reflection. "In many ways," argues Turkle, "we are forgetting the intellectual and emotional value of solitude. You're not lonely in solitude. You're only lonely if you forget how to use solitude to replenish yourself and to learn."[55] One way to "use" solitude is to sit, reflect, and write. This form of solitude is what Ralph Waldo Emerson, Henry David Thoreau, Margaret Fuller, and other transcendentalists wanted. This is not to say our troops need to move their FOBs to Walden Pond, but that they can carve out opportunities for reflection.

As a remediation of talking, Facebook chat does not offer the stillness and solitude needed for self-reflection. Knopf's analytical survey of war letters suggests that the letter home was a place where warriors could begin to renegotiate their identities. Service members often wrote about how war has changed them, for the better or the worse, and through their writing they attempt to get reacquainted with themselves as they come to terms with how they have changed, and they often brace their loved ones to do the same.

My brother's deployment coincided with a number of dramatic events. While his ship was at sea en route to Kuwait, our grandmother died. That was terribly difficult. But the event that apparently preoccupied the majority of his thoughts was the end of a romantic relationship with a longtime girlfriend. Many of his letters reflected his heartache. In others he wrote about the dreadful realities of war. In the following excerpts it is evident that the act of letter writing enables an opportunity for self-reflection.

[January 27, 2006] This has been a very hard deployment so far and a tremendous emotional strain for me. I am constantly swinging up and down mood-wise: you know how I am with break-ups. It's weird, right when I am reassured that things weren't right and good riddance, etc., the next minute I get depressed.

[January 29, 2006] One of my corpsman lost both of his legs below the knees. He was a passenger in a Humvee that hit a landmine. His legs were crushed and unsalvageable. That really hit home around here for a while. He's back in Bethesda now. Below knee is much better than above knee cause the joint is still in tact.

[February 5, 2006] Being out here really makes me think about love and relationships and makes me question myself. I'm sorry for bludgeoning you with this but you are really the only one I have to talk to. . . . I try not to think about it, but there really isn't much to think about out here. . . . Oh well that's enough of that. Figured I'd write since postage is free for me right now. Those are just some of the thoughts I've been having.

Today, troops aren't writing letters. Does this mean they are missing opportunities to process their experiences? My goal is not to wax poetic about letter writing. Letters, or even the act of writing, are not the only way to engage in self-reflection. My point is simply to suggest that what technology makes easy is not always what nurtures the spirit. In the excerpt above my brother admits, "There really isn't much to think about out here," so he spends his time reflecting.

By contrast today's warriors have a number of social network members to "think about." In his book *What It Is Like to Go to War*, former Marine and Vietnam veteran Karl Marlantes describes how too much access to the home front can be confusing for the war fighter. He writes, "Today a soldier can go out on patrol and kill someone or have one of his friends killed and call his girlfriend . . . and talk about anything except what just happened. And if society itself tries to blur it as much as possible, by conscious well-intended efforts to provide 'all the comforts of home' . . . what chance does your average eighteen-year-old have of not becoming confused?"[56]

Constant contact and immediacy promote a fixation on the "what" of right now, but *not* the "what" of a war zone. Not only does the military's social media policy prohibit personnel from talking about this above all else, but also the more serious activities associated with war would not be considered suitable for discussion on Facebook. Therefore, troops in a war zone end up participating in the give-and-take of casual civilian conversation online. This is not to say that they should be barred from communicating with their social networks. Rather, it is meant to suggest that we should consider the implications of instantaneous and efficient "chatting" from a war zone.

A gunnery sergeant in his late thirties, for example, described his most recent deployment as a veritable gluttony of contact. He compared the level of connection during the 2010 deployment to his previous deployment in 2006.

> My entire family was on Facebook, so I had them all there, and every once in a while I'd catch them, um . . . so they'd be on at the same time so I could—what is it?—IM chat with them. So I was getting real time. Plus you get your phone calls. . . . This time was a lot better with keeping up. It was really rare we went over two weeks and we didn't hear from someone.

The theme of "keeping up" surfaces again here. It resonates with Turkle's notion that when we're texting, on the phone, doing e-mail, or surfing the web, we experience a sensation of being "filled up." Yet feeling full is not necessarily the same as being nourished. Internet researcher danah boyd makes a similar argument when she describes our unhealthy "addiction" to shallow but stimulating communication. She warns, "If we're not careful, we're going to develop the psychological equivalent of obesity. We'll find ourselves consuming content that is least beneficial for ourselves or society as a whole." [57] In the context of war, communication between fronts moved from a one-to-one model marked by the handwritten letter to a *simultaneous* one-to-one model whereby troops can engage in several conversations at once. The latter enables a feeling of satiation without requiring much concentration or commitment.

Increasingly, our socio-technical structures encourage multitasking. In Turkle's words, "We live a contradiction: Insisting that our world is increasingly complex, we nevertheless have created a communications culture that has decreased the time available for us to sit and think, uninterrupted." [58] Recall the interview responses from Marines in war zones who spoke about having five Facebook chat windows open while responding to dozens of Facebook notifications. All this outward communication impedes on our inward stillness of thought. Some things, and I would think war is one of them, aren't amenable to being thought about in conjunction with fifteen other things. Perhaps this is why the Bushido required Japanese samurai to practice a daily meditative art form, such as the tea ceremony or writing haiku. Likewise, Marlantes argues that during combat tours, service members must carve out time to reflect. He writes, "It is through meditative practices that you observe your own mind." [59] We need stillness to process.

This is not to say that the socio-technical structure of social media cannot serve meditative purposes. During my online observations, I witnessed service members using Facebook as a space for communal grieving. After the death of a comrade, some Marines used his Facebook wall as a place to remember their fallen "brother." Each poster used the second person, "you," as if they were speaking to their fallen comrade directly via his Facebook page. This is not uncommon for postmortem wall posts. Using the pronoun "you" reflects both a grieving practice and the communicative norms associated with Facebook. [60] Each of the posts also includes a personal memory, for example, "I will always carry on the saying you told me that night"; "I will never forget giving you your first lager"; or, in a post from someone who recalls their final Facebook conversation, "We were talking on here," suggesting that Facebook is not just *part* of the environment, it is an environment itself. These types of posts not only allow service members to memorialize their fallen comrade but also give them access to his social network, a potential source of understanding and emotional support.

In other cases, service members who suffered severe injuries used their Facebook walls to narrate their experiences for themselves and their social network. Like the letters my brother wrote, these types of posts demonstrate an attempt to make sense of their new identities. The post in figure 6 is from a young Marine who, in his words, "was blown up in Afghanistan."

Figure 6. Anniversary of an accident

He lost both of his legs at the hip and his right arm at the elbow. He wrote the post one year following his accident. At the end he writes, "We are all in this together from the start. I love all of you. I love you too Facebook :)."

His declaration of "love" for Facebook is compelling here. He loves the affordances of the network. It is a voice and an easy method of contact for a relatively immobile person. It is also worthy of note that the post does not necessarily abide by Facebook's cultural conventions. Although he writes in response to Facebook's prompt—"What's on your mind?"—the post represents a yearlong reflection rather than an immediate "status update."

Nor do the previous responses about fallen comrades abide by the conventions associated with Facebook communication. Even graphically, it is easy to see that these types of posts "say" much more than what we typically expect from a status update. Longer posts such as these operate more closely to the way letters functioned for my brother or for the warriors in Knopf's analysis. They offer an opportunity to ruminate.

This chapter and the chapter prior demonstrated that scaring Marines into silence or barring Facebook from the front are not practical solutions to PR control or attention deficit.[61] But figuring out how to temper expectations for constant and immediate contact could make a difference. When I asked a Marine how his deployment would have been different if he hadn't had access to Facebook, he laughed and said, "I would have gotten more work done." This is a sentiment that resonates with many of us. Social media can pull us out of context: filling out Excel sheets one minute and chatting about weekend plans the next. But in the context of combat, "work" can be a matter of life and death. Lance Corporal Sutton described the discomfort he felt having "one foot over there and one foot here." It is an interesting conundrum really. Now that we have become hyperconnected, how do we recover a sense of healthy distance? This will be the unique challenge faced by this generation of warriors. What will their transition be like? Will it be more difficult to leave the world of combat behind for a civilian life they never fully left?

CHAPTER 3
Photos from the Field

Lance Corporal Pine's MOS 4641 designates him as a combat photographer. He is a soft-spoken young man who has been serving in the Marine Corps for a little over three years. He said he became a combat photographer, in part, because his father, a former infantry Marine, did not want his son becoming a "grunt" like himself. For Lance Corporal Pine, combat photography was a way for him to "be with the grunts without being a grunt." He deployed to Musa Qala, Afghanistan (with the grunts), from March 2010 to October 2010. During our interview in Okinawa, Lance Corporal Pine and I spoke about the expansion of digital photography in the field. Most US troops, whether their MOS declares it or not, are combat photographers. As a professional combat photographer, however, Lance Corporal Pine is responsible for operational imagery and intelligence imagery, as well as imagery for investigations, research, development, and recruiting.

To train as a professional combat photographer, Lance Corporal Pine attended a three-month photography course at the defense information school in Maryland. There, he learned how to use professional equipment but not necessarily how to take a photograph. Or in other words, it was unclear what, beyond the standard-issue high-resolution Nikons and Canons, distinguished a professional photo from a personal one. As Lance Corporal Pine says, "Before I joined the Marine Corps, my photography was like camera phone stuff." As result, his professional/public photos take on a domestic snapshot quality as he imports many civilian or personal photography practices to the execution of his MOS. Just like his "quick pic" camera phone days, the main subject of Lance Corporal Pine's professional photography is people. He said, "In Afghanistan I mostly took candid shots of other Marines, sometimes children and locals but mostly Marines." He describes the theme of his photography as "behind-the-scenes" images depicting Marines "hanging out" or "goofing off."

Although his professional MOS 4641 supposes a particular value set, Lance Corporal Pine's experience with a camera phone predisposed his photo-making practices. In other words, his MOS indicates a set of professional expectations, but his civilian experiences with camera phone technology informed his style and content. Because the Canon EOS 5D Mark II camera he used during his deployment was property of the Marine Corps, Lance Corporal Pine couldn't immediately share with friends and family

Figure 7. Marines talking to each other

Figure 8. Marine giving thumbs-up

any of the professional photos he took. After he returned, however, he made some of them available on his Facebook page with the requisite US Marine Corps accreditation (see figure 7). His Facebook page also features photos he took during deployment using his personal camera (see figure 8).[1]

The compositional and stylistic features distinguishing Lance Corporal Pine's professional imagery from his personal snapshots lend insight to some of the changing norms and practices with regard to photography and visual style. In both images Lance Corporal Pine focuses on people. Although the technical quality in the first is higher since he is using a more expensive camera with better resolution, the style and affect in both images are causal. Neither signifies "war" as our popular imaginings anticipate it; there are no tanks, trenches, or war-weary infantrymen. Instead, these images conjure a casual, domesticated, almost nonchalant view of combat deployment, especially the personal snapshot (see figure 8) where the photo participants engage an imagined audience. There, the participants smile at the camera, acknowledging their role in the photo-making process. The Marine on the right gives two thumbs up as his rifle hangs by his side. Presumably these Marines (inclusive of the photographer) understand that this image will circulate among a social network. In 2011, around the time Lance Corporal Pine took this photo, 50 percent of all Americans were using social media sites like Facebook. According to the same Pew research study, 76 percent of teenagers use social media, and 93 percent of those teenagers specifically use Facebook.[2]

Recognizing that your (or others') personal photography will likely circulate online is one way the mobile, networked communication environment influences contemporary photography practices. The process of making photos takes into account new audiences and contexts for sharing.[3] During our interview Lance Corporal Pine admitted, "The hardest thing is to document a Marine candidly." He went on to say, "They'll always . . . they're taught to be very aware of the media and cameras. . . . They want to look like, 'Photograph me, I want to be a hard-ass at all times,' but to get them when they're not expecting it is hard. Even me being there with them, as soon as you pull out a camera they start acting for it." This behavior is not unique to Marines. Photography's role in self-presentation and identity management is more prominent than ever before. Casually mugging or clowning for the camera suggests a new relationship to photo making and sharing.

Emergent visual and social practices of digital photography reflect a larger visual shift from what was once called a "Kodak culture," characterized by private images of family life, into a new era of visual discourses marked by ego-centered images of everyday life, or what I refer to as "Facebook culture."[4] Simply put, Facebook's social, cultural, and aesthetic logics are shaping war's visuality on the web. As US troops in a war zone filter their deployment experiences through the collegiate conventions associated with Facebook's visual culture, the visual discourse becomes a paradox of imagery such as two Marines wearing skeleton masks on a FOB in Afghanistan (see figure 9).

The photo's caption to the upper right reads "in Afghanistan." The image depicts two Marines in full digital desert camouflage posing for a picture while wearing skeleton masks. The Marine on the left looks down at his digital camera, either reviewing a photo or getting ready to hand it off

Figure 9. Marines in skeleton masks

to the "shooter." The Marine on the right leans back, turning at the waist to mug for the camera. Marines often refer to the gear in the photo (masks aside) as "Battle Rattle." It suggests that they are prepared for a combat scenario, either outside the wire or there is a high indirect fire threat, meaning mortars or rockets could hit their base at any moment. The silliness and nonchalance captured in the photo seems antithetical to their physical locale, especially a condition of imminent danger. Excepting military personnel, it is safe to assume that most audiences, judging by the rhetoric of the image, would not recognize this as a combat scenario. Photos like this reflect the ways in which our shifting visual repertoire—with emphases on friendship, domesticity, and spontaneity—modifies visual discourses for contemporary war and how those normative representations impact the way service members make meaning of their wartime experiences.

In preparation for writing this book, I reviewed and categorized around 250 digital photos from nine different Facebook photo albums. I read the imagery alongside interview responses about digital photography and online album-making practices. Although Marines' enthusiasm for taking photos varied (ranging from serious amateur photographers to casual camera phone users), they all had something in common: They carried at least one digital camera or camera phone on them at all times. Several Marines said they used the extra grenade pouch in their flak jackets as a camera case. This point illustrates the centrality of digital cameras today. They are now part of a Marine's deployment kit.[5]

In order to access a deeper appreciation for online photo practices, it was important to tune in to the *imagined context* within which the service members think they are operating. Piecing together the imagined context begins with close attention to textual indicators of who the *imagined audience* might be.[6] In other words, a critical reading of an image's form and content can offer clues about its audience. Generally speaking, the nine Facebook albums featured two categories of imagery, and subsequently two imagined audiences. The first category consists of colloquial representations of young adult life (posing with friends, playing games, and wearing costumes). These images speak to a broad, peer-based social network audience. Their style and content closely align with Facebook's visual repertoire. A second category of imagery comprises what Marines refer to as "moto," or motivational imagery. Moto-style imagery suggests a very specific, culture-laden nod to other Marines and military personnel. It is a way for Marines to communicate with and legitimate their wartime experiences to themselves and each other. Moto images include archetypal public representations of war such as guns, tanks, and artillery pieces, as well as more casual, person-centered shots of personnel posing with guns, flexing their muscles, or poking fun at each other.

Historically, service members' personal wartime snapshots rarely cross the threshold into general public consciousness; but when they do, they can cause controversy, outrage, and confusion. The infamous series of inmate abuse photos that originated in the American-run prison at Abu Ghraib are one example. The Abu Ghraib photos are nearly a decade old now. Since their creation, digital photography and social network software have proliferated to such an extent that warrior-produced imagery is becoming commonplace in our public networks. As digital photography scholars Daniel Rubinstein and Katrina Sluis point out, we have entered the age of the "networked image," an era marked by a few key paradigm shifts involving the mass-amateurization of photography and a move from broadcast media monologues to multiple, networked, community dialogues.[7] War is a particularly illuminating vantage point from which to observe this shift since war was, until recently, almost exclusively represented through traditional mass media outlets. Prior to this century, professional practitioners dominated public representations of war. These representations have largely shaped public impression over what war looks like. And although created by amateurs, the Facebook albums also include mass media–style "war" imagery. It appears that warriors draw from the models cast by their mass media predecessors as they try to make sense of and represent their deployment experiences online. Relying on existing public forms is a way to render their experiences intelligible to themselves, each other, and their social networks. In this way, the practice of assembling a photo album is an exercise in self-storytelling. The Marines featured in this book respond to conflicting demands in the condensed, instantaneous storytelling context of social network sites.

In addition to a shift from a broadcast model to a network, the changing nature of war in this century also informs its visual representation. In previous American conflicts there were visual markers of the war's progress—the raising of the flag at Iwo Jima, or the Times Square kiss on V-J Day. But today, would-be visual icons lack the narrative follow-through to become wholly iconic. The image of Saddam Hussein's statue coming down or the photograph of President Bush declaring "Mission Accomplished" on an aircraft carrier could have reached the status of icon if the war's narrative had supported them. Like other eventual icons, their potential in 2003 was only hypothetical. Now those images are iconic for their satire. These wars lack an easily identifiable narrative structure. Without icons or a master narrative to help them organize and make sense of their experiences, US troops produce their own personal markers of the war's progress and regression. A predominant example included in the albums from this study is the genre of photos documenting memorial ceremonies for fallen comrades.

Much like the hardbound albums of the twentieth century, digital albums reveal more about conventions of representation than the subjects featured in them. For the most part, the photographs in the Facebook albums reflect a dialogic tension between conventional representations of war (tanks, guns, and stiff-lipped Marines) and more mundane, everyday imagery (hanging out, playing guitar, listening to MP3 players). Although the images conflate traditional boundaries between professional war photography and personal snapshot photography, they never allow those boundaries to be entirely erased. Instead the albums speak to a much broader cultural archive that includes many types of picture making (professional, personal, digital, snapshot) as well as different codes of representation (news media, video games, Hollywood films) and alternative contexts for presentation (private albums, social network sites, public forums). All this is to say that war fighters have access to the same cultural frameworks as we do. They draw from the same reference points, the same pop culture icons, and the same modes of representation to interpret and make sense of their experiences. In other words, war is knowable only through the vocabularies and discourses available to describe it.[8]

One would think that if war could be described, it could be done through Facebook, a platform that represents a veritable surplus of sharing, an abundance of communication. But in its abundance lies a frustration. Even in excess (and access) there is inability to share. In Okinawa, a Marine who recently returned from Afghanistan described Facebook's multimodal communication platform as offering a piecemeal representation of his deployment. He said, "Even though photos might not entirely do that job . . . um, and Facebook updates might not entirely do that job, it at least gets them [civilian family and friends] a little closer to understanding a little bit of what you're going through while you're over there." The assumption is that "polymedia," the term new media scholars Mirca Madianou and Daniel Miller use to describe this new condition of multiplicity of channels, has the potential to present a fuller "picture" of twenty-first-century combat deployment.[9]

But the content troops post to Facebook reflects a culturally inflected genre of usage. Describing his Facebook photos, Lance Corporal Pine said, "I had a couple with me and my friend smiling or whatever." He went on to say, "They'd [friends and family] see that we were happy but how dirty we were." I asked Lance Corporal Pine what influenced his decision to post these particular images. He responded, "So they could see I'm all right. I still have a smile on my face even though I'm hatin' life, you know? Like, 'This really sucks but I'm doin' all right.'" In many ways Lance Corporal Pine's response reminded me of Lance Corporal Sutton, who said he felt like he had "one foot over there and one foot here." In his interview, Lance Corporal Pine described a similar duality. With one foot he is tired, dirty, and "hatin' life," and with the other he is participating in a domestic social space where he strikes a pose and smiles for the camera so that his imagined audience feels reassured.

Lance Corporal Pine's personal Facebook photos emphasize a happy-go-lucky social life, the prevailing theme inherent to Facebook's emergent aesthetic, and one that becomes more calcified as Facebook becomes the most popular picture-sharing site in the world.[10] The texture of war's visual archive begins to change when service members participate in Facebook's visual culture, uploading their deployment photos in accordance with existing norms. The new visual discourse for war contributes to a sense of disorientation.

A New Type of Snapshot: From Kodak to Facebook

Before I describe how social media culture modifies war's visual representation on the web, I want to trace some of the larger visual shifts in snapshot photography. Much of the existing literature on the evolution of snapshot photography points out that since the 1990s, and even more so since the beginning of the new millennium, cameras have increasingly served as tools for mediating everyday experience, not just rituals or ceremonial moments.[11] In the early days of digital photography, the new technology simulated and mimicked professional photographic procedures and conventions.[12] But today, as camera phone technology and social network software become ubiquitous, digital snapshots have developed their own stylistic norms and functions in line with contemporary network culture and the changing social functions of digital photography. To be sure, digital photography, mobile messaging, and social network software have contributed to the expansion of subjects deemed photo worthy, with more emphasis on the everyday and banal. But it is not just the technology that transforms practice. An accompanying sociocultural revolution with new communication values and literacies also inform what we like to show, share, and see online.

Just as Kodak advertisements shaped the cultural frames through which we interpreted our lives in the twentieth century, new discourses surrounding the use and function of digital photography produce a similar framing effect. According to cultural historian Nancy West, Kodak advertisements produced particular assumptions about the purpose of snapshots and defined the appropriate subjects for recording. Kodak culture provided a structured and patterned way of looking at the world, a framework for understanding how a "real world" gets transformed into a symbolic one.[13] By constructing picture taking as an activity devoted to preserving memory, West argues that Kodak's campaigns *changed the way people experienced events*. According to West, "Kodak taught amateur photographers to apprehend their experiences and memories as objects of nostalgia." The ability to take and keep snapshots allowed people "to arrange their lives in such a way that painful or unpleasant aspects were systematically erased."[14] The emphasis on the positive aspects of life is still prevalent in digital photography, but the *rate* at which we capture, render, and share images has increased exponentially.

Internet access ratchets up the rate of interpretive processes. Practically speaking, we produce and digest "memories" in real time. Recording an event has become part of the event, maybe even the most important part.[15] In Turkle's words, "People become alienated from their own experience and anxious about watching a version of their lives scrolling along faster than they can handle. They are not able to keep up with the unedited version of their lives, but they are responsible for it."[16] Social networks generate a compulsion to visibility that impacts a person's sensory experience of an event. Digital anthropologist Daniel Miller argues that the act of broadcasting an experience to a social network has now become central to the very experience itself. He argues that people don't feel like they are actually on vacation unless they see photographs of themselves enjoying that vacation and what is more, people don't seem to feel they have had an experience of an event unless they have broadcast it to their social networks.[17] Internal interpretive processes now require external validation and acknowledgment.

Even beyond the context of war, social media encourage an almost un-natural self-awareness, asking users to process their experiences instanta-neously, and to package life as they live it.[18] A quicker metabolism of thought is becoming second nature to a generation who has become accustomed to being "on" all the time. The process of digesting an experience now in-cludes a filter. Today we are thinking through the generalized other more than ever before. In this way, the biographical narratives constituting the Facebook deployment albums can be read as acts of deliberate improvisa-tion. They are necessarily polysemic, offering an edited mix of available meanings because they must make sense to a variety of audiences.[19]

In the space of social networking, the self is encapsulated both visu-ally and textually and is meant to serve as an indicator of a person's lived experience. In her interview research about mobile and social media uses, Turkle argues that the self has become externally manufactured rather than internally developed. The self has become a series of profiles to be sculpted and refined in response to public opinion. Turkle writes, "On Twitter or Facebook you're trying to express something real about who you are but because you're also creating something for others' consumption, you find yourself imagining and playing to your audience more and more. So those moments in which you're supposed to be showing your true self become a performance."[20] This vocabulary of inward/outward and authentic/con-trived marks my point of departure from Turkle. Humans have always understood themselves relative to a generalized other. We make meaning of ourselves through the eyes of "society." The difference now is that the feedback loop has changed. The "public" is more expansive, and we take more perspectives into account (e.g., the nightmare reader), but it's not like we were "more real" before Facebook or Twitter. Online social network-ing changes the discourses on "real" or "authentic." Turkle's concern is that the externalization of every thought (via status updates or tweets) will result in a lack of "in"-sight. By contrast I am optimistic that our insights can become more inclusive of a diversified generalized other. So, in my view, the good news is we are more inclined to think about others and take a multiplicity of perspectives into account when we communicate online. The concern, however, is that the logic of the lowest common denominator, inspired by "the nightmare reader," has a homogenizing effect where our messages become "safe" and diluted.

Today even the most mundane encounters with daily living find ex-pression on our social networks (see figure 10). In her work on digital imagery and photo sharing Susan Murray describes an emergent "every-day aesthetic" in contemporary snapshot photography. She argues, "It has become less about the special or rarefied moments of domestic living and

Figure 10. Field toilet

more about an immediate, rather fleeting, display and collection of one's discovery and framing of small and mundane."[21] Murray attributes this emerging aesthetic to the faster pace of content creation and dissemination. The integration of mobile internet technology with picture and text messaging allows for an image with caption attached to be posted on a website within seconds of the image being taken. Murray argues that we have moved away from the photograph as an "embalmer of time" toward "a more alive, immediate, and often transitory, practice/form."[22] This new form of snapshot photography introduces a host of stylistic conventions distinguishing the twenty-first-century digital snapshot from its Kodak-era kin.

Prior to this century's revolution in photo practices, an image of a Marine in Afghanistan using a makeshift toilet, or "wag bag" as it's called in the field, would likely not have been photographed let alone included in an album. Yet "toilet pics," predominantly images of young, oftentimes intoxicated, women caught with their pants down have been identified as an emergent genre of digital photography among college-aged social media users.[23] According to Christopher Mussello's description of twentieth-century snapshot photography, most people "would not consider it appropriate to photograph everyday events" since the subject matter for personal Kodak-era photography consisted mostly of "special events and people. . . . Daily events such as cleaning, eating, watching television, or rising and dressing in the morning are not shown."[24] But changes in technology and photography's new visually communicative function have altered what qualifies as photo worthy. Now people post photos of cats, dogs, babies, food, and intimate aspects of their personal life no matter how banal or inconsequential.[25]

The style of photography characteristic of Web 2.0 platforms reveals our zeitgeist. As visual scholar Wendy Kozol argues, photography "encodes social norms and privileges certain perspectives on a historical moment."[26] Evidently we live in a moment where there is a great deal of public interest in seeing photographs that were traditionally considered private. Risto Sarvas and David Frohlich point to our fascination with reality television shows as indicative of this trend. They write, "some images that would not necessarily have had public appeal a few decades ago might be interesting to a large audience today."[27] Similarly, new media scholars Michael Stefanone and Derek Lackoff describe a substantial congruence between Web 2.0's culture of personal self-disclosure and the "reality culture" dominating much of the television market.[28] So it would seem that not only do we have access to images formerly considered private, but we also have an interest in seeing them. The emphasis on sharing and the accessibility of personal snapshots to broader, more loosely connected audiences is arguably the largest transformation in photography practices today.

Sharing Is Caring

The nature of social media photo sharing inspires a level of performativity markedly different from the practices associated with twentieth-century coffee-table albums. In her examination of Western digital photography's changing roles and functions, José van Dijck argues that photography always served as an instrument of communication and a means of sharing experience but convergent mobile technology speeds up the metabolism of thought and action.[29] For one thing, digital is easy to copy. During an interview in Okinawa, an infantry sergeant said, "I never printed anything out. The platform is digital. I'm not saying actual photos are going out of style, but they kind of are. Because now I can like e-mail bomb the same ten photos to fifty different people." In the networked reality of people's everyday life, the default mode of personal photography becomes sharing. As the Okinawa infantry sergeant describes, sharing in one sense refers to distribution. He can "e-mail bomb the same ten photos to fifty different people." But in another sense of the word, sharing also has to do with communication, as in sharing feelings, emotions, or ideas (see figure 11). According to new media scholar Nicholas John, the context of Web 2.0 makes the most utility of this second sense of sharing: *sharing as telling.*[30]

Figure 11. Marine wearing "Iraq sucks" T-shirt

Similarly, Tim Kindberg, Mirjana Spasojevic, Rowanne Fleck, and Abigail Sellen's research finds that young people take less interest in sharing photos as *objects* than in sharing them as *experiences*.[31]

The emphasis on sharing immediate encounters with everyday life changes the style and content of snapshot photography. Caitlin McLaughlin and Jessica Vitak's research on Facebook's social norms describes Facebook imagery as largely ego centered, depicting users and their friends at social events and on vacations.[32] Although it may be more ego centered, snapshot photography has historically strived to capture joyful moments of celebration rather than negative aspects of life "such as pain, death, anger, and sorrow."[33] The context of war, however, complicates an emphasis on positive, life–affirming social events. Although going to war is certainly a significant life event, and one that can be framed positively through visual appeals to patriotism, sacrifice, and honor, it can also be a traumatic and sometimes fatal event that does not adhere to snapshot photography's accentuation on the positive. Another complicating factor is that deployment to a theater of war is an elongated event compared to snapshot photography's other subject matter, which typically includes shorter duration episodes such as vacations, birthday parties, weddings, and family reunions.[34]

Networked Audiences

Networked systems such as Facebook enable new presentational contexts for personal pictures.[35] Photos once intended to remain in personal archives increasingly enter the public domain through social networks. Some photography scholars such as Sarvas and Frohlich have already begun to mourn "the death of the album."[36] But I see no cause for mourning. Instead I would argue that albums get more play today than they ever did, thanks to advances in technology. It is much easier and cost-effective to create an album today—no more expensive printing, or cumbersome albums and sticky pages. Instead digital photographers can upload, edit, label, caption, and post photos into an online album within minutes. Perhaps it is a perceived hastiness in album creation that causes Sarvas and Frohlich to mourn. But again, I argue that new contexts for sharing are an add-on, a reflection of emergent cultural attitudes and values, rather than a replacement. It is easier to share our personal photos today, and we like doing it.

Much of the existing literature on personal photography, especially on photo albums, focuses on the images people present in the more private settings of the home. And scant social network site research treats photos beyond acknowledging them as elements of self-presentation.[37] Although some scholars have paid attention to the sociality of digital photography on social network and photo-sharing sites, there is a notable lack of scholarship on online album creation.[38] My work builds on existing literature by examining what new media scholar Patricia Lange describes as the "publicly private" use of personal photo albums on Facebook. Lange's compound expressions "publicly private" and "privately public" refer to the amount of identity information imparted by authors (the first half of the compound expression) and the available physical access to the media content (the second half of the compound).[39] Following Lange's distinctions, Facebook photo albums are publicly private because author identification and profile information are available, but the content they create is available only to a closed network of friends and family. In contrast, YouTube content is available to anyone, but the identity of the author remains relatively hidden. A reason to focus on Facebook photo albums as opposed to profile pictures or broad gallery collections is because albums are traditionally thought of as private media. The purpose of an album is to organize photos to share with invited visitors in the home. But the quasi-public domain of a social network site means that a handful of "visitors" are now hundreds of Facebook "friends."[40]

To be sure, the hybrid space of the internet muddies the water of context and complicates the audience question. As argued in the previous chapter, social network sites flatten multiple audiences into one, a phenomenon Marwick and boyd refer to as "context collapse."[41] This concept speaks to the coexistence of "ideal readers" and "nightmare readers" in the same social space causing communication in networked environments to operate in response to the lowest common denominator. This means that users create content for the most sensitive audience members.[42] Many of the Marines I interviewed cited their mothers as the "nightmare readers" for their deployment photos. They spoke about carefully selecting images that were "safe for mom" and would not cause her discomfort or alarm. In an interview at Okinawa with a Marine who deployed to Afghanistan in 2010, he described two primary audiences for his photography—his parents and other military personnel. The way he speaks about his Facebook photos suggests that he imagines other Marines as "ideal" readers and his parents as "nightmare" readers. In his words, "Anything that I knew my parents thought was a dangerous situation, I maybe took a photo of it, or several photos of it, I just didn't share it. So like if I thought that a background, they might think was a less than safe place, I didn't send it to them. Depending on what the photo was I might send it to some people but not to others." I asked if the "some people" he was willing to share his "less than safe" looking pictures with were other Marines. He said, "Yes and maybe other military service members but not my parents." The Marine describes an awareness of multiple audiences, distinguishing between two "types" of potential viewers.

Visualizing War on the Web

The Facebook photo albums featured in this book are audience-centered texts. They reflect a pastiche of existing modes of representation. Characterized on the one hand by familiar, traditional, and synecdochic representations of war with emphases on guns, gear, and artillery, the Facebook albums also feature more colloquial representations of young adult life in line with Facebook culture's visual repertoire. Service members' photo albums effectively participate in a rich, complex visual archive. In doing so, they represent a publicly inflected private media. As visual anthropologist Richard Chalfen argues, "Ordered collections . . . repeatedly [tell] the same 'stories' according to some master scenario" as they "deliver culturally significant tales and myths about ourselves to ourselves."[43] Private pictures are entangled within and influenced by larger cultural stories about community, family, and gender, or, in the case of this book, cultural stories about war.

People choose objects to shoot based on their cultural schemata.[44] In other words, we see things using conventional notions. We even tend to view abstract or artistic images in terms of ordinary understanding. To communicate an abstraction like war, then, it would need to be photographed according to visual discourses already in existence. This is how private pictures come to reaffirm "culturally structured values."[45] In this regard, Facebook photo albums documenting a combat deployment are particularly complex. They rely on an intricate threading of professional war imagery—a public medium—through the private medium of personal snapshot photography. What is more, their presentational context is a publicly private communication platform. In the following section, I examine the production of online albums as a sense-making ritual where personnel situate their war experiences within the everyday discourse characteristic of Facebook culture. I attend to both the content and processes of production carefully, tacking back and forth between specific textual details and the "big picture." The goal is to understand how deployed personnel might use this particular visual space to make meaning of their wartime experiences.[46]

The Facebook Aesthetic on the Battlefield

A majority of the photos in the albums depict participants mugging for the lens, posing with friends, causally hanging out, or goofing off. Participants in the photos are usually physically close and interacting with the camera in some way. Informal behavior and physical closeness suggest the primacy of human relationships. These types of images represent Facebook's association with youth culture. Owing to the accessibility of this subject pool for most media scholars at large land-grant universities, the existing literature on social media centers mostly on college students' uses and gratifications. Mapped onto another college-aged population—service members deployed in Iraq and Afghanistan—it is not surprising that many of their photos adopt a similar aesthetic and that they use their photos for similar purposes. Andrew Mendelson and Zizi Papacharissi's analysis of college students' Facebook photo galleries suggests that the photos therein allow college students to speak to each other visually and play out their college lives for each other. According to Mendelson and Papacharissi, these photos establish proof of an "authentic" college experience, one filled with friends and the rituals of college life such as drinking, sports, and the closeness of a peer group.[47]

The young Marines featured in this book illuminate productive differences from their collegiate kin. Although their age range might be similar, Marines on deployment represent a group with fairly rigid institutional identities existing in a geographically and ideologically distant context. Their interaction with Facebook from a theater of war represents a clash of cultures, events, and modes of representation. Facebook's emphasis on carefree college life appears antithetical to the existing visual episteme of war. So when Marines participate in Facebook's cultural repertoire from a theater of war, rather than a college campus, the resulting photographic archive includes a visual discourse unique to this generation of warrior. For example, I identified two forms of imagery that particularly reflect norms we associate with social media visual culture. The first is a new style of posing with comrades, and the second is the self-shot photo, the selfie.

The Buddy Pose

Posing with buddies has been a long-standing fixture in warrior-produced imagery since the American Civil War (see figure 12). The images depicted in the Facebook albums, however, reveal a new form of the buddy pose. Visual media scholar David Perlmutter argues that during the Civil War, battlefield photography was a way for individual soldiers to "own a vision of war (or warriorhood) for the first time in history and that vision's implicit message was one of camaraderie." In many ways, argues Perlmutter, those images of camaraderie served as "a metonym for the most positive experience of the war."[48] According to the online Facebook albums I saw, visual representations of camaraderie remain a mainstay for this generation. A key difference, however, is that Facebook culture's emphasis on parties and social experiences promotes an iteration of the buddy shot wherein the focus shifts to capturing a fun-filled social moment more than the relationship among comrades.[49] As one can imagine, it would be rather difficult for service personnel in a war zone to replicate a visual style that emphasizes a happening social life. Nevertheless, they do their best to adhere to Facebook's visual norm.

The image in figure 13 depicts a group of Marines clowning around in front of the camera. Most of them are in full combat gear, evidently preparing to go out on patrol or just returning from one. The Marine in the far back appears to be singing or shouting with outstretched arms. In

Figure 12. Comrades posing arm in arm

Figure 13. Marines performing for the camera

front of him, a Marine holds a cigar to his mouth. In the front row we see a Marine playing air guitar, and a Marine extending both middle fingers as the Marine to his immediate left embraces him. In the far back right corner we can see a Marine lifting his leg in the air and smiling broadly. The style and content of this image are jovial. The participants' physical proximity to one another and unencumbered outward expression suggests intimacy and friendship. But the central feature in this image is the social scene. The exaggerated "fun" in this photo emphasizes its performative quality. As sociologist Erving Goffman argues, the very act of photography inspires performance: "People give a 'performance' when they allow themselves to be photographed, in the sense that they make allowance for a public that will ultimately see the photograph."[50] It is more than likely, as Lance Corporal Pine pointed out during his interview, that the aim of the camera initiated the rock star posturing depicted in this image.

Because photos play a large role in the way we present our identities online, we transform ourselves before the camera in order to portray a particular version of ourselves to our social network.[51] In an interview at Camp Pendleton, a very young-looking lance corporal who had just returned from his first tour in Afghanistan smiled as he talked about his deployment album. "I think my Afghan album is funny," he chuckled to himself. "It shows that we like to have fun even in 140-degree weather. You know, like a 'work hard, play hard' kinda thing." The goal of "showing" that they "like to have fun" in even the most dire of circumstances aligns with the ways in which people use social network sites to present aspects of themselves to their "friends." As Mendelson and Papacharissi argue, "These expressions can simultaneously express uniqueness and connection to others."[52] For military personnel, uniqueness resides in their physical locale (e.g., "140-degree weather"), but at the same time they express connection and similarity with others by showing that they too have a fun and vibrant social life. The twenty-first-century buddy pose is a hypersocial iteration that depicts squad members actively posing for the camera to create some sort of social scene. Sometimes they smile, make silly faces, give the finger, or perform other lewd gestures.

Another compositional format unique to this era of social media war imagery is the self-shot, where the photographer holds the camera out to capture himself and, at times, his comrades. This style of image, often called a "selfie," has become increasingly prevalent in personal digital snapshot photography. Digital cameras allow for immediate review, deletion, and recapture. Consequently there is less risk involved trying to reach out and take a picture of oneself. Owing to its relative "newness," this style of photography practice and posing is distinctively "youthful."[53] We rarely overhear young people in campus bars or on tourist vistas saying, "That's going to be a good one" because the concept of waiting for film development is lost on them.

Selfies

The self-shot image is a good example of photography's shifting cultural practices. Photography scholar Madeline Jenks argues that "people use these selfies to document moments of their lives and share quick updates with their friends and family."[54] In a similar vein, Barbara Harrison's ethnographic study of how people connect personal photos to memory and narration found that self-presentation rather than family presentation is the major function of photos today. She describes a shift from the personal photo being bound up with memory to its role in identity formation.[55] Today, personal photography plays more of a role in the affirmation of personhood and personal bonds than it does in the documentation of family life.

Figure 14 is a self-shot image of a Marine inside of an MRAP, a mine-resistant ambush protected vehicle. The designed purpose of an MRAP is to survive IED attacks and ambushes. In spite of the context requiring the MRAP and his Kevlar helmet, the Marine presents himself with a smile. In the comment box to the right of the image we see a message presumably from a romantic partner saying, "☺ This smile will always cheer me up baby I LOVE YOU!!!!!" The Marine who posted the image responds one minute later with "I know I smiled for you. ☺" The nearly live communication initiated by this photo, and the selfie genre more generally, serve as

January 15, 2012

in a MRAP — with

Like · Comment · Share

likes this.

This smile will always cheer me
up baby I LOVE YOU!!!!
January 15, 2012 at 11:05pm · Like

Lovin the goggles ;D
January 15, 2012 at 11:06pm · Like

i know i smiled for you.
January 15, 2012 at 11:06pm · Like

muah
January 15, 2012 at 11:13pm via mobile ·

Write a comment...

Figure 14. Selfie in an MRAP

evidence that sharing (in the sense of telling) is the primary communicative function for digital photos in the internet age. The instantaneous nature of these postings influences their content insofar as there is a degree of spontaneity and immediacy to the image—a desire to capture and share the moment.

Within Facebook's fast-paced communication economy, images are as fleeting as the ephemeral moments they capture. Given the speed of exchange, comments tend to occur instantly before the "moment" is passed and the image becomes obsolete. This is in comparison to older photo practices, where the context for the image remains relatively fixed. A photograph in a twentieth-century album is a timeless artifact. Its historical context feels more fixed. In a digital world, *we exchange images as experiences*. The selfie signifies both technological and sociocultural evolution. It speaks to photography's growing role in identity affirmation, documentation, and verification.

The next major genre of imagery consists of "moto" photos. Conceived of as a subculture's selfie, moto photos are a way for troops to affirm bonds with one another, present themselves, and communicate their experiences in ways they would like to be seen and understood. Moto photos rely on widely understood cultural expectations for what war (and warriors) should look like. Generally speaking, moto photos depict a stiff upper lip. Perhaps surprisingly, the primary intended audience for moto imagery is other Marines or service members. Exchanging moto imagery is a cultural practice that has been around for decades, but because of social network software, moto imagery has gained broader audiences. Many Marines describe the practice itself as having increased in popularity because of the availability of digital photo technology. But perhaps another reason moto imagery has taken a greater hold among contemporary US troops is because the wars in Iraq and Afghanistan are so complex that performing moto is a way for them to authenticate and legitimize their deployments to themselves, each other, and their social networks.

Moto Photos

Making up nearly half of the photos in the albums, moto shots constitute the largest category of imagery. As one Marine sergeant in Okinawa explained, a moto shot is "any picture of you in gear looking badass." For the most part, the participants in the photograph are posed, and, as the sergeant went on to explain, "Almost 90 percent, if there is gear involved and no one is smiling, it's a moto shot." These types of images boost morale for the participants, but many of the Marines I spoke with also said the reason they take moto shots is "for the guys in the rear," the personnel who have yet to deploy. Beyond a handful of photographs depicting artillery hardware itself, the majority of these photos show personnel informally posing with their guns or casually engaging with them in some way. After I learned the term "moto," I asked a gunnery sergeant in Okinawa about this type of image. He said, "Oh yeah, you know grab your gun, flex, grab your Ka-Bar, flex."[56] These images differ from buddy poses because the positioning of the guns, Ka-Bars, grenades, and so on suggests that the *weapons*, rather than the people, are the central focus.

Like most personal photographs, the images depicted in figures 15 and 16 reflect a level of interaction between the subjects and the photographer. In snapshots like these, particularly in the context of a combat zone, one can assume the photographer and subjects know one another intimately. Furthermore, as the buddyhood photos demonstrate, photography is a social activity where participants commonly share a goal of making photos that emphasize how they would like to be seen. Most participants pose directly for the lens, looking straight ahead, highly aware of being photographed. The intimate social process of making these types of images both reflects and shapes their intended audiences.

The moto image falls in line with photography's verification goals. Civilian family members, "the guys in the rear," and peer groups within the social network likely imagine guns and other weaponry to be an important aspect of the war experience. It follows, then, that personnel would want to visually enact those expectations. Not only is this a way to verify their experience to others, but it also allows them to make sense of and authenti-

Figure 15. Group moto photo

Figure 16. Marines posing in a moto photo

cate their own experiences to each other and themselves. While these types of moto images tend to highlight martial superiority, they also emphasize a sociality in line with the norms of Facebook culture, through the physical closeness of participants, their interaction with the photographer, and the friendly banter in accompanying captions and/or commentary.

The composition and content of digital photos, especially in the presentational context of social network sites, are tools for conversation and peer-group building. According to the interviews, service members emphasize

Figure 17. "Look at you all moto"

photography's documentary function by claiming that they value photos as permanent records of their lives. But their behaviors on Facebook and some of the more indirect interview responses show that photos serve as part of a conversation, a way of speaking to each other visually and verifying their experiences. Sidebar commentary from comrades, and to a lesser extent friends and family, confirms social bonds.

In figure 17 we see a stiff-lipped Marine in full gear wearing dark red–tinted sunglasses standing in front of a Humvee. His arms rest on the ammo pouch strapped to his chest. Just above his hands you can see the butt of a pistol emerging from its holster. The first comment posted in the side bar, presumably from another Marine reads, "Look at you all moto." Referencing the well-known culturally specific genre of representation is a way for the poster to demonstrate his insider knowledge. He may also be poking fun at the participant in the image. The tone of his comment, "Look at you all moto," could have been a condescending jab as in, "Look at you all dolled up."

In keeping with archetypal representations of war, all the moto photos contain a masculine inflection. In a literal sense, nearly all the participants in the photos were men. Women were marginal, if present at all. This is an authentic reflection of my interview pool, the US military demographics, and the fact that women serving on deployment were usually relegated to supportive roles in the rear echelon.[57] Until 2013, women were restricted from serving in combat roles.[58] Beyond the literal gender disparity, in favor of men, the Facebook photos also performed a hegemonic masculinity at the semiotic and ideological levels as well. The military has always been stereotyped as a bastion of masculinity.

The Marine Corps especially conjures an image of elite brotherhood.[59] In his autobiographical war memoir *One Bullet Away: The Making of a Marine Officer*, Nathaniel Fick writes that "hardness" was the supreme virtue among Marines. "The greatest compliment one could pay to another," writes Fick, "was to say he was hard. Hardness wasn't toughness, nor was it courage, although both were part of it. Hardness was the ability to face an overwhelming situation with aplomb, smile calmly at it, and then triumph through sheer professional pride."[60] Most of the images in the Facebook albums, particularly the moto shots, which constituted the majority, performed this hardness.

A growing bulk of communication scholarship examines impression management and the role of performativity in social media presentations of the self.[61] Some of the literature considers the role of audience, particularly the way(s) in which users assemble a networked self and perform to a variety of actual and imagined audiences and publics.[62] The practice of assembling a photo album is an exercise in self-storytelling. The Marines who create these albums participate in an autobiographical performance that reflexively employs performativity to traverse from private to public, but also potentially from the personal to the political or from the individual to the collective, and back.[63]

The consistent use of military acronyms, nicknames, references to inside jokes or past events, statements of affection, and occasional teasing reinforce group cohesiveness and belonging. Moreover, the context of friendship (as in Facebook "friends") allows for statements that those outside of the social group, or who lack the requisite cultural knowledge, would find offensive.[64] The image in figure 18 shows a Marine holding a grenade and sticking out his tongue.

The caption reads, "POG!!!!" The acronym stands for "person other than grunt." A Marine sergeant twice deployed to Iraq and stationed in Okinawa during our interview explained the social function of the term. He said, "There are subcommunities in the Marine Corps . . . a big separation between grunts and POGs. A POG is kind of a derogatory word we use because grunts think we're better than everyone else."[65] The album creator tagged two people along with the word "grenade," which serves to personify the grenade and/or dehumanize the POG. One network member clicked "like" beneath the photo, and a third person commented, "DAMN FUCKING STRAIGHT," suggesting agreement over the POG label. Since other Marines constitute the primary imagined audience for moto imagery, a full interpretation usually requires insider knowledge.

Figure 18. The POG and the grenade

Sidebar comments also allow participants to relive the pictured events, emphasizing the shared experience. The image in figure 19, for example, depicts a Marine engaged in a firefight. This photograph is representative of a related moto subgenre, which reflects a less exaggerated, less hypermasculine style. It is an action shot, reflecting what war media scholar Michael Griffin would consider "frontline" (as opposed to "backstage") activity. It also more closely aligns with mainstream representations of war.[66] The album's author writes in the commentary box, "Im actually getting shot at during this picture, its crazy because I didn't realize I even had this picture for a long time. I wonder who took this photo?" He goes on to write in a follow-up post, "I cant remember who that was on the roof with me that day either." According to the commentary's time stamp, two hours later someone responds with, "I took this picture bro, it was the day that hellfire hit real close." The original author responds within moments (twelve minutes later), writing, "Oh yeah I forgot. I got a close up front seat on that roof too. It was pretty awesome." Snapshots help us affirm our identities within social groups, they provide documentary evidence in service to our memories, and they communicate cultural values and ideals.

The photograph in figure 19 and the accompanying exchange reinforce a number of the themes touched on so far. First, they highlight the process of picture making as a significant component to experiencing the event. Second, the composition of the image and the accompanying commentary, particularly the reference to "hellfire," authenticate expectations of a traditional "war experience." And third, they offer an opportunity for conversa-

Figure 19. An action shot

tion and strengthening of social bonds. These themes fall in line with those of Sarvas and Frohlich, who argue the three values of snapshots are their contributions to identity, memory, and communication.[67]

Although the subjects in the photo are comrades and the comments emphasize human relationships, I categorized images like this one as "motivational" because the Marine positioned on the wall is actively engaged with the enemy and the upward angle presents a power dynamic situating the viewer in a position to admire his courageous defense.[68] These visual tropes align more closely with the conventional representations of war found in traditional news media coverage. I also categorized this style of image as "motivational" because the personnel I interviewed described a sense of satisfaction derived from both creating and reviewing these types of images. One Marine said, "Even though media representations are distorted, the closer we get to those representations, the better they [social network members] can relate." He went on to say, "[It] makes us feel better—the myth is where we get some of the satisfaction." The composition of the photos in figure 20 and figure 21 draw on iconic imagery of war.

Similar to the image in figure 19, which depicts American "watchmen on the wall," the images in figure 20 and figure 21 reflect and refract our collective consciousness about war. They look like scenes from a movie and serve a motivational function for other personnel because they fulfill cultural expectations for what war should look like. This is especially important since US involvement in Iraq and Afghanistan has been a confusing melodrama from the start, publicly criticized for its costs, legality, con-

Figure 20. Marines lining a wall

Figure 21. Marines on a hilltop

sequences, and impact.[69] Civilian audiences also find these images to be pleasing since they do not challenge popular imaginings of war.

According to my interviews and online observations, the primary cultural function for moto photos, however, is not to satisfy civilian audiences. Rather, moto photos are for the personnel themselves to verify and authenticate their war experience. To do so, they turn to existing visual discourses of war. And for many young Marines, some of the most popular visual discourses they have access to are war-themed video games. Even if they don't play video games themselves, the video game aesthetic has become more prevalent in recent news media war coverage,[70] not to mention the fact that the military often uses video games for recruiting and training purposes.[71] As figures 22–25 demonstrate, the composition bears an uncanny resem-

Figure 22. Video game screen capture

Figure 23. Video game aesthetic

blance to some of the most popular war-themed video games. Mimicking the style of presentation found in some of the most popular video games like the Call of Duty series (see figure 22) helps troops legitimize their deployments to themselves and their social network.[72]

If there is any doubt that their experiences in Iraq or Afghanistan are authentic, these images provide reassurance that what they are doing

Figure 24. First-person shooter video game simulation

Figure 25. First-person shooter

sure looks a lot like "war" as our popular imaginings would have it. Evan Wright, author of *Generation Kill*, argues that many of today's war fighters were raised in an "ultraviolent culture" of warfare films and video games.[73] Indeed, much of the digital imagery they produce mirrors their popular culture counterparts, yet they do not share the bulk of these images online, because they want to protect the sensibilities of their network members. As an infantry Marine explained, "There's a certain type of censorship that we would . . . uhm kinda buffer for the stuff back home. We're not gonna send certain images back home. We're gonna send everything back home that makes everyone feel, you know, kinda good about what we're doing." He went on to say, "We're not trying to scare anybody. We wouldn't send pictures of firefights, because they don't need to see that, especially while we're still over there." His comments indirectly reference Marwick and boyd's concept of "the nightmare reader." The idea that he is acutely aware of how his images could be interpreted by the most sensitive audience members speaks to a new level of self-consciousness introduced by the social network era. What ends up appearing in these albums, then, is a pastiche of Facebook-friendly visions of war.

When I asked a corporal in Okinawa who had just returned from deployment in Herat Province, Afghanistan, to describe the theme of his Facebook photography, he said it was "personal" and "not military related" because he didn't want to post anything that would "benefit the enemy." He made a specific reference to OPSEC, which makes me think that the institutional pressures I discussed earlier coalesce with the visual norms of Facebook in fascinating ways. Chapter 1 demonstrated how social media policy expects Marines to be twenty-four-hour PR agents for the Corps. Marines achieve this by visually omitting the professional side of their war experience. In other words, as this Marine describes, his Facebook imagery is "personal." He said, "I put up pictures of me smiling at salsa night." When I asked him how he imagined his social network might interpret his photos, he said, "Sometimes they can say, 'Whoa, were you on vacation?' because I only posted stuff I had fun in. I was always smiling, you know, I never posted anything of the bad stuff on Facebook." Avoiding the "bad," "risky," "dark," or "revealing" images of war was a common theme among participants and reflects one of the ways Marines manage their identities online.

Like their collegiate counterparts, Marines primarily take and post photos to share with each other. It allows them to compare and/or legitimize their wartime experiences and to gain a sense of "perspective." An infantry sergeant who deployed to Iraq and was stationed in Okinawa at the time of our interview said:

It's for perspective. Just say my squad went out and did something, and you know second squad went out on foot patrol and did something. I wanna see where they went. I wanna see what they did. We can talk about it, but I want to see it. If first squad went out and got to meet people in this village or that village . . . like there were other villages I never even got to go to because that was second platoon or the mobile section that would go out there. Once we would get back [to the patrol base] and people are telling war stories. . . . We always tell war stories to each other. I'd go to my buddy like, "Hey man, what was it like wherever the hell you were." And he'd say, "Oh man, well I got pictures right here."

This commentary is significant for a few reasons. First the Marine describes a desire to "see" as many fragments of "the war" as possible. Anyone can tell a war story, but as he says, "I want to see it." He is reflexive about his limited perspective, recognizing that other platoons and other sections experience deployment differently. But he also shows an interest in learning those perspectives. He said, "There were other villages I never even got to go to." Later in the interview he said that his desire to take and post photos came from the idea of "knowing you are part of history and you're trying to piece it together as you go."[74] Small units of squads and platoons carry out patrols. These patrols are a part of a mission. Missions make up operations. And war is an amalgamation of operations and offensives.

Framed this way, it is easy to see the network structure of war. Their "mission" is not just on the ground, and they express a responsibility to represent that mission for others. In this interview, the Marine sergeant recognizes his contribution to the larger picture of war. Social network sites, made up of a constellation of individuals, present similar opportunities to acknowledge interdependency by prompting users to imagine a broad canvas of mutual relationships and to situate themselves as part of a historic, ever-evolving web. Just as it is for Marines on a patrol base, sharing experiences is part of the social economy on Facebook.

Although album creators appear to organize their albums chronologically from oldest to newest, they generally lack an overarching narrative.[75] As Chalfen argues of twentieth-century albums, "The narrative remains in the heads of the picture makers and on-camera participants for verbal telling and retelling during exhibition events."[76] But the presentational context of a social network doesn't allow for verbal accompaniment beyond a brief caption. Moreover, as the infantry sergeant made clear, it can be rather difficult to cobble together a story out of a series of disjointed missions. During another interview in Okinawa, a sergeant who deployed to Iraq for a second time in 2008 described his photo captioning practice: "In the captions I'd try to write things like 'This is us showing up, this is us, you know, this is what we had to live in.' It's almost like we're trying to share our experience in some way with the people that care about us the most back home." He went on to describe his minimal use of captions as a way to create and maintain insider/outsider attachments and belongings. He said, "Yeah we'll post up pictures on Facebook but that doesn't mean we explain what they mean to the general population. I have friends on my Facebook page that I wouldn't explain what a picture means to them." In this way, photo sharing on Facebook seems to operate according to the idea that people should not need explain what they share.

In a similar vein, the title of Robert Hariman and John Lucaites's book *No Caption Needed* references the easily identifiable content of iconic photographs and the way popular images become signposts for collective memories.[77] By contrast, my interest is with the context and practice of publishing *personal* snapshots on Facebook (rather than professionally produced iconic images existing in public forums) and how the technological structure, visual norms of representation, and relational context of "friendship" inform habits of capturing, editing, and sharing. As the Marine explains above, there are some "friends" he does not want to explain a photograph to.

Although digital technology has expanded photo-worthy events to include the everyday, the motivations to take personal photographs have largely remained consistent.[78] Although Facebook photo albums include new iterations of the personal snapshot with emphasis on self-affirming sociality, their general model remains the family albums of the twentieth century, which, according to West, "take photos of almost exclusively happy moments" and use those photos to turn complex histories into "narratives of timeless pleasure—striving for a pain free recollection."[79] In light of the deployment albums, this begs the question as to whether one can "bear witness" to what's not there.[80] Are images of smiling Marines on a patrol base an invitation to imagine what lies outside of the frame? Does Facebook's here-then-gone, phatic form of communication inhibit opportunities to take the time to think about what's not shown? My main concern is best encapsulated by the old adage "what the eye doesn't see, the heart doesn't grieve over." Therefore the issue appears to be a matter of *quality*, not quantity. We don't need more photos of war. We have plenty. The question is about the types of photos currently circulating.[81] It is only when we see things we don't normally see that we are reminded of the constant condition of not seeing.

Bridging the Gap: Ceremonial Imagery

Some personal snapshots do achieve a more public, or iconic, quality in their readily identifiable content and adherence to familiar norms of representation. Photographs depicting ceremonial events are one such example. Events such as graduations, birthday parties, weddings, and family

Figure 26. Marine receiving a promotion

reunions have remained a linchpin in personal snapshot photography since the days of Kodak.[82] The accessibility, in terms of intelligibility, of ceremonial events makes them a productive point of conversation between US troops and civilian social network members. Seven of the nine albums included two types of ceremony: Photographs depicting a promotion in rank or photographs depicting a memorial service.

Of all the photos in the albums, the promotion photos seem to invite the most sidebar commentary from members of the social network (see figure 26). The larger quantity of comments could be due to the fact that these types of images do not require too much interpretive work on the part of the audience, or perhaps because such events invite congratulatory messages. With only slight variations, the promotion photos depict service personnel in desert camis (camouflage) standing at attention, facing one another. Accompanying the photo is usually a caption indicating that the depicted event is a promotion. With the help of a caption, viewers can fill in the narrative and quickly identify the roles of the participants in the image.

The comments' time stamps show that they occur almost immediately after the album is posted. In many cases, the album's creator responds to congratulatory messages instantly from his post in Iraq or Afghanistan. These are significant exchanges because they represent a relational moment where civilians reach out over the threshold between fronts. In contrast to the other, more Facebook-friendly images of shiny happy people holding guns, the promotion photos allow personnel to keep both feet planted in the deployment situation. This time it is the civilian social network members

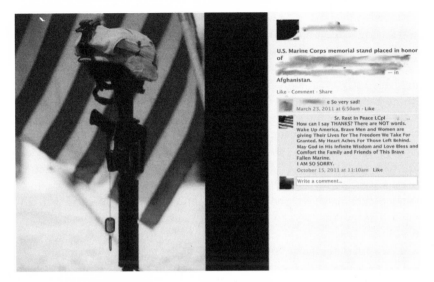

Figure 27. Battle cross

who must build a bridge of understanding. In this way, these images are satisfying to both parties. Service members derive a sense of social capital from sharing these images, and social network members get an opportunity to participate in the war effort by demonstrating their support.

Like the promotion shots, the memorial photographs document a highly ritualized event. However, they represent a ceremony to which civilians find it more difficult to relate. For the most part, the memorial photographs depict what troops refer to as a "battle cross," a pair of standard-issue boots with an inverted M-16 rising out of the sand, dog tags hanging over the pistol grip, and a helmet on top (see figure 27). Several albums included this style of image, but they did not receive nearly as much sidebar commentary from network members. Instead, the memorial photos appeared to be an opportunity for service members to build and sustain relationships by communicating shared values and stories among themselves.

Some of the photos reflected different components of the memorial event, but most focused on the boots, helmet, and gun display. During this impromptu memorial, troops hold formation as an officer and a close friend of the fallen speak, and then afterward they break formation and individually pay their respects to their comrade by placing their hands on his helmet or boots. The memorial ceremony and its accompanying photographs mark a genre unique to this century's style of war fighting. Today dying is much more individualized, with warriors subjected to IED blasts more often than aerial bombs or ambush attacks. As a result, the death of a comrade warrants more undivided ceremonial attention.

One particular image depicts the moment before the troops break formation to pay their individual respects. The album's creator posted this image and tagged another Marine, presumably one shown in the picture. I did not include the screen capture out of respect for the participants and the sanctity of the moment. The Marine who was tagged responded hours later to say that it was "one of the saddest days." Generally speaking, as Pierre Bourdieu argues, "The ordinary photograph, a private product for private use, has no meaning, value, or charm except for a finite group of subjects, mainly those who took it and those who are its objects."[83] It appears that the Marine who was tagged revisited his emotional state during the photo's creation.

Lange uses the term "media circuit" to describe how sharing content online enables some members of a social group to stay connected or interact in qualitatively meaningful ways even if geographically dispersed. To illustrate her point, Lange gives an example of an aunt of two boys she interviewed who posted a comment on one of the boys' YouTube videos. Although the aunt lives several states away and the boys rarely see her, viewing and posting comments allows the aunt to reaffirm her position in a familial social network. When the boys read her comments, they complete the media circuit.[84]

Following Lange, much existing literature discusses the social and emotional benefits of online social network sites. Nicole Ellison, Charles Steinfeld, and Cliff Lampe, for example, discuss content sharing and friendship practices on Facebook in terms of social capital, arguing that "sharing time and space with others supports relational development in multiple ways."[85] Their research highlights two forms of social capital derived from online social membership: "bridging capital" (establishing new or weak ties) and "bonding capital" (strengthening existing ties).

Synthesizing Lange's theory of media circuitry with Ellison, Steinfeld, and Lampe's research, we can deduce that the semipublic, peer group display of photo albums on Facebook plays an important role in enabling both forms of social capital. Service personnel can create *bridges* with geographically and ideologically distant friends and relatives while at the same time reaffirming existing *bonds* with squad members they have been or currently are deployed with. Once posted, these albums create *memories of now*, allowing service personnel to reminisce and feel nostalgic, even if they still have several months left on their tour.

In this way, creating a photo album is less about documenting the past and is more about demonstrating faith in the future. This is especially evident when the event being documented is still in progress. Critical memoir scholar Thomas Larson examines technology's influence on memoir writing practices. He identifies an increasingly popular subgenre of the memoir unique to the late twentieth and early twenty-first century known as the "sudden memoir" whereby the memoirist writes about "the immediate past, even the still corruptible present, not waiting for time to ripen or change what they know."[86] When troops upload a photo album from the field, it is not unlike writing a sudden memoir. One of the album creators suffered serious injuries from an IED blast shortly after posting his album. Needless to say, the autobiography presented in his Facebook album changed dramatically after the incident.

Facebook Photo Albums as Personal Narratives

All the Marines I interviewed had been deployed at least once to Iraq or Afghanistan. Reviewing habits varied, but most participants described the photo albums as playing an important role in perpetuating memories for a group, calling up moments for reflection and reminiscence. Cultural scholar Marita Sturken considers photos "artifacts used to conjure memory, nostalgia, and contemplation."[87] As I repeatedly found during interviews and as evidenced through the Facebook albums' commentary, the albums primarily served as a point of remembrance and communication for the participants in the photos and to a lesser extent close friends and family back home.

Combat photographer Lance Corporal Pine said of his Facebook photo album, "I like looking back at it just 'cause, uh . . . there are some photos that I have that are of some funny times, and . . . there are like, some photos of some people, like, for memories of people who didn't make it back and stuff like that." He paused and then launched into a story. "I got a picture of one of my friends like maybe two or three weeks before he got killed out there. He uh . . . we were on a patrol for a little Shura meeting with some Afghan elders, and we were . . . the important people were going to talk to them, and the less important people, like us, we were going to hold security." As Lance Corporal Pine was speaking, I noticed that I was holding my breath. I assumed he was recounting the moment of his friend's death. But to my surprise, Lance Corporal Pine broke into a smile and described in great detail the moment he took the photo. For Lance Corporal Pine, the photo symbolized a significant bonding moment. He and his fallen comrade created this image together. Preserving the photo helps keep that moment, that relationship, alive.

For the most part, the Marines I spoke with demonstrated a sophisticated awareness about how their personal photos contribute to or contradict existing visual discourses of war. On the one hand, they derive a sense of satisfaction or "motivation" from images that align with dominant representations of war. But, on the other hand, they recognize that these images don't necessarily do justice to the complexity of their experiences either. In September 2012, a Marine lieutenant and public affairs officer took to her personal Facebook page to decry her frustration with the news media's representation of the war in Afghanistan (see figure 28). She wrote, "So in the last 3 days, one reporter asked me to make sure he got to embed on a patrol that would be in a firefight so that he could take a picture of a Marine with 'dirt on his face and blood on his collar . . . ' and another asked me to arrange a joint ANA [Afghan National Army] patrol specifically so she could go film it. . . . Who do they think they are? We are fighting a war, not on a movie set!" Her Facebook status drew a lot of support in the form of "likes" and commiserating commentary.

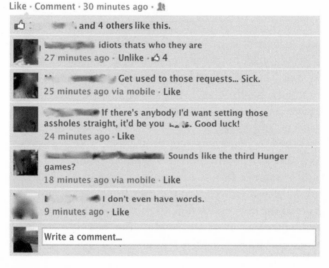

Figure 28. Frustrated post about reporters

The military's discontent with broadcast news is a longstanding attitude that developed in response to what the military perceives as negative, morale-deflating coverage in American conflicts prior to the new millennium.[88] As war scholars Thomas Rid and Marc Hecker point out, "For a long time the press and other forms of journalism were the only vehicles of public information emanating from a conflict zone."[89] Because of this, the branches of the military, politicians, and even members of the increasingly pessimistic public held professional reporters and photographers responsible for public morale.

However, around the dawn of the twenty-first century, broadcast media monologues gave way to multiple, dynamic, networked dialogues where laypeople had access to public platforms of expression. The decentralization of authorship changed relationships between the news media and public morale. For instance, a warrior's self-produced footage could become the content for a five o'clock news broadcast. As a result, accountability for bad PR or dwindling war support shifted inward from the professional reporter to the military personnel themselves. This promotes a heightened self-consciousness on the part of individual service members.

In one photograph, a Marine in desert camouflage holds a young Afghan child close to his chest. The Marine and the child appear content, studying each other's faces while the Marine pats the child's back (see figure 29). In the comment bar to the right a person writes, "They dont ever show any of this on the news." A second comment from a Marine who is tagged in the photo, presumably the Marine depicted, reads, "LMAO! Where did you find this!? I'm sure this is prolly in some Marine Corps propaganda film!"

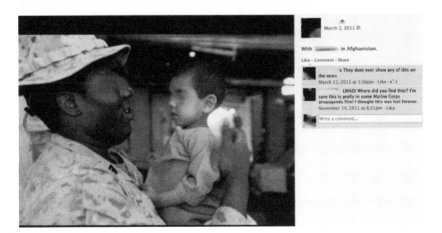

Figure 29. Marine holding a child

The comment speaks to a perceived dialectic between the news media and a "Marine Corps propaganda film."

The accompanying commentary also speaks to the individual war fighter's awareness of his position within a web of competing discourses about war. On the one hand, the Marines I interviewed perceive the representation of their experiences by the mainstream news as an exaggeration, emphasizing active, frontline conflict. During an interview with a Marine sergeant, he made it a point to clarify this impression. "It's not just about kicking doors in," he said. Yet, on the other hand, many Marines recognize that visual representations of their humanitarian efforts can also appear generic. This is evident in the above commentary about USMC propaganda. The "clean" and "dirty" snapshots of war are not oppositional representations of "truth" or "falsehood," but rather they are two sides of the same coin. They each reduce and condense war to isolated moments of entertainment and spectacle. The Marine sergeant in Okinawa who made the door-kicking comment went on to say, "We did a lot of good stuff over there, you know, like building schools and setting up the Iraqi police station." Indeed, several Marines cited "the good stuff" as their favorite deployment memory. In speaking about the humanitarian side of war, the sergeant at Okinawa continued: "We didn't like it at the time, we were like, 'Ooorah, we're death-dealing war fighters, we don't want to hand out soccer balls.' But you know, I look at it now, and I bet that's part of the reason why that area quieted down. Because we went in there and did some good stuff." His comment speaks to the duality referenced in the PAO's frustrated post. Initially imagining himself as the news media would portray him, a "death-dealing war fighter," his experience did not quite align with that characterization, so he calls up another generic representation of a humanitarian aid worker "handing out soccer balls." It's more than likely that neither of these representations adequately captures the myriad of roles he had to play. But in this moment we can hear him caught between the two, groping for a vocabulary to approximate the richness of his experience.

Social media promote such an awareness of audience that war fighters often make sense of their deployments through existing popular discourses. The photo albums discussed in this chapter represent audience-centered texts, reflecting an amalgamation of existing modes of representation. On the one hand, we see familiar archetypes for war—guns, gear, and trenches. On the other hand, we see more colloquial representations of young adult life more in line with social media's visual repertoire. The albums reflect a tension, then, between conventional representations of war and more mundane, everyday imagery.

War's perpetual, persistent force in our everyday lives is at issue in the next chapter as well, through an examination of how service members commandeer pop culture to elicit engagement from civilian audiences. By invoking popular internet memes, US troops establish a sense of copresence and maintain cultural relevancy among their social networks. Although social media allow contemporary warriors to remain active participants in civilian culture, the same cannot be said of the inverse. Civilians cannot participate in war culture. The next chapter considers the space of the internet meme to be a middle ground for military and civilian audiences.

CHAPTER 4
Marine Corps Video Memes

Internet accessibility at the front allows US troops to stay culturally connected with their civilian counterparts. Not only can they observe what their social network members are talking about on their Facebook pages, but they can also participate in the conversation. During an interview in Okinawa, a gunnery sergeant explained how access to various media platforms gave him a sense of copresence with his civilian social network back home. Keeping up with pop culture trends was key to feeling tuned in, and it also gave him something to talk about with his wife.

> MARINE: Most of the time Marines would honestly look on YouTube and look up like . . . music videos 'cause when you're out there you don't . . . we didn't have cable . . . where we were . . . we didn't have TV . . . we had *nothing*. So for us it was like try to get it all in at one time. You'd have a Marine with a window open watching a video, he's got Skype down here, YouTube up here, he's got Facebook in the corner, he's got a head set on . . .
>
> SILVESTRI: So YouTube was for entertainment?
>
> MARINE: Yeah, mostly for entertainment, looking up videos . . . or like once in a while I'd use it for the new movies coming out, to see what the new movie—'cause you know we didn't have a clue—my wife, "Hey, the new Batman trailer's out" or something stupid, and I'd go look at the trailer. So it definitely keeps you up in the world—all those media outlets kept us up-to-date.

Looking at this transcript, it is hard to tell what exactly the gunnery sergeant finds to be "something stupid." Is it the Batman trailer? It is all movie trailers? Is it his wife's interest in the movie trailer? Is it using YouTube to look at movie trailers? Regardless, he ends up participating in the "something stupid" by lending it his attention.

As the last two chapters demonstrated, for the first time in the history of modern warfare, troops and civilians share a social sphere of affectivity in real time. Interacting with content, in most cases pop culture content, and oftentimes user-generated pop culture content, has become a fundamental part of what participants experience as this digital social space, or what media scholar Limor Shifman calls "the digital sphere."[1] In fact, as I mentioned previously, sharing is Web 2.0's "central cultural logic," contributing to composite "sharing economies."[2] A major premise of the sharing economy is that *what we share reflects what we value.* That's why scholars like Shifman have begun paying attention to seemingly trivial popular culture artifacts like internet memes as a way to access our "deep social and cultural structures."[3] Simply put, memes are units of culture—ideas, symbols, or practices that spread through imitation and appropriation in the form of writing, speech, gestures, rituals, or other imitable phenomena. Biologist Richard Dawkins defined the concept of a meme in his 1976 book *The Selfish Gene.* Dawkins's goal was to use evolutionary theory to explain the way cultural information spreads by tracing the flow, flux, mutation, and evolution of memes.[4] Following Dawkins, Shifman argues, and I agree, that, in this century, the internet meme is a useful concept to understand contemporary cultural trends.

A first step is to consider which units of culture we most like to share in the present moment. In other words, what captures our attention today? According to an aggregate of the top YouTube videos for the year 2013, the year I stopped collecting data for this book, the top ten included a Harlem shake video, a Volvo commercial, a fictional rap battle between classical composer Mozart and digital composer Skrillex, and Miley Cyrus's "Wrecking Ball" music video.[5] From this perspective, the gunnery sergeant's "stupid" sentiment takes on new light. If what we share online is indicative of our cultural values and interests, what do these texts say about us? This is a downside to US troops' constant connectivity with the home front. They can perceive public disengagement with war. They can see that broadcast journalists no longer cover the war's progress on the news and that presidential candidates barely mention it on the campaign trail; civilians aren't discussing it on their Facebook pages, and no one clicks on military-related YouTube links unless it's a hilarious meme video or a sentimental homecoming video.[6]

In an attention economy where visibility equals status, if troops want to participate, they first need to find out what draws public interest and then construct their contributions accordingly. In other words, they need to keep up with popular culture in order to compete for public attention. By learning how to proficiently create, circulate, and transform multimodal texts, military personnel—as cultural participants—can have more stake and say in the broader discursive community.

Social Presencing

The creation and dissemination of user-generated pop culture content, namely, YouTube videos of well-known internet memes, mark an attempt to convey a voice to a collective (and collapsed) civilian audience. They are a way for deployed personnel to claim social presence.[7] Typically used to describe the psychological involvement of interlocutors in an interpersonal setting, "social presence" refers to "the feeling of 'being with another' or the degree of salience of the other person in the interaction."[8] In this context, I use the term "social presence" to draw attention to what I perceive as a lack.[9]

Collectively, we are not psychologically involved with the subjectivity of deployed service members. Journalist James Fallows points out, "As a country, America has been at war nonstop for the past 13 years. As a public it has not. A total of about 2.5 million Americans, roughly three-quarters of 1 percent, served in Iraq or Afghanistan at any point in the post-9/11 years, many of them more than once."[10] Fallows' critique goes on to describe the United States as a "Chickenhawk Nation," a sardonic phrase meant to label those who are eager to go to war, as long as someone else is going.

Not only are few Americans willing to go to war, but a majority have lost interest in lending it their attention altogether.[11] In her essay "No One's Looking: The Disappearing Audience for War," Susan Carruthers argues that dwindling TV airtime devoted to war has caused many independent filmmakers to produce documentary films on the subject. However, as Carruthers notes, "These films have significantly failed to attract viewers."[12] Even Hollywood films with blockbuster budgets like *Stop-Loss* experience a lack of box office draw. With a budget of $25 million, *Stop-Loss* grossed only $11 million.[13] The Marines I spoke with echoed Carruthers' concern that "no one is looking," so they take it on themselves to corral an audience and command a social presence. One way they achieve this is through active engagement with popular culture—meeting us in the symbolic community of the meme-o-sphere.

The ability of service members to cultivate a sense of social presence amid their social network is significant since, demographically, they are a small minority in the United States. As I mentioned by way of Fallows' report, roughly 1 percent of the US population serves in the armed forces. Of that 1 percent, an even smaller portion deploys to a war zone. This demographic, then, and the personnel featured in this book represent a small and distinct discourse community—a group of people who share a common way of thinking and talking about social reality. The few Americans who deploy to a war zone have their own ways of communicating about particular social realities that may not be translatable to contemporary dominant discourses. Although social media offer opportunities for deployed personnel to stay current, in order to meaningfully participate in the broader discursive community, they must render their discourses intelligible to a wider audience. According to YouTube's global head of content, Robert Kyncl, making the most of social media is "about leaning in. . . . You have to participate in cultural moments."[14] But is it reasonable to expect our fighting forces to "lean in" from a war zone?

The current attention economy demands that they do. Conceptually speaking, the attention economy suggests that as content has become more plentiful and easier to access, we lack the human attention to deal with it all. In other words, *attention* becomes the scarce commodity over which we must compete. Being able to successfully compete in the attention economy requires a new form of literacy—*social media literacy*. To be social media literate, one must be technologically proficient, be well versed in pop culture discourses, and demonstrate a sophisticated understanding of audience.[15] In other words, social media literacy requires familiarity with subcultural standards—recognition that the right way or the wrong way to employ intertextual digital discourses is never definitive and is under constant negotiation. Yet with the help of the Like button (introduced by Facebook in 2008) and the Share button (introduced by Facebook in 2009), it is easier to track popularity. The bottom line is that the attention economy will let you know where you stand.[16]

Over the course of my research, I learned about four different types of warrior-produced videos (meme, combat, comic, and deployment). Each reflects different values and serves unique cultural functions. The central focus of this chapter, however, is the meme video because it is a distinct cultural artifact and practice that, in many ways, can best represent the unique in-between-ness experienced by this generation of warrior. In other words, the space of the meme is a symbolic portal between worlds, home and away.

Social Media Literacy

Generally speaking, all the video types demonstrate a sophisticated level of social media literacy—a careful negotiation of geographical, institutional, ideological, and technological constraints. They also suggest an appeal to two different audiences, or discourse communities. According to my interviews, one imagined audience consists of other military personnel, or members of the same discourse community who share common ways of thinking and talking about social reality. Another audience is the civilian public. When speaking about an imagined audience beyond their comrades, many Marines invoke an "us versus them" framework by making vague references to groups like "civilians," "America," or "the people back home." This language divides their social worlds up into "us" (in-group) and "them" (out-group). While meme videos in particular attract a broad base, Marines dog-whistle to one another through specific visual referents like the use of moto imagery, a trope that also appears in the photo albums discussed in the last chapter.

For the most part, however, the biggest audience concern remains the "nightmare reader." Earlier I referenced an infantry sergeant who described the importance of self-censorship by saying, "We're not gonna send certain images and stuff back home. We're gonna send everything back home that makes everyone feel, you know, kinda good about what we're doing. We're not trying to scare anybody." Networked communication environments have encouraged communicators to be more audience oriented. Recognizing the networked structure of one's audience and avoiding content that sensitive members could find "scary" demonstrates a sophisticated level of social media literacy. Not only does the infantry sergeant avoid content that would alienate audience members, but he also actively sends content that will encourage them to feel "kinda good" about military operations in Iraq and Afghanistan.

In addition to a desire to make their audiences feel assured, in some cases, the troops also seek to establish a common identity with them. In another interview at Okinawa, a combat engineer sergeant described his online identity management as an attempt to show that he is just like everybody else. He said, "I see a lot of focus on hardships of deployments, hardships of being in a military environment. It's there and it's relevant in my stuff [video footage] too. But I wanted to make a point to show that we're not just all about that. It's not like that every single day. You know? We can laugh and have a good time out there just as well as everybody else." The impulse to distance himself and his fellow Marines from the "hardships" associated with "a military environment" and to present deployment as a fun social event, as in, "we can laugh and have a good time," "we're not just all about that," is an effort to connect with civilian values, especially the values of a social media climate that places a premium on coolness and popularity. An aspect of social media literacy involves knowing how to perform those qualities.

A way Marines try to communicate a sense of humor and appeal to perceived civilian values is by participating in internet video memes. Meme videos allow Marines to demonstrate social presence and argue for cultural relevancy. For fellow Marines, the meme videos serve to parody and critique what they perceive to be America's trivial fetish-du-jour. The gunnery sergeant I cited earlier described his wife's excitement over a new movie release as "something stupid," yet he was compelled to watch the trailer regardless so he could continue absorbing the pop culture lexicon. So even though internet access and the invocation of internet memes can

connect deployed troops to civilian culture, they can also serve as stark reminders that troops in a war zone are *not* on the same plane as their civilian
counterparts—geographically, institutionally, and ideologically.

A Historical Overview of Video Sharing

Until recently, video production required expensive cameras and recording
media (film, VHS). Distribution required bulky and fragile physical media
(cartridges, tapes). And playback was possible only by using further specialized equipment (projectors, televisions, and VCRs). Advances in digital
imaging technology have made recorded video ubiquitous. Additionally the
expansion of high-speed data networks across the globe and the increased
availability of internet-enabled smartphones have helped to connect billions
of people to the internet, fuelling growth in social media and video-sharing
websites. In March 2013 YouTube reported one billion unique visitors to the
site each month. What is more, the recent popularity of music videos such
as South Korean singer Psy's "Gangnam Style" has contributed to an explosion in viewership and meme participation on YouTube.[17] What is special
about YouTube is that it decentralized apparatuses of production, making it
possible for nearly anyone to contribute to the symbolic cultural landscape.[18]

Even before the rise of YouTube as a central hub for video, the practice
of sharing funny or surprising videos with friends was common among
middle-class Americans. Taking cues from television shows like *Candid
Camera* in the 1950s, or *That's Incredible* and *Real People* in the 1970s, middle-class Americans, armed with camcorders, began visually documenting
the rituals of everyday life in the nuclear family.[19] In the 1990s the hit television show *America's Funniest Home Videos* (*AFHV*) capitalized on the
explosion of camcorder technology, asking viewers to send in their "funniest home video" for a chance to win weekly cash prizes. Media historian
Steve Fore describes *AFHV* as a "fascinatingly contradictory cultural document." He writes that the show's format simultaneously "demonstrates
the apparent ease with which camcorder technology may be used to create
an expressive record of everyday life," while at the same time it defines
"a limited range of suitable subject matter and treatment."[20] In this way
AFHV establishes a paradigm for personal videos, much like Kodak did for
the personal snapshot. A notable difference between the two is that *AFHV*
showcased the unexpected and oftentimes clumsy moments that would
have been edited out of a Kodak family album. Imagine a father and son
throwing a baseball in the yard. The Kodak moment would capture their
smiling faces as they play catch. The *AFHV* moment would be the baseball
hitting the father in the groin. *AFHV* encouraged us to laugh at ourselves
and offered a free pass to laugh at others. As the theme song declares, "We

are the red, white, and blue. Oh, the funny things you do! America, America, this is you." *AFHV* invokes a national identity based on a commonly shared humor associated with aspects of the home and private life.

Audiences of *AFHV* tacitly understood the difference between home-mode production and professional TV production and were therefore forgiving of the videos' lack of technical polish. In fact, the technical deficiencies in the home videos actually enhanced the product when placed in the broadcast context. Juxtaposed with the professionally produced programming that came before it, the home videos featured in *AFHV* carried an appealing aesthetic of authenticity.

By the start of the twenty-first century, digital camcorders were on their way to replacing analog video recorders. Although they were expensive, handheld video cameras were widely used in skateboard communities to document tricks and stunts.[21] In 2000, MTV debuted the television show *Jackass*, which extended the skateboarding community's "extreme sport" formula to include "extreme behavior." Simply put, *Jackass* took *AFHV*'s groin shot to a whole new level. Instead of capturing accidents, *Jackass* was predicated on an intention to fail. The show featured stunts and gags performed by a variety of individuals, the most popular of whom were Steve-O (Steven Glover), Chris Pontius, Bam Margera, Johnny Knoxville (Philip John Clapp), and Ryan Dunn. Their antics included lighting farts on fire, stapling butt cheeks together, and crashing into each other while riding in shopping carts.[22] Before each show, MTV asked viewers not to replicate the stunts, but, of course, many did. To the chagrin of suburban parents everywhere, the *Jackass* aesthetic was both easily accessible and easily replicated. Young people were both behind the camera and in front of it.

Drawing from the funny and amazing videos they saw on *AFHV* as well as the self-documentary model presented by *Jackass*, American youth generated a meme that would eventually spread from their camcorder's playback screen to the World Wide Web. In 2005 the video-sharing website YouTube went public with the video "Me at the Zoo," featuring the site's twenty-six-year-old cofounder, Jawed Karim, standing outside the elephant exhibit at the San Diego Zoo. He says, "The cool thing about these guys [the elephants] is that they have really, really long, um . . . trunks." He pauses. "And that's pretty much all there is to say."[23] The "cool," casual, carefree style presented by Karim set a precedent for what types of videos to expect on YouTube. Soon videos depicting sky-high geysers created by mixing Mentos mints with Diet Coke became YouTube sensations and further solidified the site's cultural repertoire.[24]

YouTube's slogan, "Broadcast Yourself," encouraged users to think big about audiences. Taking cues from mass media, individuals could now produce their own content. Whereas *AFHV* told Americans, "You *might* be a star tonight, so let that camera roll," YouTube circumvented professional filters to give users direct access to their audiences and the possibility of stardom. Teen pop sensation Justin Bieber is a great example. As a twelve-year-old, Bieber posted homemade videos of himself singing on YouTube. Hundreds of views turned into thousands, then millions, and by age fifteen he was a superstar.[25] Of course, Bieber's story is an exceptional example. A vast majority of videos receive a couple views and then fade into the background.

The key to YouTube success is to make the video entertaining. Media studies scholar Aaron Hess observed that YouTube videos appear to rely on "infotainment" production logic, accomplished primarily through techniques such as parody, spoof, and irony. Lei Guo and Lorin Lee are less optimistic about users' interest in information, however. They describe YouTube's principle operating logic as more exclusively entertainment, labeling it "LOL or Leave" and arguing that on YouTube, uploaders strive for view counts, and viewers come for entertaining rather than educational experiences. Additional studies have shown that YouTube videos with the most views include entertainment-oriented content.[26]

The Making of a Meme

Occasionally a successful YouTube video will become a "hit" and go "viral" or even inspire an internet meme. The difference between a viral video and a meme video is that a viral video does not necessarily inspire derivations or alternative versions. In a viral video, the original idea and content stay intact as it circulates through social networks. By contrast, a meme spreads through imitation and mutation. As Shifman describes, "mimetic videos" are popular clips that generate extensive user engagement by creative repetition.[27] An illustrative comparison would be the videos entitled "Evolution of Dance" and "The Star Wars Kid." "Evolution of Dance" features a dancer performing a live rendition of several popular dances to their accompanying songs.[28] Although this video was wildly popular, accumulating millions of hits within months, it did not spawn any creative imitations. It is therefore considered a viral video. By contrast "The Star Wars Kid" is a meme video because several people created their own renditions of the original, which featured a high school student awkwardly wielding a golf ball retriever to imitate a light saber.[29] This is not to say that viral videos and meme videos are totally separate. The viral video is usually the foundation for a meme. Shifman argues that the inherently flawed or incomplete attributes of a viral video are what make it so ripe for reproduction and further creative engagement.[30] In the case of "The Star Wars Kid,"

for example, thousands of viewers uploaded their own versions of the awk-
ward light saber–wielding teen to YouTube. Even television programs like
Arrested Development and *Family Guy* demonstrated their "coolness" by
making references to the meme on their shows.

In this way, the internet meme is a genre of participatory culture. Some
scholars are uncomfortable with the idea that video memes qualify as cultural participation, worrying that this mode cheapens public discourse.[31]
Arguing along the lines of Clay Johnson's "Information Diet," which holds
that we are consuming too much unhealthy "comfort food" in the form
of pop culture, Olga Goriunova describes "the mumbling, instant, repet-
itive, easy, playful, junk, worthless creativity" as a form of "new media
idiocy."[32] Goriunova uses French philosopher Gilles Deleuze's definition
of the idiot as a private thinker preoccupied with personal thoughts and
ideas. Yet I contend that every member of a social collective participates
in culture when he or she engages with others, negotiates representations,
and makes use of artifacts. Cultural anthropologists Richard Bauman and
Charles Briggs, for example, stress how we *perform* culture.[33] Of course
they were writing long before the contemporary Web 2.0 climate, but the
performative perspective still applies. As Shifman argues, the "new arena
of bottom-up expression can blend pop culture, politics, and participation
in unexpected ways."[34] So whether or not we perceive internet memes as
pop culture junk food, they are still worth examining as instances of cultural performance and participation.

Although this chapter explores the way US troops use video memes as
a method of participating in civilian culture while at war, it is important to
note that this is not the first time in history memes have appeared on the
battlefield. A well-known meme among World War II veterans, "Kilroy
Was Here," featured a simple drawing of a bald man with a long nose peer-
ing over a wall (see figure 30). Kilroy, as he was called, was often drawn
with his fingers gripping the wall or with one or two squiggles of hair on
his head. Kilroy appeared everywhere—on the sides of tanks, planes, and
ships, scrawled on halls, walls, and even underneath toilet seats.

Kilroy created an invisible bond among servicemen, offering membership in a privileged and mysterious brotherhood. An important difference
between Kiloy's analog existence and the digital memes of today is that Kilroy primarily stayed within military culture. By contrast, the digital memes
of today are much more widely circulated. Not only that, but they are far
more visual, creating the potential for multiple meanings through inter-
textuality.[35] Another key difference is that Kiloy's presence in a war zone
inserted bizarre and unexpected humor into a bleak environment. Conversely, the warrior-produced video memes of today introduce the context

Figure 30. "Kilroy Was Here." Drawing provided by Peter James Silvestri

of war into a digital space already teeming with humorous and nonsensical whimsy. Therefore a central point of interest in this chapter is the way troops capitalize on the digital meme format to highlight the context of war. But before I move to that, I want to supply the reader with background on the military's relationship to YouTube and some of the existing scholarship on warrior-produced content.

Video Sharing and the Military

Initially the Pentagon allowed video posting, believing that the videos could increase morale by allowing troops to blow off steam and overcome boredom.[36] In the summer of 2007, however, the military enacted a policy that restricted troop access to social networking sites such as YouTube, asserting two primary reasons for the restriction: "to enhance and increase network security and protect the use of the bandwidth."[37] The policy "created a blanket ban on sites many troops use to share news, photos, video and audio with their family and friends."[38] Upon implementation of the restriction, service members' video posting decreased, although many existing videos remained available for viewing. As I explained earlier, the Defense Department lifted the ban in 2010, allowing access to YouTube and other social media sites. As of this writing, access remains open, and US troops can upload videos.

Both popular and academic sources have treated the phenomenon of warrior-produced videos since their emergence in 2005. *Rolling Stone* journalist David Sax offered in-depth coverage of the technological abilities of contemporary soldiers and their application in combat videos.[39] Evan Wright, author of *Generation Kill*, notes the degree to which soldiers live and breathe mediated popular culture and how it influences the type of content they produce.[40] In a similar vein, academic researchers such as Kari Andén-Papadopoulos argue that the warriors producing YouTube clips "fall back on contemporary popular culture and its broad repertoire of war as entertainment."[41] A majority of the analyses consider the reach and prominence of what has been called the "YouTube War" within broader discourses of popular culture, arguing that the phenomenon highlights the growing conflation of war and entertainment.

The popularity of warrior-produced videos stemmed, in large part, from public frustration with what was perceived as highly limited mainstream media coverage of war and conflict. Writing about the public value of war fighters' footage on YouTube, journalists James Poniewozik and Karen Tumulty describe:

> Most of the videos are poorly lit and badly composed. And they convey the confusion of war far better than expensive, competent TV. Journalists are trained to make sense, to frame stories and order facts, smoothing over random happenings and odd twists. In Web video, war is not a playing out of political-historical forces. . . . In a terrifying, seven-minute YouTube clip, it's riding in the cab with a civilian driver as his truck takes fire and breaks down. "Come help me out!" he shouts to his military escort as the camera dives under the dashboard with him. "I'm going home when this s——'s done. When this s——'s done I'm f—— out of here!" On YouTube, war is also, appropriately, unbleeped.[42]

What Poniewozik and Tumulty celebrate here, it seems, is an aesthetic of authenticity that holds war's horror to be synonymous with its reality. Within this formula, an authentic experience hinges on violence and bloodshed. But as photography historian Cara Finnegan points out, it is an illusion to think that texts are capable of offering transparent representations of the material world, because realism itself is a set of conventions and norms grounded in rhetorical purposes.[43] This is not to deny nondiscursive material conditions, but rather to say that they cannot exist outside specified discursive systems. All war reporting, despite convincing appearances of authenticity, is a rhetorical construction. This is why I argue that instead of writing off warrior-produced memes as fictitious or frivolous, we should consider them to be another way to learn about war.

Traditional war reporting has gone the way of the dodo. This is in part because war itself has become difficult to narrate. A war on terrorism is not conducive to a linear narrative structure. Even after we capture "the bad guy," the game of Whack-a-Mole continues. The fall of Saddam Hussein or Osama bin Laden would have been the climax of a conventional war story. But today our world is becoming less conducive to familiar forms of narrative. The twenty-four-hour news cycle of fragmented coverage from disparate sources including the Associated Press, Facebook, and Twitter makes it almost impossible to create a traditional story. Media theorist Douglas Rushkoff describes this phenomenon as "narrative collapse," a symptom of what he calls "presentist" culture.[44] According to Rushkoff, we exist in a perpetual state of emergency brought on by anxiety-inducing, anachronistic coverage of current events on a never-ending news cycle. It is as if we have lost a sense of eventfulness altogether. Traditionally conceived, an event or a narrative presumes a beginning, middle, and end. But today, as Rushkoff argues, "We occupy, we freelance, and we trade derivatives. Everything happens in the now. . . . The challenges of a post-Industrial society are less like conquests with clear endpoints than they are steady-state concerns. Oil is spilling. The climate is changing. Terrorists are plotting. The hard part is that they are never quite solved for the future so much as managed in the present."[45] So even if journalists had the authority they once did, they would not be able to make sense of the unedited flow of reporting. As a public, we are becoming more used to the impossibility of a ready-made narrative structure. In fact, we anticipate multiple perspectives and alternative story lines. This is not to say we seek them out, but we are aware they exist. For example, another reason warrior-produced footage draws public interest is because it depicts a more humane side to war fighting. This perspective offers a counterpoint to broadcast news media, which has been perceived as focusing almost exclusively on "the car bomb of the day."[46] As war media scholar Christian Christensen describes:

The volume of footage shot by coalition troops in Iraq and Afghanistan, and then posted to the YouTube site, is substantial. There is no way to accurately measure exactly how many clips exist, but suffice it to say that countless hours can be spent locating and watching such material. It is important to note that the majority of clips posted to YouTube do not show soldiers engaged in war crimes, violence or anti-social behavior, but rather taking part in the mundane, day-to-day activities one would associate with military personnel during free time: sitting around in tents, talking with colleagues, eating, singing songs and sending messages to loved ones back home.[47]

Most scholarly treatments of US troops' YouTube videos imagine them as vernacular discourses. They argue that service members in combat have largely lacked a voice uncontrolled by the military to shape, influence, and participate in the public deliberation of war. Christina Smith and Kelly McDonald, for example, consider the way personnel represent themselves online, arguing that warrior-produced videos offer an alternative to the military-media control over information.[48] To an extent, this book joins that conversation, but I want to resist an overvaluation of YouTube's voice-granting potential. Unlike my father's generation, the means of production and distribution are accessible to US troops. However, the troops cannot necessarily participate in meaningful public deliberation about war without constraint. What is say-able for them on YouTube is restricted by a number of factors: institutional, technological, and ideological.

A warrior's discursive subject position is significantly different from the average civilian YouTuber's discursive position. A poignant example of this disconnect surfaced during an interview in Okinawa. The interview was with a combat engineer sergeant who had already deployed to Iraq, and, during the time of our interview, was gearing up for a tour in Afghanistan. As he explained it, his job was to "basically search for IEDs and use demolitions to blow things up." He spoke about his deployments in a way that resonated with my father's anecdote about the Beatles. He said:

> The nice thing about it, the weird thing about it . . . you'll have a best friend or a really good friend of yours die and like two days later it's like nothing happened. It's because you put it away because you know you can't deal with it there. You have to wait 'til you get back. You know when you get back you have to take that time to actually remember them and go through the grieving process, but while you're there. . . . Time stops everywhere else. The US doesn't change. The world doesn't change. The only thing that you know is that days come and days go in Afghanistan.

Like my father's description of the lapse between "I Want to Hold Your Hand" and "Hey Jude," the sergeant talks about nothing mattering beyond his own survival in the war zone. In this quote it seems as if both his feet are firmly planted "over there." He initially describes deployment as "the nice thing," presumably because he can put tragic events like the death of a comrade "away" until he gets home.

Deployment, then, is largely an exercise in stress management. One way Marines de-stress is by making and sharing videos. The combat engineer sergeant described video production as a favorite pastime among many Marines. He even goes so far as to say that he has become so good at distracting himself on deployment that he prefers deployment to home.

[Making and posting videos] shows that we joke around and kid. A day over there is just an average day. Most days are normal days. We wake up. We do what we need to do. We go to sleep. You know. . . . Everything in between . . . is just like, you know like anyone else's nine to five, you know? It's just that you're always on that high alert stress-wise a little bit more, but you joke more because of it. You do things that take away that stress more so because you are that way. So you actually enjoy yourself, in a sense, more so on deployment than when you're home.

Entertainment media are a way to cope with an unyielding state of high alert. Popular culture marks an escape from war culture. Similar to the function of the United Service Organizations (USO) tour, producing and sharing videos has become a momentary reprieve from war-related activity. Videos have also become central to social bonding and group cohesion. And in the particular case of the video meme, they present an opportunity to participate in public conversation.[49] As this Marine sergeant said, his videos "show" civilian audiences that they can adopt the values and attitudes of the home front in spite of being in a war zone.

Participating in Meme Culture
The idea of escaping war through a shared sphere of affectivity does not necessarily mean that troops are moving closer to home. At home, pop culture represents the sociocultural backdrop, communicating a society's norms, values, and attitudes. Invoking popular culture artifacts within the context of war has the potential to make deployed personnel seem even further removed from home-front ideology. To recall the gunnery sergeant's thoughts at the start of this chapter, watching reality shows, movie trailers, and music videos might be perceived as "stupid" to service members in Iraq and Afghanistan, but they participate nonetheless. The creative uptake of video memes, for example, offers US troops the opportunity to engage in domestic public discourse about popular culture. Seen this way, the videos represent a liminal space. When troops engage with internet memes, they do not experience "one foot here and one foot there" but rather a *suspension* of footing altogether. In the space of the internet meme, US troops *create* culture.

Participation in meme cultures is not as simple as deciding you want to engage and then doing so. It requires a sophisticated level of literacy—

knowing how to read the texts and how to create your own. As media scholars Jean Burgess and Joshua Green argue:

> YouTube is a potential site of cosmopolitan cultural citizenship—a space in which individuals can represent their identities and perspectives, engage with self-representations of others, and encounter cultural difference. But access to all the layers of possible participation is limited to a particular segment of the population—those with the motivations, technological competencies, and site-specific cultural capital sufficient to participate at all levels of engagement the network affords.[50]

Agency and literacy go hand in hand. To participate as a global citizen, you not only must have technological and cultural access to the digital sphere, but you must also be able to meaningfully participate in its discourses. To do that, you need to be social media literate; and you must be able to keep up.

There are two key facets of social media literacy—technological literacy and ideological literacy. The difference between ideological literacy and technological literacy is roughly a distinction between content and medium. Simply put, ideology is the body of ideas reflecting the attitudes, values, and aspirations of an individual, group, class, or culture. To be ideologically literate, one has to be reflexive about "what" is being communicated in terms of norms, attitudes, and values. Ideology circulates via media. Technological literacy, then, refers to the means of communication—the technological aspects, the repertoire of competences that enable people to analyze, evaluate, and create messages in a wide variety of media. Technological literacy involves more than knowing how to use a particular medium. The process of selecting a channel among polymediated platforms is accompanied by a host of complicated, oftentimes ethical decisions.[51] Communicators need to consider which media are most appropriate for communicating a specific message to a particular audience.

The internet, with its immediate and infinite connectivity, causes memes to evolve faster and spread further than ever before. Every new social network is another incubator of memes.[52] Twitter offers a useful illustration of the dizzying rate of meme proliferation. The Twitter-sphere uses a hashtag system (which has become a meme in itself) to attract individual users to unmoderated, ad hoc discussion forums. Any combination of characters led by a hash or pound sign, such as "#dontyoulovethisbook," can become a topic for discussion. If enough individuals promote the hashtag, it appears as a "trending topic" on a user's homepage and can attract even more commentary. At issue, however, is the fleetingness of hashtag topics. They momentarily corral our attention before disappearing into digital oblivion.[53] The hashtag has become a metaphor for our evanescent attention.

Keeping up with the flow of public discourse requires a great deal of time and effort. And listening to the garble of popular culture requires a kind of dexterity. One can imagine how arduous it would be for a service member, both geographically and ideologically removed, to keep "one foot" involved in the musings of our popular culture. My father's anecdote about the Beatles represents our conventional understanding of a war experience. You go away for a period and then come home. But today, going away is a matter only of geography. Now people can use the manifold connections afforded by digital media to stay engaged in public discourse. Digital media ethnographers Patricia Lange and Mizuko Ito argue that youth are particularly adept at using social media to exercise their voices, even as they do banal things like post photo albums or create video memes.[54] Young adults are the most voracious consumers of online video. Three quarters of the eighteen-to-twenty-nine age demographic report that they download or stream video.[55] Two-thirds of active-duty military personnel fall within this age bracket.[56] It is less of a surprise, then, that US troops use video memes to speak back to civilian culture.

If there were ever any doubt whether war fighters can stay culturally engaged while on deployment, the video memes they post online are proof not only that they're literate in this social space but also that they have something to say. Video memes serve two primary functions for deployed personnel. First they allow service members as a social collective to define themselves against outsider groups (usually civilians but sometimes other service branches). Second, video memes are a method of social presencing.

US Marines and Internet Memes

Several warrior-produced video memes have surfaced over the last few years. The ghost riding meme, for example, which peaked in popularity around 2007, usually involves a car coasting in neutral while participants dance alongside or on top of it with musical accompaniment by Mistah Fab's "Ghost Ride It." According to the meme reference site Know Your Meme (knowyourmeme.com), there have been many ghost riding parodies on YouTube, including a video of service members dancing on top of an MRAP carrier that has received over a million and a half views (see figure 31).[57]

The Harlem shake meme is one of the more recent examples. In February 2013, DJ Baauer's heavy-bass, instrumental song inspired a dance video meme that spread like wildfire on YouTube. The formula involved a masked individual dancing alone in a public setting before cutting to a wild dance

Figure 31. Ghost riding an MRAP

party featuring a large group dancing in the same setting. Throughout the second week of February 2013, more than four thousand Harlem shake videos were uploaded to YouTube each day. By February 13, approximately twelve thousand Harlem shake videos had been posted, gaining more than forty-four million views.[58]

The screen capture in figure 32 depicts a Facebook page with an embedded YouTube video of Marines doing the Harlem shake. An active-duty Marine posted the video February 9, 2013, at the height of the global Harlem shake phenomenon. In the commentary to the right, one person writes: "This needs to be on YouTube," to which the Marine who posted it said, "It is," and then listed a few other websites where the video exists.

Evidently the concern for this Marine and his social network is access and circulation. The Facebook friend wants to make sure the video can be seen and circulated beyond a semiprivate Facebook page. Next the exchange turns to view count. The number of views is a way to gauge social impact. In the attention economy, metrics such as "likes" and comments are indicators of worth. A third commenter requests the YouTube link, presumably so he can share the video with people beyond his social circle. These points are demonstrative of an idiom of practice that speaks to the functional relationship between YouTube and Facebook.

Facebook and YouTube appear to have a symbiotic relationship. YouTube's popularity increased when Facebook became a public platform. Facebook allows people to draw a specific audience's attention to a particu-

Figure 32. Harlem shaking in the barracks

Figure 33. Harlem shake commentary

lar video through sharing, tagging, and posting. On Facebook, as digital media scholar Nancy Baym argues, no two users have "access to the same set of people or messages, giving them each an experience of the site that is individualized yet overlapping with others."[59] This is why the Facebook friend in the commentary in figure 32 requests the YouTube link. This person wants to share it with his or her own circle of "friends." In fact, the Marine who posted the Harlem shake video depicted in figure 32 was doing the same thing. He admitted (see figure 33) that he was not an original participant in the video: "I wasn't in the room, just had this sent to me." He also said, "I'm only leaving this up for a little bit." The underlying assumption is that he has some control over his audience's attention and their access to the content. From this perspective, once he takes the video off his page, it dissolves into YouTube's archival abyss and will be lost forever. This is a hasty assumption, of course, especially in light of the number of "shares," which was 3,049 at the time of this writing.

It might be useful to think of Facebook as YouTube's hashtag. But instead of tagging a topic, a Facebook user tags a person, a specific audience member. In other words, YouTube is a place for storage and Facebook is a means of circulation.[60] I deduced this media ideology from the idioms of practice described by the Marines that I interviewed. For example, a Marine sergeant described YouTube as a place for storage and Facebook as a method of sharing.

> SERGEANT: A lot of my Marines have put a lot of videos on there.
> SILVESTRI: Is that how they share things?
> SERGEANT: That's one way, but I usually get on their Facebook and that's how I find their videos 'cause I can't find things on YouTube.

Simply put, YouTube's value is in its archive. Facebook's value is the ability to draw others' attention to relevant clips within YouTube's expansive archive. Following Lange's conceptual distinctions between "publicly private" and "privately public," Facebook represents the former category, where the producer's identity is available but the content is not widely disseminated, and YouTube represents the latter, where the content is widely disseminated but the producer remains relatively anonymous. In other words, YouTube, for the most part, is a broadcast site. Everyone has access to the same content. Most people search for videos with specific keywords instead of openly browsing for new content. They arrive at the site knowing what they are looking for, if they haven't already been funneled to the video by clicking on a link from a friend's Facebook page. US troops recognize and exploit Facebook and YouTube's symbiosis in order to demonstrate their meme proficiency. They remain actively engaged with meme culture even from their posts in a war zone.

A Marine-produced meme that has received extremely wide public attention is a lip dub to Canadian singer-songwriter Carly Rae Jepsen's summer 2012 hit "Call Me Maybe." Jepsen's song inspired homemade lip dubs from fans the world over, including the US Olympic swim team, pop singer Justin Bieber, the University of Florida baseball team, a group of Canadian Air flight attendants, the Miami Dolphins cheerleaders, and, of course, the US military.[61] In fact, YouTube listed Bieber's lip dub among the top ten most searched for videos during the year 2012, an indication of this particular meme's popularity at the time of my research.[62] Shifman traces the origins of the lip dub, a performative genre where voice and body are split, to Dennis Potter's 1978 TV series *Pennies from Heaven*, which featured a 1930s salesman who avoided the agonies of his life by escaping through lip-synch to the magical world of music.[63] In this way, it's rather fitting that service members in a war zone, a presumably agonizing experience, would choose to replicate a lip-synching meme.

"Call Me Maybe": The US Marine Meme

In July 2012, members of the US armed forces stationed in Kandahar International Airport, Afghanistan, performed a "Call Me Maybe" lip dub video that showed US troops happily singing and dancing to Jepsen's hit single. An article for *ABC News* said the goal was to "show troops in a more positive, light-hearted way" and to create distance "from the controversies that have dogged the US mission for the past several months." The article went on to cite the Quran burnings on a US base near Kabul and the leaked video of Marines urinating on Afghan corpses. The lip dub project was a USO undertaking by USO employees Eric Raum and his friend Randy Moresi. In other words, it was an institutionally sanctioned meme. Raum described the project as offering a "human side" to the military: "It's a side of the military that you don't get to see."[64] The video depicts fun-loving Marines singing on a shooting range, an airman doing the robot, and other cheerful dance scenes (see figure 34). One YouTube commenter writes, "This should be a recruitment video." And I would argue that it most certainly is.

Raum and Moresi produced the video with permission and support from the military. The commanding officer gave explicit orders that everyone on the air base was to follow Raum and Moresi's instructions. The result is a professional-grade three-minute video complete with lighting kits, expensive dollied camera moves, and polished choreography. It makes military life look like summer camp. The military used to be sold as a career. Now it is sold as an experience. This video marks an evolution in the type of experience being sold. It is not the brave paratrooper or the adrenaline-pumped Marine diving into a fighting hole. Instead, it is a domesticated social experience, emphasizing casual friendship sociality as service members dance and lip-sync to a pop song. Currently the rights to the video are owned by

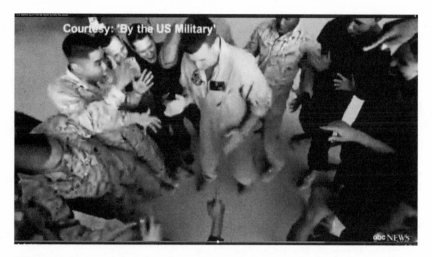

Figure 34. Airman doing the robot

Great video guys, LOVE the Mortar scene! I took and cut it side by side with the original Dolphins one, take a look if you like!

Miami Dolphins Cheerleaders "Call Me Maybe" By Carly Rae Jepson Military Tribute
by Andrew Stupfel
2 years ago • 3,007,543 views
This is a military tribute video to the Dolphins Cheerleaders. We do the video scene for scene the same as their video.

Figure 35. Marines parodying Dolphins cheerleaders

the US military. At the time of this writing, the video has received over 2.5 million views.[65]

A few months later, in September, Marines on an undisclosed FOB in Afghanistan posted another version of the "Call Me Maybe" video. This time it featured a group of dirty, sweaty, shirtless Marines performing a near-perfect shot-by-shot remake of the Miami Dolphins cheerleaders' version of the Jepsen lip dub video (see figure 35). By contrast with the USO production, the FOB Marines' video reflected vernacular rather than institutional discourses.

The Miami Dolphins cheerleaders produced their "Call Me Maybe" video while on a calendar photo shoot in the Dominican Republic. Abiding by the principle that imitation is the best form of flattery, the Marines dedicated their rendition to the cheerleaders with a final screen that read: "To the Dolphin Cheerleaders, thank you for the inspiration. —Your fans in Afghanistan."[66] The Marines were so confident in their imitation that

hahahaha wow

Feb 17, 2013 3:01pm
A side by side of the original Dolphins Call Me Maybe
along with the latest Military Version!

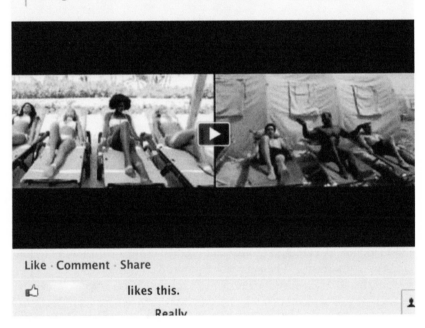

Figure 36. Side-by-side Marines and cheerleaders

versions were posted using split screens so the audience could make more direct comparisons (see figure 36).[67]

What is significant about the FOB version is that it defies expectations for a meme video. Most memes propagate an idea. For the "Call Me Maybe" strain, the focus is on the close synching with Jepsen's hit single. By contrast, this video is a *meta*-meme. The Marines mimic the cheerleaders' mimetic performance of Jepsen's song. They lip-synch Jepsen while they video dub the cheerleaders. The second layer of parody allows them to carry out more cultural work through the video. For example, the close

Figure 37. Split screen

replication of the cheerleaders' video serves to highlight the war zone context. When looking at duplicates, the impulse is to point out differences. What becomes blatantly obvious, in this case, is the backdrop of war.

In order to foreground their unique context, the Marines need to match everything else as closely as they can. They achieve this through skillful media literacy, revealed in the end product and made even more impressive by their lack of resources. They use mop heads as pompoms, fold their shorts to look like bikini bottoms, and use makeshift field showers to imitate sexy water scenes. Their choreography and editing are spot-on, in perfect synchronization with the music *and* the cheerleaders (see figure 37).

Every detail is accounted for. Even the Marine participants reflect careful casting. Their age, race, hair color, and relative body type reveal an attempt to match their cheerleader counterparts. The technical precision is what makes this video so compelling. Therefore, when they present viewers with incongruences like a pistol sliding up the hairy leg of a Marine rather than a pompom sliding up the smooth, tanned leg of a cheerleader, it serves to highlight their presence in a war zone. An attention to detail extends, perhaps unsurprisingly, to OPSEC concerns. Eleven seconds into the video, a blurred box appears over the right shoulder of one of the Marines. The box was likely placed there to obscure the name of the base or some part of the base that could identify where they are located.

This video is a testament to the Marines' multivalent literacy. It appeals to a broad audience because it draws from dominant ideology. The cheerleaders represent the ultimate objectified femininity. They shimmy and shake on the beach in bikinis. They playfully toss their hair and wink at the camera. And as is the case with all lip dubs, they literally have no voice. Although Americans are familiar with this commercialized image of womanhood, when US war fighters, commonly imagined as the mythos of masculinity, invoke these qualities, it is an unexpected and highly entertaining twist. Employing the gender flip trope, which has been a staple in American popular culture for decades, shows that the Marines are ideologically literate. They recognize how the public imagines them and they play on it using a timeless pop culture trope. They demonstrate that they understand what the public finds entertaining. The video participates in public culture's comedic repertoire, while at the same time resisting it and poking fun at it. In this way, the Marines in this video position themselves against civilian popular culture, even while participating in it.

More than that, they position themselves against other branches in the military as well. Interservice rivalry is part and parcel of military culture. Although this rivalry may seem counterintuitive (and perhaps counterproductive) during wartime, these rivalries intensify and even multiply to include intrabranch resentments as well. For example, the slang term "POG," which I mentioned earlier, stands for "person other than grunt." It is a derogatory moniker that infantry Marines give to fellow Marines who are not stationed in combat outposts (COPs) or FOBs. The discrepancy is a deep-seated, culturally inflected battle over legitimacy, over who qualifies as a "real" warrior. As I mentioned, one of the earliest and most widely disseminated military versions of the "Call Me Maybe" lip dub was the product of a USO effort on a large air base in Kandahar. To forward operating or infantry units like the ones featured in the cheerleader-inspired version of the "Call Me Maybe" lip dub, the service members stationed at Kandahar have it "pretty cushy," as one infantry sergeant described. In this way, the Marines in the second "Call Me Maybe" video reach out to an audience beyond the sea of generalized others constituting the domestic pop culturescape.[67] They also speak to each other.

The second "Call Me Maybe" video should be read as a response to the USO's project, and it offers an opportunity to consider the tiered aspect of Marine meme audiences. First, the video appeals to a broad collective. Presented in the format of a meme, its overall style and content are ideologically salient with contemporary American popular culture. By adopting dominant discourses and creatively reminding the American public that there is a war in Afghanistan, the video makes an argument for social presence. Second, the video speaks to those affiliated with the armed forces. Memes allow social collectives to come together and define themselves as a group, and set themselves against other outsider groups. For example, other participants in the "Call Me Maybe" memes share affiliation through their profession, sports teams, or even celebrity status. In memes produced by US troops, they largely define themselves against civilian others. But even within the military community, there are further subcommunities to which the video memes speak.

The insider-outsider dynamic animating the second "Call Me Maybe" video is what makes it such a rich text worthy of study. For viewers in the know, the text reflects a gesture toward solidarity with other service members. Read as a response to the USO's project, the second "Call Me Maybe" video pits Marines in COPs and FOBs against service members in more supportive roles in the rear echelon, or on air bases in Kandahar, for instance. While they parody the cheerleaders' video, on the one hand, they also parody the idea of making such videos, on the other.

It takes a great deal of time and effort to produce these videos. In comparison with the expensive USO production, the gritty, handheld version produced by the forward operating Marines comments on the relative luxury and resources enjoyed by personnel at Kandahar. Read this way, the meta-meme takes on more significance too. Imitating the cheerleaders' lip dub suggests that the forward operating Marines are calling personnel in the rear echelon "cheerleaders" for the war effort. By contrast they are the key players. The video's final scene is highly significant in this regard (see figure 38). The final shot parallels the cheerleaders' version, but instead of a Miami Dolphins logo, the Marines place an American flag suggesting that the nation, rather than a football team, is the object of their cheers.

Figure 38. American flag and Dolphins logo

Replacing the Miami Dolphins NFL logo with the American flag also serves to critique the civilian public's preoccupations with trivial pop culture (like sports) during a time of global conflict. This perception, expressed by many service members during interviews and on Facebook pages, derives from their lived realities in Iraq and Afghanistan.

The Marines' parody of the Miami Dolphins cheerleader video is a multileveled critique. They poke fun at what they perceive as trivial American pop culture fascinations while asserting their legitimacy as "real" war fighters relative to their rear-deployed comrades on the air base in Kandahar. Understood within this second frame, it is easier to identify some of the details that communicate the fact that these men are "on the field" rather than "on the sidelines." One significant moment, in particular, is the release of a 120 mm shell from a mortar. The participants in this particular scene are different from the other "main characters." For one thing, they are not Marines; they are soldiers, distinguishable by the type of camouflage they wear. Yet they are an infantry unit, so their forward position in theater grants them a wartime prestige that supersedes their branch affiliation. Simply put, in wartime, grunts identify with grunts ahead of the rear echelon regardless of service branch loyalties.

In the mortar scene, two soldiers in full gear load a 120 mm mortar, a system used by mechanized infantry, armor, and cavalry units. Audiences can hear the deep "thumph" sound of the powerful mortar leaving the M298 mortar tube above Jepsen's audio track. This is the only snippet of external audio included in the video. Service members flag this moment as their "favorite" when they post or share the video on their Facebook pages.

The post in figure 39 highlights the two-second mortar scene: "My Favorite piece, the Mortar guys are dancing before and after firing! LOL." The Facebook post extracts the mortar scene from the original three-minute video so it can be watched in exclusivity. The bottom right of the screen capture in figure 39 shows that this brief clip was "liked" by 243 people and shared, or reposted, by 93 others. The mortar scene as well as a few others, such as the pistol instead of the pompom, the ammo belt instead of a cheerleading skirt (see figure 40), and a final group shot showing a Marine holding an M249 squad automatic weapon (a really big gun), serve as moto imagery. In the previous chapter I explained how images of weaponry function within military combat culture as sources of empowerment and insider knowledge. References to artillery in the cheerleading video serve similar functions. They are a way for warriors to bond with one another as well as a way for them to boast about the authenticity of their war experience to "the guys in the rear."

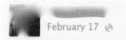

February 17

Feb 17, 2013 12:35pm
My Favorite piece, the Mortar guys are dancing before and after firing! LOL

Like · Comment · Share   👍 243 💬 1 📤 93

Figure 39. Army soldiers in the mortar scene

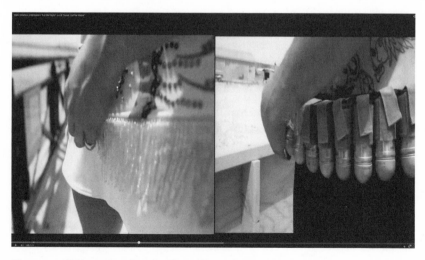

Figure 40. Split screen cheerleading skirt and ammo belt

The thing about memes is that anyone can participate in them. If you can do the Harlem shake at a dentist's office, then you can do it on an aircraft carrier. That is why memes work so well as a mode of public participation. For troops in Iraq and Afghanistan, memes offer the opportunity to speak to civilians on a shared plane. Participation hinges on a rich repertoire of both media and ideological literacy in order to adopt the familiar discourses that allow them to be heard. Although meme videos can connect war fighters to civilian culture, they can also serve as stark reminders that they are *not* on the same plane as their civilian counterparts—geographically, institutionally, and ideologically. Returning to the "one foot over here" and "one foot over there" conceptualization of the twenty-first-century deployment, memes reflect a suspension of footing. Their meaning resides in a liminal space of both/and. As texts, "Marine memes" participate in both discourse communities—the dominant public discourse of popular culture as well as the localized discourse(s) of the war fighter community.

Marine meme videos are multifaceted texts with multidimensional audiences. They are a way for troops to argue for their relevance and social presence to an American public who has lost interest in the war. Meme videos are about participating in, not merely connecting with, popular culture back home. Compared to my father's experience of "going away" to Vietnam, troops don't "go away" anymore. In fact, their participation might be amplified *the farther* they are away from home. The more distant they feel, the more they seek to close the ideological gap. Contemporary service members do not exist outside of social media's attention economy. They participate in it. Chapter 2, for example, introduced a Marine who equated feeling cared for and loved with receiving "likes" and comments on his Facebook page. It follows, then, that the troops would perform the popular culture discourses of the home front in order to receive public attention even if only in the form of view counts.

Meme videos are also a way for service members to bond with one another and configure insider/outsider boundaries. Moto moments cultivate cohesion and group identity and visually perform expectations for an "authentic" war experience. Appealing to moto helps war fighters make what they are doing seem meaningful, at least to themselves, amid a public who is bored with war fighting.

Generally speaking, a sense of public apathy informs warrior-produced content and sharing habits. During an interview at Camp Pendleton, a lance corporal said he didn't include any "disturbing" imagery on his Facebook page because "it's a side of war no one wants to talk about. No one wants to see that. Everyone knows that's going on." It may not always be the case that the troops avoid capturing "disturbing" content, but they most certainly avoid sharing it with civilian network members who do not care to see it and who lack the embodied knowledge required to interpret it accurately. A second genre of video, the combat/comic video, marks a retreat from public discourse and becomes an important in-group ritual among US troops. Meme videos, on the other hand, represent an extension outward. They allow service members and civilians to meet on a shared plane of affectivity. Evidently US troops shimmying and shaking to a pop song *is* a side of war that everyone wants to see, share, and talk about.

Combat Videos and Comic Videos

As I pointed out in the introduction to this chapter, the demographic of Americans who go to war is miniscule. The group who experiences combat is even more exclusive. A second major audio-visual genre circulating among personnel is "the combat video." Whereas nearly everyone can participate in a meme, few participate in combat. For this reason, videos depicting combat scenarios like firefights and IED blasts hold a lot of cachet in military culture. The combat video and its inverse, the comic video, work to further develop the boundaries between insider and outsider groups and function as a bonding activity for deployed personnel. The level of bonding promoted among personnel through these types of videos is different from the participation afforded by meme videos. Through meme videos, personnel suspend their footing and participate in civilian culture. By contrast, combat/comic videos circulate internally, building stronger intimacy ties among members of the exclusive combat culture, and keep both feet more firmly planted in the deployment situation.

Combat Videos

Between 2005 and 2007 YouTube videos of troops engaged in conflict received a lot of public attention.[69] YouTube was a new and exciting technology. It offered a boots-on-the-ground view of war.[70] By 2007, YouTube's novelty was beginning to wear off, and so was our endorphin rush from the Iraq invasion four years before. Audiences for these types of videos were disappearing. It seemed as if the wars in Iraq and Afghanistan had "jumped the shark."[71] We appeared to be suffering from a national affliction of media malaise, image fatigue, and/or empathy drought.[72]

But combat videos continued to play an important role for troops on deployment. Their pattern of circulation is just different. According to my interviews, Marines said they mostly made and watched combat/comic videos together in real time, or they shared them person-to-person via hardware devices. Because fewer videos of this kind circulate through networked platforms, I cannot include as many screen captures. Instead, I describe their content based on how the Marines talked about them during interviews and the handful of videos I've seen, as well as the existing scholarly literature on the subject.

Scholarly conversations about how the wars have played out on YouTube peaked around 2009 and focused almost exclusively on the combat video. Kari Andén-Papadopoulos, Christian Christensen, Jonathan Pieslak, Kevin McSorely, Jessica Ritchie, Christina Smith, and Kelly McDonald have all studied the combat genre—videos containing pictures of combat operations, weaponry, destruction, explosions, and death. On the whole, these authors describe the genre as heavily edited videos, including camera shots spliced together in tandem with rap or heavy metal music. They argue that the videos contain nationalist and/or Orientalist discourses and reinforce long-standing notions of hegemonic masculinity, heteronormativity, and/or discourses of control in US military culture.[73]

Combat videos mostly consist of firefights, battlefield interactions, and masculine displays of prowess as troops hold and discharge their weapons. The videos are stylistically shaky, unfocused, and grainy—a result of handheld, helmet-held, and dashboard-held amateur efforts. Taken together, the content and style play on cultural logics surrounding aesthetics of authenticity, as well as mainstream warfare photography and videography.[74] For the most part, the Marines I spoke with describe a tacit way of knowing what to capture with video as opposed to still photography. On a practical level, the discrepancy seems to hinge on "action" versus "nonaction."

I wouldn't take still photos of a firefight. If I was in a firefight, that's something that is very action oriented, so I would take video of it if I could help it. You know, obviously sometimes I can't, but I had a camera that I hooked up to my flak jacket on a patrol one day, and I had planned on, you know, just taking little bits and spots and pieces, and when we got into a firefight, I just recorded the whole thing. That worked a lot better than, you know, me running around with a camera instead of my weapon taking pictures.

Ease of use and safety (wanting to have his hand on his weapon rather than his camera) coincided with a propensity to videotape action. Another infantry Marine sergeant said:

When you take a [still] picture it's a single point—you are focused on a single action, a single thing that's happening at that point and time. When you are taking a video, you can cover much more ground, much more area, faster, and capture all the craziness that's going on at that point and time. It takes more attention to detail to take a still photo, where video is a simpler application.

Action, sound, and movement are important to good video footage. A corporal stationed at Camp Pendleton said he took video rather than still photos of certain things because video allows for a "fuller picture" and gives an impression of "the whole sequence." He said, "One time a truck got blowed up so I have a video of a forty-foot-long truck picking up a thirty-thousand-pound truck, lifting it up, and putting it up on like a trailer. It's like . . . a lot of power there. I thought it was pretty cool. In a still picture you couldn't see the one truck pick up the other truck. In the video you can see the whole sequence." The desire to capture movement makes riding in a convoy one of the best opportunities to videotape. As one Marine put it, "It was more available to . . . it was easier to videotape, you know, driving down the highway or driving to a city, and it was easier to videotape, you know, 'cause it's like some guys would have helmet cams, they'd mount 'em to their helmets, and turn 'em on, and be like behind a gun in a turret just looking around or whatever. I only saw a couple guys with the helmet cams though; they were pretty expensive." Because helmet cams were expensive, many Marines placed their personal cameras on the Humvee's dash and hit the "record" button. It is a strange practice since they do not want the Humvee in front of them to roll over an IED, but they press record on their cameras just in case it does. When an IED doesn't go off, they are left with a visual documentation of what transportation during deployment was like. A lieutenant who returned from Kabul, Afghanistan, in June 2012 valued his driving footage because it captured the dynamism of the experience. He said, "I didn't actually post any video, but I took a lot from like helicopters or driving through. We actually made a little video of us driving through Kabul and put it to music. Kabul is crazy. It's nuts. People driving the wrong way. That place is nuts. . . . You can capture the movement, sound, or sights—video is so much cooler [than still photography]."

Generally speaking, combat videos are more like video clips than they are like movies. They are short fragments, ripped from context, lacking a narrative structure or storyline. Outsiders would have a difficult time decoding the video's meaning—one of the reasons the lieutenant did not post any of his footage on Facebook. Sometimes, as he mentioned, these types of videos are spliced together and edited to music, but they are still a series of decontextualized fragments. A Marine at Okinawa described the genre as follows: "You know, they'll take a bunch of stuff of like guys shooting rockets into buildings and stuff, and they'll put a compilation of, you know, action scenes together and be like, '1/6th in Nasiriyah' or 'Marjah' or whatever. . . . . They'll be like guys sitting behind a wall rattling off machine gun fire or shooting a rocket into a building or watching a tank drive over a car." McSorely's research describes combat videos as "somatic," disorienting montages that depict an emotionally visceral, first-person, embodied experience. McSorely's specific interest is with helmet-cam footage. He writes about the sounds, describing some moments as powerfully silent except for the deliberative breathing of the camera operator, and argues that the natural, bodily sounds add to the sense of being there—the (corpo)reality of war.[75] However, most of the existing literature on combat videos, and the examples I've seen, emphasizes an accompanying soundtrack—usually masculine, aggressive rap or heavy metal songs that evoke feelings of ferocity and righteousness. In contrast to the lack of audio editing described in McSorely's texts, the accompanying rap and heavy metal music serves to disembody the experience. Drowning the brutality of war with a heavy bass track allows service members to watch the scenes from an emotional and psychological distance. Arguably, the accompanying music encourages viewers to feel tough, rugged, righteous, and brave. As an infantry rifleman and fire team leader explained the movie-making process:

> We had ample free time between missions while on deployment, and one of the first large purchases I made at the exchange was a laptop with Windows Movie Maker (I think that's what it was called). I had never used it before, but since I had a small digital camera I carried on patrol, I became sort of the unofficial photographer for our squad. I had a lot of still photos and nothing else to do, so I started experimenting with WMM and piecing them together into a slideshow, with music in the background. I'm sure I'd taken inspiration from the videos the prior battalion had shown us, and the guys in my platoon liked what I came up with enough to request a copy, and a few started making videos of their own.

This is how the genre replicates itself. It becomes a hobby and a way to promote group cohesion. Regardless of public interest, combat videos have always circulated among troops during these wars. Evidently the troops continue to make them whether the civilian public is looking or not. Combat videos appear to represent a local discourse for the Marines in this study. This is not to say that combat videos are unintelligible to a broader public audience. Most viewers can identify the genre of "combat" mimetically as it has been borrowed from news media footage and age-old war stories ranging from Homer's *Iliad* to *Saving Private Ryan*. Thus although audiences can interpret what they are looking at, they are not interested in seeing it. Carruthers describes our "reluctance to see" as a "yawning public aversion" stemming from our privileged distance from war's destruction. War "fails to puncture the surface of everyday life in the USA." She goes on to argue that "while civilians snooze, their uniformed counterparts in Iraq are busily shooting everything in sight—digital cameras having become an essential piece of the 21st-century kit. Over here no one may be looking. But over there it seems that everyone is snapping and filming."[76] Combat videos allow war fighters to distinguish themselves and assign meaning to what they are doing. Since the audience for combat videos is primarily other service members, it is unsurprising they don't garner broad public attention. For deployed personnel, the combat video is part of a larger experiential narrative. They can fill in the blind spots in ways that the civilian public cannot. To a civilian, it's a video of someone getting shot at. But to a Marine, it is a comrade engaging the enemy so his brothers can safely advance.

Comic Videos

Gallows humor has always had its place in a theater of war. In his memoir about disarming bombs in Iraq, Brian Castner describes how he stumbled across something so disturbing he had to laugh. He writes:

> I noticed an erect table to one side, out of place among the destruction, with an intact cardboard box on top. The box had to have been put there after the detonation; there was no way it could have survived the blast intact. I looked inside, and did not know immediately what I saw. The thing, it had been human at one time, or at least part of one. There was a sandal . . . was that a foot, in the sandal? I peered closer, and got my first whiff as flies started to buzz around me. I found toenails . . . and a tuft or two of hair, and eventually counted five protrusions. . . . Yes, I had figured it out. It was definitely a foot lying in this cardboard box. A foot in a box. Someone had put a foot in a box. I laughed. I couldn't help it. . . . "Does anyone know how this foot got in the box?" I called out. I took a picture of the foot in the box to save for the report. The guys at headquarters in Baghdad would get a kick out of it.[77]

Earlier in this chapter I quoted a combat engineer sergeant who said that because of the severity of the situation, he finds himself joking around more on deployment than he does back home. If combat videos communicate the danger of war, comic videos emphasize the inverse.[78] They serve a similar bonding function for Marines—perhaps more so since the audience for funny videos is even more exclusive. Most of the humor relies on the logic that "you had to be there." Most viewers, then, beyond the participants in the video, lack the requisite insider knowledge to decode its significance.

Bonding humor assumes that groups who share a body of knowledge, rituals, experiences, and values also share a sense of humor. Some call it "I-get-it humor," where the listener must bring some kind of specialized knowledge to the joke in order for it to act as a powerful tool to produce and/or strengthen a shared social bond.[79] I refer to it, here, as "you had to be there" since there is so much emphasis on physical location and proximity in discourses about war. This can be seen in arguments over legitimacy—how "forward" or how "rear" a person was stationed, for example. The emphasis on locale is also present when personnel talk about being "over here" and "over there." And so it goes with humor. In order to "get it," oftentimes "you had to be there." During an interview in Okinawa, an infantry sergeant tried to describe one of his favorite funny videos.

Our radio operator was sittin' behind the gun in the turret one time, and I don't even know how this came up, and it's probably a lot funnier in my head than I'm gonna say it, but. . . . It was just . . . they were talking about ice cream or something, and . . . our radio operator was like, "Sergeant [Paulson] likes ice cream. . . ." It was just . . . the situation . . . you'd have to be there, but it was really funny.

For those who are there, reviewing these videos extends and strengthens social bonds. For the most part, personnel watch the combat/comic videos together, in a shared space, oftentimes immediately after filming. In many of the interviews, the Marines cited a specific individual from their unit who was the unofficial "video guy," the person who was most adept at using the editing software and would produce videos for the group. During an interview with a lieutenant at Camp Pendleton, I asked about the "video guy."

SILVESTRI: Did he make it to post it? For his social network?
LIEUTENANT: No. He made it for us. He made it, and we all got around and watched it.
SILVESTRI: Did you watch it while you were there?
LIEUTENANT: Yeah. Yeah.
SILVESTRI: What were the themes of the videos?
LIEUTENANT: Uh. The one I'm thinking of was just like driving around Kabul and like crazy stuff that happens there. There's just like so many people and the weirdest stuff going on. Goats walking through the road. Trash everywhere.

SILVESTRI: So the environment?

LIEUTENANT: Yeah. Just the environment.

SILVESTRI: But why would you watch it while you are there? If you're in the environment, why are you watching a video of the environment?

LIEUTENANT: [*Smiling*] Well, 'cause you're driving, and like you almost hit that guy, or you're driving, and you're like, "Oh, remember that?" Or whatever.

SILVESTRI: Remember it? It was like yesterday, though, right?

LIEUTENANT: Heh heh. I don't know. That's what people like to do. People take photos on their camera and look at it right afterwards.

SILVESTRI: Do you watch it now?

LIEUTENANT: Nah. Nah. I would but. It's like the experience is a bonding thing and then afterwards it's funny to look back at it. [Reviewing] it is like a follow on to the bonding session.

SILVESTRI: And if you were to show those videos to family and friends?

LIEUTENANT: It probably wouldn't be as funny.

The bond appears to exist within a feeling of belongingness and togetherness. The brief, nonlinear, hastily edited (if edited at all), nonnarrative structures of combat/comic videos serve their purpose in country as opportunities for bonding. It is more about reliving the event together than it is about the event itself. They use videos to actively construct opportunities for bonding and memory making.

During my brother's deployment to Iraq, for example, the Marines sung deployment-inspired Christmas carols for the video camera while "burning shitters," a well-known and widely hated task among US troops.[80] As the name suggests, it involves incinerating human excrement for sanitation purposes. The process is long, the smell is putrid, and, to be frank, the job is "shitty."

Later on they would watch their performance as a group. On the bottom right of the screen capture in figure 41, the number of views is only eighty-six compared to the thousands of views for the meme videos. The low view count serves to support the idea that this type of humor is intended for in-group members who have specified knowledge. It also derives from the fact that this particular video was not shared by using Facebook as a distribution platform.

The event experienced, captured, witnessed, and remembered forms a bond among personnel. It keeps both feet in the war zone and among their comrades, even if the activity is not directly related to the mission. When the troops come home, the opportunities for interpersonal connection in a shared space dissipates except for its disembodied existence on social net-

MEU xmas

slyvestri

▶ Subscribe 151

86 views

Figure 41. Marines singing Christmas carols

work platforms. A young private first class in Okinawa who returned from Afghanistan in July 2011 said watching self-produced footage was a favorite and frequent pastime while in theater, but now that he is home, he doesn't watch his videos anymore.

> PRIVATE FIRST CLASS: If I was with a group of guys that I went out with, I would just go over it with them. We'd probably sit around looking at 'em and go, "Oh yeah this is when that happened . . ." or we'll probably just put the video recorder on the TV and just watch the whole hour of something that we just [did], rambling on, and everybody rambling on.
>
> SILVESTRI: Even though you're still there?
>
> PRIVATE FIRST CLASS: Yes! [*Laughs*]
>
> SILVESTRI: Now that you're home do you still watch it?
>
> PRIVATE FIRST CLASS: No. Not as much as I did when we were there. When I was there, we did it like almost every other day. If we did something we'd just go through and laugh at all the stupid stuff that we did. But not so much now since it's just kinda like me and not the guys I was with.

Once home from deployment, squads disperse. Personnel go to separate bases or transition out of the military entirely. Individual service members find themselves surrounded by people, even their most intimate kin, who lack the requisite discursive knowledge to understand what they have experienced. They are left to make sense of their deployments for themselves. This is an anxiety-inducing episode that service members begin preparing for long before deployment ends. It is a period of transition undertaken by every warrior and has been documented as a confusing and troubling experience as far back as Homer's *Odyssey*.

One of the ways US troops prepare for both feet landing back home is by creating what they call "deployment videos." The deployment video is a chronologically organized video detailing the good, the bad, the ugly, and the mundane of an individual service member's deployment. The deployment video is the most personal of texts. It is from the perspective of an individual Marine among his unit on deployment. So far this chapter has moved from texts with broad discursive access to more locally inflected texts. The deployment video is a unique combination because it draws from familiar cultural discourses to communicate a relatively personal experience.

Deployment videos function as we imagine a twentieth-century photo album to function. A key difference, however, is temporality. Most personnel produce their deployment videos before they've even processed out of country. In other words, they commemorate their tour of duty before it has ended, not to mention before the war, itself, is over. A Marine at Camp Pendleton who had recently returned from his first deployment to Afghanistan said deployment videos serve educational, preparatory purposes. "Some of the members from the battalion we relieved [showed] us a few of the videos from their deployment, just so we could get an idea of what they had faced," he explained. The deployment videos preemptively collect experiences into coherent, digestible narratives so troops can begin memorializing their deployments before they've left. And, as the Marine's comment above suggests, they can also provide incoming units with a visual itinerary for what to expect.[81]

Deployment Videos

Troops use deployment videos to prepare themselves for finding their footing when they come home. This practice becomes even more significant as advances in transportation have shortened the transition time between being in theater and being home from weeks to a matter of days or even hours. The troops are being slingshot back to the States, leaving less opportunity for them to smoothly ease back into their previous lives.

Much like the brief, mediated mental and emotional shifts enabled by so-cial media communication, the physical shift now is nearly instantaneous too. Earlier I cited a combat engineer who described coming home, or back "over here," as worrisome because he knows he will have to deal with the emotional baggage he has been stockpiling while he was "over there." The deployment video becomes a sense-making apparatus. It promotes a linear, chronological narrative with a beginning, middle, and end. Largely emphasizing the positive and picturesque, the deployment videos keep just enough of the "dark" or "disturbing" images to give a sense of hon-esty and authenticity. Overall, the storyline is familiar and tidy, and easily recognizable. According to the Marines I interviewed, most deployment videos begin with a unit's arrival in country. The majority of the content consists of still photos strung together chronologically and edited to music with video clips interspersed throughout. As with the combat videos, the musical accompaniment imposes affect. The story is usually told from the perspective of an individual service member since the majority of the con-tent is from his personal snapshot or video collection. Since many Marines make their deployment videos prior to exiting theater, they do not include the anticipated homecoming ending to the war story. For example, the screen shot in figure 42 depicts a deployment video that closes with the words "United States of America" scrolling across the screen in lieu of a

Ar Ramadi Iraq. Fox Co 2/5 2004

Figure 42. Deployment video final screen

clearly demarcated ending. The video in figure 42 is from a 2004 deployment. The person who posted the video is also the video's creator as the
caption below reads, "Most Pictures are taken by me. Made during one of
my tour[s] in Iraq."[82] He did not upload the video to YouTube until 2009.

Deployment videos take on the generic traits of self-representation.
Media scholar Nancy Thumim describes self-representational texts as
emphasizing "ordinary people, ordinary people in community, community, emotion, experience, interior worlds, personal history, idea of a
personal journey, individual perspective, speaking to camera, home-made
DIY scrapbook style, family photos, and personal artifacts."[83] As self-
representational texts, deployment videos help personnel see and understand themselves and their deployments the way they would like to be seen,
understood, and remembered. However, sometimes they need assistance
constructing this narrative.

In many of the letters my brother wrote to me, he referenced a desire for
some sort of commemorative video. I didn't know it then, but he was asking
me to help him assemble his deployment video. During his first month in
country, he wrote, "I have lots of good pictures and footage of the trip so far
that you could sort through and put together a nice DVD for me!!!" A few
months later, he wrote, "I have a ton of pictures that will make a nice DVD
esp. the x-mas ones, which you can set to Stevie [Nicks'] 'Silent Night.'"
One month later he wrote again, "So I have a ton of great pictures and
video clips I'll let you sort through and artistically create a DVD for me!"[84]
It is clear to me now that what my brother wanted was a narrative. He sent
me hundreds of digital images on compact discs. The files were entirely
disorganized. My only clues to chronology involved opening each file and
tracking his weight loss and mustache gain. The video is approximately
twelve minutes long with a definite structure—his unit's arrival by ship in
Kuwait, some imagery of camaraderie set to Ram Jam's "Black Betty," and
some photos of combat operations set to Imogen Heap's "Hide and Seek."
The video concludes with his unit's retrograde back to the States. He was
home about a month before I completed the video. To this day, he cherishes
it, though he doesn't watch it anymore. I think it served its purpose. The
wars in Iraq and Afghanistan are confusing. They are perpetual and without clear boundaries. The enemy is an ideology rather than a uniformed
militia. The American public can enjoy the privilege of opting out, and give
up trying to understand what the news media labeled a quagmire. But for
the troops, being able to understand their deployment and assign a narrative to their experience is critical.

Perhaps the wars' ambiguity is what inspires deployment videos to follow such a generic formula. The adherence to chronology and traditional

tropes of war makes my brother's outsourcing the work of building a narrative less surprising. Although deployment videos capture an individual's wartime experience, they draw from well-known public discourses about war to do so. In this way, the deployment video is similar to a Kodak-era family album in that it is a relatively private text, relying on public narratives and patterns of communication. The deployment video draws from iconic tropes of the war story—the departure, the arrival, the hard times, the camaraderie, and so on. The desire to order the world, to put seemingly disparate or confusing events into a narrative, is a universal human impulse. A lance corporal in Okinawa described his deployment video as a bizarre mnemonic device for an experience, most of which he would rather not remember. He said, "I think it's just the simplest way to summarize what we went through, for those who aren't sure how to describe it. Words don't do the experience justice. The videos don't either really—you don't get the unpredictability, the smell, or the intense fear that you have no choice but to suppress—but for some people the videos probably come closer."

There is a common assumption that trauma brings people together. And war, as a temporally extended traumatic event, is said to form the tightest of bonds. That is partly why the combat videos work as a vehicle of cohesion among troops. Warriors can bear witness to one another's trauma. But while they can bear witness to their own experiences and the experiences of their comrades, they aren't always able to talk about what they've seen or done. A sergeant in Okinawa gearing up for his fourth deployment said his inability to explain his experience was what motivated him to capture video.

I just wanted to grasp, I wanted to have something to be able to say, to show people and say. . . . They ask me all the time, "What did you do?" You know? And I can explain it to them or I can show them. It's easier to show somebody because even if I explain what I've been through, or what I've seen, or what I've done, people I've found that don't have like the experiences, or haven't actually been to those places, won't fully grasp what I'm talking about, and it's not because I think that they're stupid; it's just because they haven't been in those experiences before. I want them to be able to understand them fully 100 percent.

He begins by saying, "I just wanted to grasp" and "I wanted to have something to be able to say." These comments suggest that the deployment video arms him with intelligibility—it allows him to "grasp" what he went through, to make sense of a long, fragmented experience. Additionally, he cites a desire for his audience to understand "fully 100 percent" what his experiences were like. He thinks people will understand if he "show[s]" them the deployment video. The problem, however, is that most people are not interested in seeing those experiences. Sometimes even a service person's closest of kin resemble Carruthers' yawning public, disinterested in war—even a war fought by their own child. During an interview with a baby-faced private first class at Okinawa, he described his family's boredom with his deployment video:

> PRIVATE FIRST CLASS: [My family] actually gave up watching after about twelve minutes. They're like, "All you're doing is looking at your feet." I was like, "Just wait! There's a part that's about to come up."
> SILVESTRI: Do you think that's what they expected Afghanistan to be like?
> PRIVATE FIRST CLASS: Not really.
> SILVESTRI: How do you think it surprised them?
> PRIVATE FIRST CLASS: I think they'd think it was going to be like more gunfire and me running and ducking under some kind of tent. I don't know what they thought. But this is what I did.

During deployment, making, sharing, and watching videos is an important bonding ritual among troops. When they watch videos together they relive shared experiences and derive a sense of mutual respect and understanding. It makes sense that when they return home they would try to recreate a similar bonding activity with friends and family by sitting down and reviewing their deployment video together. But it does not have the same affect. Even when civilian kin are attentive audience members, their engagement with the narrative is anticipatory. They have ideas about what a war story should look like, and if the deployment video doesn't meet their expectations, they may, as the private first class's family did, "give up watching." This encourages the troops to present, make meaning, and potentially remember their deployments with age-old public discourses about war. It may not be the most fitting model, however, to understand the wars of the new millennium.

Stick a Flag in It: Yearning for the End

The wars of the new millennium are perpetual. They resist narrative's conventional markers of a beginning, middle, and end. As a case in point, the 2011 troop withdrawal from Iraq signified closure to be sure, but not necessarily a definitive end. Neither victory nor defeat was clear. The fog of the Iraq War still hangs low and thick—its meaning is still muddled, especially as we send American forces back again.[84] And over a decade later in Afghanistan, Osama Bin Laden is dead, but the war continues.[85] It is of little wonder, then, that Carruthers identifies a disappearing audience for war. From the audience's perspective, there is no payoff for their attention. Following the story through the climax doesn't lead to a satisfying sigh of resolution. In their confusion and frustration, audiences lend their attention elsewhere.

As a result of our nonnarrative, "presentist" culture, our attention structures have changed. Our collective interest in internet memes is indicative of this shift. Whereas narratives inscribe motivation and logical understanding, this is not the case for memes. In memes, there is no clear narrative, and it is arguable whether they have an ending at all. In fact, memes might be the perfect metaphor for an age that no longer declares war.[87] A critical point, however, is that memes require attention to propagate. With war, the inverse seems to be true. Without our attention, war perpetuates.

For the American public, war has become a naturalized context—a backdrop for the latest meme video. Our shallow understanding and engagement with war comes at the expense of bearing moral witness to it. As I've argued elsewhere, whether we choose to acknowledge it or not, war is a collective, political, public trauma. It is a social ill. We are all morally implicated in acts of war.[88] But what does it say about our commitment to ending the trauma of war when we shoulder boots on the ground with the responsibility of reminding us that one is taking place?

Liberal democracy depends on the willingness of strangers to be sufficiently attuned to the existence of others so that their positions might be considered.[89] What happens if we do not acknowledge others' positions where they reside but instead expect them to meet us in the depoliticized social sphere of affectivity? This chapter focused on the differences between participating in public discourse through widely intelligible meme videos, and retreating from public discourse through the internal sharing of locally inflected texts. In the former, Marines and civilians meet on a shared social plane, accessible through popular culture discourses. In the latter, Marines communicate to each other through culturally specific discourses whereby interpretation relies on embodied ways of knowing.

Meme videos require literacies that position troops in a liminal space between "here" and "there." Combat/comic videos favor a mentality that keeps "both feet" in the deployment scenario. Although I am hesitant to make a wholesale evaluative claim about which subject position is better for the health, morale, and safety of our troops, I will say that Marines describe the former subjectivity, a veritable social straddle, as a source of stress during our interviews. The critical point, here, is that service members must compete in the same attention economy as everyone else. Get in line and make a meme. If war does not permeate everyday existence for most Americans save for its visualization as the context for the latest meme video, can we say that we are sufficiently attuned to the trauma of war? Or will we allow it to persist and be lulled into believing that everything is under control? If the loss of human life is the sin qua non of war, where's the evidence of it? It is certainly not on Facebook or YouTube.

CONCLUSION

This Means War

At first glance, social media appear to be a morale boost for the troops since they can stay in touch and receive emotional support from loved ones back home. That perspective is not incorrect; the situation is just a little more complicated than that. Although social media present opportunities to create digital intimacy, doing so requires a great deal of time and attention. Platforms like Facebook are built on architectures of active participation. Users are the content. Having a presence on Facebook, for example, requires participants to update personal content, actively contribute to threads and discussions, and share personal information with other network members.[1] Social media's association with everyday civilian culture promotes casual norms of conversation with emphases on constant connectivity, immediacy, sociality, and self-promotion.

Generally speaking, social media's unspoken codes of decorum do not leave much room for serious deliberation over hard-hitting political affairs. As Todd Gitlin quipped during a lecture at the University of Iowa, "Can a medium used to post pictures of cute kittens also be used to overthrow a dictatorship?"[2] Save for the widely publicized Kony 2012 Facebook campaign and the Arab Spring's Twitter Revolution, social media are more commonly spaces of lighthearted popular culture banter. Moreover, the alleged success of the Kony and Arab Spring cases has come under much public debate recently.[3] All this is to say that social media culture informs what we talk about among our social networks, and it's usually more popular than it is political, although one could argue that those categories are becoming one and the same. My central point is that in spite of constant connectivity and social pressure to post about themselves, for service members in Iraq and Afghanistan, the topic of war is unfitting for discussion on social media.

When service members filter their wartime experiences through the norms of Facebook, the result is something of a visual paradox—a social media–friendly version of war—shiny happy people holding guns.[4] Instead of iconic images of war-weary soldiers silhouetted against a sunset, we see video clips of Marines dancing along to the latest stateside internet phenomenon.

This is because, for the most part, US troops adopt social media discourse when communicating with their social network from Iraq and

Afghanistan. Marwick describes social media discourse as predominantly "embedded in the everyday life and conversations of people."[5] As a result, the Facebook posts, meme videos, and albums service members make on deployment emphasize a more casual and domesticated vision of war, a perspective troops adopt as they make sense of their own wartime experiences. In other words, the way the Marines communicate about their deployments via social media impacts how they think about those deployments. Performing a nonchalant, cavalier attitude for the sake of the "nightmare reader" influences interpretive frameworks for war. Simply put, connection and participation in social media culture from Iraq and Afghanistan shape not only how the personnel perceive their deployment experiences but also how the public sees them.

If we assume discursive authority rests on eye-witnessing, then the troops in Iraq and Afghanistan should be able to give us a fairly precise account of the Global War on Terrorism.[6] I asked one service member if he kept a journal documenting his deployment to Iraq. He explained that, in his view, nothing was worthy of documentation. In his words, "I started one, and it only went through Kuwait, and then by that time it stopped, you know, it was just like, 'Oh, I'm gonna write a book someday,' you know, and—I don't have enough actions in my career path to write a book—the same boring day-to-day activities." I asked why he didn't think day-to-day activities in Iraq were worth documenting. He said, "It's the same thing over and over and over again. What are you gonna do? 'Now it's Tuesday, and I'm doing the same thing I did yesterday. . . .' Why would you want to write that every single day? I wouldn't. And I didn't. Because there's nothing—most of the time there's—most of the time there's nothing. Who's gonna want to read that?" At the most basic level, his comments suggest that "actions" are requisite for documentation, and that if one were to write a book about his "career," presumably in the military, one would want to encounter sufficient "actions." Unfortunately I did not follow up as to what he meant by "actions." But his plan to write a "book" about his deployment to Iraq suggests he anticipated his experience would match an existing frame of reference for war, and when it did not, he abandoned his book project altogether. In other words, it's likely that the situated meaning of "actions" refers to a prior understanding of "war."

Although thoughtful critics have spent much of their ink on negative critiques of the war metaphor as applied by politicians, presidents, pundits, and protestors, I want to lend my attention to the terms the troops themselves use to talk about their experiences in Iraq and Afghanistan. How do they negotiate their world through language? Understanding how service members most directly involved in these conflicts define them can enrich our collective social imagination about war. Although my inquiry begins at the individual level, my focus is not on psychology. Rather, I use individual, boots-on-the-ground accounts of "war" to trace a larger cultural shift in definitions of war.

The Myth Makes Us Feel Better

During interviews, Marines rarely used the term "war" as a frame of reference for their deployments. Instead they invoked discourses associated with everyday life and used "war" to describe *specific moments* during their deployments.[7] Frames of reference are symbolic structures that allow people to impose order on personal and social experiences. Frames of reference provide perspective for the interpretation of events as well as a chart for deciding what types of action should be taken. For the contemporary service member, a deployment to a war zone is not "war" itself but may be punctuated by *moments of war*. It reflects a compelling inversion of the old adage that imagines war as "long periods of boredom punctuated by moments of sheer terror."[8] Instead, my interviews suggest that contemporary service members imagine sheer terror (or at least visual evidence of it) to be the constitutive content for war. As a case in point, I asked a service member if his digital photography reflected war. He responded that he did not think it did and went on to describe some of the images he captured that would qualify as war. In his words:

I mean, some stuff you know, because we have pictures of . . . we were . . . at the time that we came in, there were still a lot of tanks, enemy tanks sittin' on the side of the road smokin', you know, so we take pictures of that. Or there's one tower, I can't remember what town we went through, but there's . . . it is not a roundabout, but you had to drive, you had to curl around this monument type thing in the road, and then there was also a big tall electrical tower there that had been I guess bombed or something, but it was all just crushed down. So I have pictures of that, and so yeah, that would be uh, you know, pictures of war. I mean like, "Oh wow look at this," and you know . . . some of the destruction, yeah. There's a building on, at the time we called it Highway 1? I think it might be Tampa now? I don't know what it is; anyway, going to Ballad, probably twenty minutes before you get to the turn before going to Ballad, there's a building that looks like the Oklahoma City bombing, you know what that looked like? The whole front of the building was wiped out, and it reminded me of the Oklahoma City bombing site, so I got a picture, and I was like, "Wow," so I mean those types of things were pictures of . . . in Baghdad, where the missile come down into the Baath

Figure 43. Crumbling building

party, so yeah, you know . . . some. But I would say the majority of the pictures were just everyday stupid stuff going on, and you have a camera, so you click a picture.

There is an illuminating juxtaposition between "war" and "everyday stupid stuff." When he invokes "war" as a frame of reference for his experience, he flags visual markers that align with tropes of Hollywood war films. He could literally point to these *scenes* (often with his camera's lens) to declare them signposts for war (see figure 43). There are no such specific markers for the everyday. His conceptual filter for war seems to align with a common mythic understanding of war—"enemy tanks," "missiles," and "destruction." World War II apparently remains the archetype in our collective consciousness.

Although many are quick to point out that Iraq and Afghanistan represent a *new kind of war*, calling it everything from "postmodern," to "hyper modern," to "third wave," the archetype of classical warfare with nations squaring off against nations, positioning artillery piece against artillery piece, persists in the national imaginary.[9] This archetype of war is a symbolic construction sustained, in part, by popular media. To save the reader's time, I will avoid recounting the lot of Hollywood war films, but I will note that even highly praised documentaries like *Restrepo*, which hold the promise of a more complicated representation of twenty-first-century warfare, fall back on conventional tropes of war film. And apparently, first-person witnesses to war, the US troops themselves, are not beyond these tropes either.

Marines describe a sense of pleasure in visually recreating war's mythos. The pleasure derives from fulfilling expectations. As one service member explained, "People would video the convoy. I don't know if you're hopin' for some explosion to go off, or what." It is morbid to think that a service member would wait with anticipation (or "hope") for an IED blast. But his comment begins to make sense when we consider that he was deployed well after the initial 2003 invasion of Iraq, where the most traditional warlike activity occurred. He wants his experience in Iraq to reflect our cultural expectations for war. In this way, he is waiting for an IED blast so that he has proof of war.

Troops recreate the fiction of war in part for their social network audiences and in part for themselves. Myth is appealing because it allows for troops (and social network audiences) to make sense of a long, complicated experience. The myth of war also helps justify experiences—the beautiful, the mundane, and the terrifying. Earlier I referenced a combat engineer who said he recognized the heavy hand myth plays in media representations of war, but the closer he matched those tropes in his own documentary efforts, the better he felt. "[It] makes us feel better—the myth is where we get some of the satisfaction." Myths work as sense-making apparatuses. They offer ready-made narratives; they are plug-and-chug formulas to organize chaotic life encounters. A problem arises, however, for the troops when their experiences don't align with cultural expectations for war. And often, because of the style in which these recent wars are fought, they don't.

According to some war scholars, it is arguable whether "war" is even the best word to describe the prolonged international military campaign against terror. This is in part because military engagement in Iraq and Afghanistan was poorly defined from the start. As counterinsurgency strategist David Kilcullen notes, the United States has

never formally sat down with allies and determined which theater in the current conflict should have priority, how to prioritize our competing resource demands and strategic threats, and what our common, agreed-on political goals should be. Individual campaigns in Iraq and Afghanistan, of course, have been the subject of numerous Coalition conferences and formal meetings. But the overall "War on Terrorism" has not, and this has led—among other things—to sharp differences between allies over relative priorities, and indeed the conceptual basis for the war.[10]

If, at the level of strategy, there is no clear-cut conceptualization for what these wars should look like, it's less of a surprise that the troops aren't sure either. It is trickle-down confusion. Like the policy for social media, "war" also appears to operate by a "we'll know it when we see it" logic. Even boots-on-the-ground are making post-hoc judgments about whether or not they experienced "war" during their deployments.

According to my interviews, it appears the Marines are discursively and therefore conceptually caught between conventional understandings of "war" and "everyday life," wherein war consists of tanks, missiles, and destruction, and everyday life refers to work and social realms. Even as sensory witnesses to war, their thought processes appear to rely on mythic understandings of "over there" and "over here."

Part of this disorientation has to do with the fact that they are communicating on social media, a semipublic platform that requires communicators to rely on discourses familiar to a general audience. Although we would expect eyewitnesses to have more nuanced perceptions and be able to tell us that war is actually very complicated, messy, and even boring, US troops on deployment are restricted by institutional guidelines, communication infrastructure, and cultural convention. The result is a version of Iraq and Afghanistan that is a representational hodgepodge. On the one hand, there exist messages and images readily interpreted as "war," and on the other hand, we see texts more fitting to the norms of social media culture, invoking an image of everyday life in the United States.

When "Over There" Is "Over Here"

Practically speaking, the Marines in this book maintain sharp distinctions between "war" and other "everyday" aspects of deployment. For the rest of us, however, it seems that the lines distinguishing the contexts of war and everyday life are blurring. Perhaps most notably, advancements in drone technology have introduced a number of important questions in this regard. Psychologists, technology researchers, and legal experts have recently begun paying attention to the emotional disturbances drone pilots experience as they shoot at targets seven thousand miles away and return home a few hours later to eat a lasagna dinner with their family.[11] The context of war, it seems, is bleeding into everyday life. And the inverse of that phenomenon is already well underway in war zone contexts. If the study of drone pilots shows us how the context of war is introduced into everyday life, then this book shows us how the context of everyday life is introduced into a war zone. The problem is that when "war" is conflated with the "everyday," an exit strategy becomes unimaginable. What is the exit strategy for something that has become "everyday"?

Deployments to war have become perpetual at both operational and individual levels. In decades past, war for the individual service member was an *isolated* event. First, it was isolated in space and time—communication with family and friends was rare and irregular. The home front and the war front felt temporally and spatially distant. This is no longer the case. US troops can stay in constant contact with home, causing them to occupy an in-between mental and emotional space with one foot "over there" and one foot "over here." For example, chapter 2 emphasized social media's potential to be a distraction by introducing a senior enlisted NCO who admitted that he ironically felt happiest and most secure on a small patrol base outside the wire because his men did not have access to the internet. He said, "As bad as it may sound, there are a lot of issues that arise when young guys have unlimited communication access to their loved ones. . . . I needed the Marines to remain focused on their mission and not left wondering what their young, newly married wife may be doing." Although one could imagine that the troops always wondered what was going on back home, social media access from the battlefield now provides a tempting opportunity to find out. And beyond the opportunity, there is an underlying social pressure from the civilian side to remain in touch. Lance Corporal Sutton's girlfriend, for example, felt it was logical for him to stay in contact while on deployment. After all, Facebook use is sanctioned by the US military. Yet Sutton thought quitting Facebook to be logical; he felt too removed and distracted from his missions. Sutton, however, is an outlier. In spite of the dangers associated with a lack of focus, most troops feel compelled to keep up and remain copresent with friends and family.

War also used to be isolated in its occurrence. Today's service members spend significantly more time at war than those in the past. During draft wars, personnel did not typically deploy as frequently. Today the cycles of combat have been so long and so frequent that, according to a 2007 RAND study, unmarried Marines deployed an average of 311 days during a four-year enlistment period. That means if an average deployment lasts approximately six to eight months (not including predeployment training or "work-up," which lasts three to six months), then Marines are deploying to combat twice in a span of four years. In other words, Marines today spend the majority of their service lives either on deployment or preparing to deploy. We are sending the same group of nineteen-year-olds to fight our wars over and over again. To illustrate this point on a broader scale the *Marine Times* cited Defense Department data that showed that as of October 2009, American troops have deployed almost 3.3 million times to Iraq and Afghanistan. The article goes on to point out that within the eight years between 2001 and 2009, more than two million men and women have deployed, and 793,000 of them deployed more than once.[12] Simply put, for the average enlisted Marine, war is acquiring something of an "everyday" quality.

Indeed, a very small portion of the American public has been on perpetual deployment calendars for the last decade and a half. Long-term, widespread war fought by a small, distant portion of the nation's population gives way to an apathetic American public. As Paul Taylor, executive vice president of the Pew Research Center points out, "Typically when our nation is at war, it's a front-burner issue for the public. But with these post-9/11 wars, which are now past the 10-year mark, the public has been paying less and less attention."[13] As I've argued throughout, the troops are neither ignorant nor immune to our collective attention economy. With frequent and recurring deployment cycles, they are constantly moving between worlds home and away. And with constant connection and access, they perform dual identities as both members of the public audience and members of the armed forces. As active members of the public audience, they know what garners attention and have learned how to play the game. In the last chapter, I introduced a Marine at Camp Pendleton who told me that he didn't put anything "disturbing" on his Facebook page because "it's a side of war that no one wants to talk about. No one wants to see that. Everyone knows that's going on." And he's right. Our collective attention economy doesn't want to see that.

Informed by low public interest and constrained by OPSEC and the norms of decorum associated with social network site communication, US troops tend to film and photograph "stupid stuff," or things "people don't care about." In spite of the fact that these wars have been mediated more than any other in history, we are hard pressed to come up with one image that will stand in as the future collective visual recall for what Iraq or Afghanistan looked like. The lack of iconography despite a documentary surplus says something about contemporary social media culture; it appears to be the antithesis of icon culture. Our fixation on moment-to-moment experiences of the immediate present reflects Rushkoff's diagnosis of "narrative collapse," an impatient impulsiveness and loss of linear story.[14] The chaos of the present compels a search for icons to serve as punctuation marks or signposts for an unfolding story.

Nonchalant Boredom

In an analysis of an Associated Press photograph of four Marines listlessly playing a board game at their post in Afghanistan (see figure 44), John Lucaites argues on his weblog, *No Caption Needed*, that the photograph "may be something of an allegory for our own, larger cultural relationship to war . . . our boredom channeled (and in some measure legitimized) by their nonchalance."

Figure 44. Marines playing Risk in Afghanistan. Brennan Linsley, Associated Press.

In the commentary following his post, Lucaites and I discussed the possibility that apathetic, "nonchalant boredom" is a reason the conflicts in Iraq and Afghanistan persist. Lucaites writes, "Maybe it's one of the reasons the war goes on. . . . In a way we are all bored with war . . . but in that nonchalant bourgeois way that we get bored, which never really animates us to do anything about it."[15] In my view, and as I've argued throughout, the new media environment unique to the wars in Iraq and Afghanistan contributes to this "nonchalant boredom."

The nonchalance pointed out by Lucaites emerged in several of my interviews with military personnel. It stuck out with particular salience during the interview I referenced earlier with the service member who described his images of war looking like the Oklahoma City bombing site. When I asked for a summative statement about his deployment, he said, "It's just a big pain in the butt because it's a whole lot of just ridiculousness that just goes on, and goes into it." In a more lengthy comment he went on to say:

People ask you, "How did your deployment go?" and you're like, I don't know, it wasn't, we've been very fortunate we haven't had anybody hurt or killed, so it's, for us to say, most of us would be like, "It wasn't that bad," you know. Did it suck? Yeah, it's a hundred-plus degrees and sandy and dirty, and you know, you have to go to the bathroom in an outhouse, and you have to eat, you know, whatever. It's better now, it's getting better and better all the time, but at the same time, it wasn't all that bad.

He describes his deployment to Iraq as "a big pain in the butt" full of "ridiculousness." His language, especially in the first comment, is casual and evokes irritation. Out of context, it might sound like he was describing a Saturday afternoon at the Department of Motor Vehicles. In the second, fuller explanation, he begins to say that his deployment "wasn't that bad" but stops himself to disclaim that no one (presumably US troops in his unit) was hurt or killed. Then he goes on to describe the rugged living conditions, and hedges once again to explain, "It's better now, it's getting better and better all the time." He is caught between two frames of reference: war and everyday life. If he imagines war to be what he described earlier—missiles and destruction—then he certainly was, as he said, "very fortunate" not to have any of his comrades hurt or killed. He also describes harsh living conditions, which were evidently improving "all the time." Apparently for service members, the model for improvement is the ability to approximate "everyday life."

In the same set of interviews and in a host of others, Marines told me that while on deployment they constantly worked on their bases in terms of both security and comfort. For example, they use generators to power their forward operating bases, they "tactically acquire" couches, satellite dishes, and TVs, and they build furniture out of scrap wood.[16] Like the drone pilots who experience war in their otherwise everyday life, the US troops in Iraq and Afghanistan try to literally construct everyday life in a war zone. During my brother's deployment to East Hit in 2005, he built a sun deck attached to the FOB (see figure 45).

Tours of Duty

The spectrum of what constitutes war as opposed to everyday life in Iraq and Afghanistan is broad and indefinite. And deployments are certainly not uniform. Depending on whom I interview, there are varying shades of gray. Beyond "everydayness," many interviews and Facebook posts included references to "vacation" or "tourist" discourses. The Facebook photo albums, for example, used labels like "Afghanistan 2010," which sounds similar to the way we might label a vacation photo album. In fact, a Marine at Camp Pendleton describes his photography habits similarly to how we imagine a vacationing tourist would. He said, "I would take photos of just the ter-

Figure 45. OIF sun deck

rain, the countryside, anything I thought would be unique, that you just definitely couldn't see in Atlanta, Georgia, where my parents live. A house, some sort of structure . . . anything I thought they would be interested in." This Marine's response explains the logic of most tourist photography—find an iconic visual representation in a subjectively exotic locale and capture it to share with friends and family "back home."

The image in figure 46 depicts a mountainous vista in Afghanistan. Most of the Operation Enduring Freedom (OEF) albums in this study include imagery of the mountain ranges. During interviews with Marines who deployed to Afghanistan, many mentioned how beautiful they found the country to be in spite of their reason for being there. Even in Iraq, a decidedly less picturesque environment, a discourse of tourism emerged. For example, a Marine who deployed to Iraq in 2008 as part of Operation Iraqi Freedom (OIF) described his motivation to take digital photos as follows: "If you were kinda like sightseeing, going to a new location, and there was something like a palace or some historical figure [or] object there, you'd hand your camera over to someone so you could get your picture." He went on to say, "Like when we went to Babylon, you get to go on a tour of the

Figure 46. Mountain range in Afghanistan

castle for a dollar and get a picture by the entrance there." In the context of photography, travel, and album creation, it makes sense for a vacation discourse to emerge, not to mention the fact that we refer to deployments as "tours" (see figure 47).[17]

Although "vacation" was not necessarily the most fitting frame of reference, it appeared to operate as a referential placeholder for many troops. Sometimes they used "vacation" to express an important distinction, as in: "It's nice to remember the good stuff—I wouldn't say it's like a vacation of course, but it's nice to reminisce and . . . you know, there's a difference between going to Mexico and going to Iraq." Although this Marine never went on to explain what the difference was, it appears to be significant to him that a distinction is made.

For the rest of us, however, where war seems distant yet pervasive and perpetual, the tension between "war" and "work," which is arguably a trope of the "everyday," collapses. This point is exacerbated by the fact that the current conflicts employ a professional military whose deployments are becoming more and more regular. Recently an issue of the *Boston Globe* featured a photo essay of a National Guardsman returning from Afghanistan to surprise his daughter for her birthday. A caption reads, "Between the long shifts he works overseas and the flight back home . . . he was exhausted by the time he arrived."[18] Referring to an Afghanistan deployment in terms of "shift work" reflects a nonchalant, bourgeois attitude about war. It reminds me of a joke by comedian Daniel Tosh, who says, "Bring the troops home tomorrow and continue the war here. Because we owe it to our troops to let them sleep in their own beds with their families, wake up in the morning, have a delicious breakfast, drive to war."[19] Laughter aside,

Figure 47. Tourist-style photo

Tosh's satirical quip prompts audiences to reflect on the current "work-as-usual" attitude toward war in our collective consciousness.

There are surely different investments informing service members' definitions of war versus civilians' definitions—most notably, bodily risk. The distinction between war and work is much more crisp for a Marine in Iraq or Afghanistan. For him, the division is *practical*. But there is also something *ideological* at stake in maintaining war as an exception. Americans might never experience another World War II–style war. Like it or not, Iraq and Afghanistan represent what war looks like today. In the words of President Obama, speaking to the National Defense University on May 23, 2013, "We must define our effort not as a boundless 'global war on terror,' but rather as a series of persistent, targeted efforts to dismantle specific networks of violent extremists that threaten America."[20] The president's remarks call for a literal redefinition of the Global War on Terrorism. According to the new definition, war is "persistent." It is a part of everyday life.

On the thirteen-year anniversary of the September 11 attack, President Obama announced the expansion of the US campaign against the Islamic

State. He said, "We will degrade and ultimately destroy [ISIS] through a comprehensive and sustained counter-terrorism strategy."[21] Two days after the president declared "a comprehensive and sustained counter-terrorism strategy," Secretary of State John Kerry tried to assuage public anxiety with the clarification that "what we are doing is engaging in a very significant counter-terrorism operation, and it's going to go on for some period of time. . . . If somebody wants to think about it as being at war with [ISIS] they can do so, but the fact is it is a major counter-terrorism operation that will have many different moving parts."[22] Kerry's remarks suggest that the distinction between "war" and "counter-terrorism" is a matter of semantics. Yet the critical point is that vocabulary informs action. Different frameworks of interpretation lead to different conclusions about reality.

Memories of Now

The fact that evolving realties in Afghanistan do not match commonly held expectations for what war looks like causes personnel to introduce alternative discourses such as "everyday," "vacation," or "work." The emergence of competitive, incongruous discourses is a cue that the dominant discourse for war is shifting to account for its evolving constitution. For the most part, however, the service members that I interviewed appear to be caught between two discourses—war and everyday life. Neither is exactly right; hence the feeling of having one foot here and one foot there. The negative space between "war" and "everyday" marks a virtual groping for a meaningful way to talk about the twenty-first-century deployment.

Not only do these emerging tropes affect interpretations of war at the moment it is being waged, but they also contribute to the memory of war. I asked Marines if they ever reviewed their social media content from their deployments once they were home. Several responded that they had, and when I asked them how it made them feel, a majority of them said it made them want to redeploy. A contributing factor for this surprising response is that Marines' Facebook communication, thanks to institutional expectations, social norms of communication, and media-specific conventions of representation, tends to be relatively nondescript and does not include negative details about deployment. As one Marine described, "My wall posts are like real vague, you know, like 'Really miss the wife right now, can't wait to go on vacation with her this summer' or like stuff like that." In another interview, a lance corporal described using a Facebook application that summarized his year's worth of deployment posts. He said, "I did one thing like it summed up all your statuses for like that year and my top three statuses were like . . . 'Coming home,' and 'I'm home,' and . . . something else about being home." Even though the themes of their Facebook posts were roughly about homesickness, they do not contain details about the pain or drudgery of deployment.

In other cases, Facebook content can actually promote a positive view of the deployment owing to the culture's emphasis on affirmative life experiences and the fact that many Marines use the platform as a way to reassure friends and family of their safety. As one corporal described, "They can hear it from my voice all day, you know, 'Oh, I'm safe, don't worry, I'm fine,' but I can be . . . you know . . . anyone can say that, so I send them pictures of me happy in my chair and say 'Hey, I'm safe. Look, I'm fine.'" Later in the same interview I asked him if he ever imagines reviewing these photos in the future. He said, "Yeah, I think for future deployments I can look back at the pictures and video and just kinda refresh my memory on how it was and how it really is out there so I can be better mentally prepared than when I initially went there." I don't want to get caught in a discussion over what deployment is "really" like, but it is worth pointing out that Facebook communication frames deployment in a particular way.[23] And if these posts, photos, and memes become the digital artifacts that are representative of Iraq and Afghanistan, we should recognize that "the nightmare reader" informs our memories too.

Declaring War

At present, media outlets continue to use the term "war" to describe our military involvement in Iraq and Afghanistan.[24] Some critics denounce the term's persistence in light of ongoing developments, especially as December 2014 brought a symbolic end to combat operations in Afghanistan with a flag-lowering ceremony.[25] Despite evolving realities in Iraq and Afghanistan, I believe that "war" is the most fitting term to describe the continuous armed conflict, political strife, and tragic deaths occurring every day. Denying use of the term "war" resists redefinition.

The argument against using the term "war" to describe the current conflicts in Iraq and Afghanistan is that it creates a specific lens through which we view events, necessarily directing our attention to certain aspects of the situation while obscuring and distorting others. Some scholars argue that using the term "war" places possible topics of debate, and policy decisions, squarely "out of bounds."[26] The concern is that invoking the term "war" "block[s] the way to peace." I argue, however, that retreating from the term "war" severs a potentially productive ideological tension between war and peace. If the mess in Iraq and Afghanistan is not called "war," will we stop striving for peace? "Occupation," the word most commonly recommended by critics, implies a settled homeostasis, a condition the United States currently maintains in 150 countries worldwide.[27]

This line of reasoning causes me to favor "war" over existing alternatives. However, my advocacy of war as a conceptual lens is not narrowly conceived. My objective is rehabilitation and redefinition with the goal of redirecting public attitudes about US military engagements around the globe. Thinking in terms of "war" versus "occupation" reproduces the attitude of war as an everyday occurrence. Instead we need to construct a working notion of peace toward which we can meaningfully strive in order to keep the tension in place between this war-weary world and a better one yet to be constructed.

In peace studies there is a distinction between negative peace and positive peace. Negative peace is simply the absence of armed conflict, an "aimless peace."[28] Conversely, positive peace is a condition where military engagement has stopped and a just peace exists, a state of political stability actively working toward the reduction of structural violence.[29] A just or positive peace describes a rhetorically engaged, agonistic affair, where conflict is not eliminated but managed constructively and nonviolently.

The notion of a just peace offers a conceptual alternative to war. But first we need to get clear about the meaning of war. In his book *War Is a Force That Gives Us Meaning*, journalist Chris Hedges argues, "Until there is a common vocabulary and a shared historical memory there is no peace in any society, only an absence of war. The fighting may have stopped in Bosnia or Cyprus but this does not mean the war is over. The search for a common narrative must, at times, be forced upon a society. Few societies seem able to do this willingly."[30]

One of the things I've tried to demonstrate through this book is that the narrative for war is changing. War's forms of representation are changing. War looks and feels a lot different than it used to. The fact that evolving realties do not match commonly held expectations for what war looks like causes personnel to introduce alternative discourses such as "everyday," "vacation," or "work." These terms offer new insights. They generate what rhetorical scholar Kenneth Burke calls "perspective by incongruity," an instance when a conventional way of seeing the world is disrupted or met with an alternative vision that alters the original perspective in some way.[31] Instead of resisting or ignoring this shift, let's hold ourselves accountable for it. What does it reveal to us about ourselves?

Feel the Network

The universe existed as a living network long before our fascination with social media. We have always been part of a world wide web, even before the internet told us so. My enthusiasm for social network sites derives from my belief that they can bring our awareness of this fact to the fore. Social media platforms enhance our capacity to see and feel the network—to expand our moral imagination—perceiving ourselves as positioned within a web of relationships intimately, intricately, and infinitely linked.[32]

Indeed, social networks connect us globally; yet our tendency is to think parochially. A narrow scope is not necessarily a negative thing, especially if we can remain vigilantly aware that when we tug at a single point, we find ourselves attached to the rest of the world. Trouble arises, however, when we forget our attachments and become self-involved. Eli Praiser quotes Mark Zuckerberg, the founder and CEO of Facebook, as saying, "A squirrel dying in your front yard may have more relevance to your interests right now than people dying in Africa."[33] It is difficult to debate personal relevance. But I refuse to lose my optimism over social media's potential to reveal ourselves to each other. We must be willing to share, not just information about ourselves but also resources with ourselves—the very least of which is our time, attention, and mutual concern. But it will take courage and tolerance both to reveal and to see, shifting the emphasis from quantity to quality and forcing us to raise the standards of our engagement with one another as global "friends."

Notes

Introduction: New Faces of War

1. During my brother's deployment to Iraq in 2005–2006, the chief mode of communication was still pen-and-paper letter writing. Toward the end of his tour, the Marine Corps introduced an electronically printed mail service called "MotoMail," where electronic letters were downloaded, printed, and delivered to designated forward operating bases within twenty-four hours. But as I discovered by the bewildered looks of the eighteen- and nineteen-year-old Marines I interviewed for my research, this system of communication is antiquated. The site is still active, and from what I can tell, the service is still available, but many of the Marines I interviewed had never heard of it. Of course many of them were only ten or eleven years old when MotoMail came out. I can't help but feel nostalgic about MotoMail since I remember using it to connect with my brother who was in Iraq while I was in college at Indiana. See "MotoMail," last modified January 1, 2012, https://www.motomail.us/login.cfm?CFID=4067925&CFTOKEN=89b5e9e359 8333f6-4668547B-9625-466B-A040E991E7694AAB.

2. Deven Friedman, ed., *This Is Our War: Servicemen's Photographs of Life in Iraq* (New York: Aritsan, 2006); Liam Kennedy, "Soldier Photography: Visualizing the War in Iraq," *Review of International Studies* 35 (2009): 817–833; Janine Struk, *Private Pictures: Soldiers' Inside View of War* (London: I. B. Tauris, 2011).

3. Quotes appearing without attribution are from the author's personal interviews.

4. The increasing trend in internet studies is to use lowercase for the initial letter *i* in *internet*, to remove from it the status of a proper noun, with agency and autonomous power.

5. The portable satellite units developed the nickname "Cheetahs," for their mobility and speed. See Elaine Wilson, "'Cheetahs' Offer Swift Connection Home for Deployed Troops," *Defense.gov*, February 4, 2011, accessed February 5, 2012, http://www.defense.gov/news/newsarticle.aspx?id=62707.

6. Harvard student Mark Zuckerbueg launched Facebook on February 4, 2004, with restricted access. At first only Harvard students, and then only university-affiliated people with ".edu" e-mail addresses, could become members. Facebook opened to the general public in 2005.

7. Clay Shirky, *Here Comes Everybody: The Power of Organizing without Organizations* (New York: Penguin, 2008), 106.

8. Shirky, *Here Comes Everybody*, 17.

9. Jay David Bolter and Richard A. Grusin argue that remediation is a defining characteristic of new digital media in "Remediation," *Configurations* 4 (1996): 311–358.

10. Roger Silverstone, "What's New about New Media?," *New Media and Society* 1.1 (1999): 10.

11. For essays on the way technology shapes relationships, communities, and spaces, see danah boyd, "Friends, Friendsters, and MySpace: Top 8; Writing Community into Being on Social Network Sites," *First Monday* 11 (2006), accessed December 9, 2012, http://firstmonday.org/htbin/cgiwrap/bin/ojs/index .php/fm/article/view/1418/1336; danah boyd, "None of This Is Real," *Structures of Participation in Digital Culture*, ed. Joe Karaganis (New York: Social Science Research Council, 2008), 132–157.

12. Langdon Winner, *The Whale and the Reactor: A Search for Limits in an Age of High Technology* (Chicago: University of Chicago Press, 1986), 6.

13. According to Winner, politics are "arrangements of power and authority in human associations as well as the activities that take place within those arrangements." Technology is "all of modern practical artifice." See Winner, *The Whale and the Reactor*, 6.

14. Michel de Certeau, *The Practice of Everyday Life* (Berkeley: University of California Press, 1984).

15. Christian Lundberg and Joshua Gunn, "'Ouija Board, Are There Any Communications?': Agency, Ontotheology, and the Death of the Humanist Subject, or, Continuing the ARS Conversation," *Rhetoric Society Quarterly* 35.4 (2005): 83–105. The question of agency has been a topic of recent interest to rhetorical scholars. For a synthesis on a 2003 gathering at the Alliance of Rhetoric Society's discussion of agency, see Cheryl Geisler, "How Ought We to Understand the Concept of Rhetorical Agency? Report from the ARS," *Rhetoric Society Quarterly* 34.3 (2004): 9–17. Geisler's essay opens with John Lucaites's assertion that "every rhetorical performance enacts and contains a theory of its own agency—of its own possibilities—as it structures and enacts the relationships between speaker and audience, self and other, action and structure." See Geisler, "How Ought," 9.

16. By 2016, the US deployment to Afghanistan will have lasted just over fifteen years—one of the longest continuous military operations in US history.

17. Office of the Press Secretary, "Statement by the President on Afghanistan," May 27, 2014, http://www.whitehouse.gov/the-press-office/2014/05/27 /statement-president-afghanistan.

18. Safa Haeri, "Concocting a 'Greater Middle East' Brew," *Asia Times*, March 4, 2004, http://www.atimes.com/atimes/Middle_East/FC04Ak06.html.

19. Author's personal e-mail correspondence.

20. I use the verb "thrown" here in the Heideggerian sense of the word. Martin Heidegger, *Being and Time*, trans. John Macquarrie and Edward Robinson (New York: Harper & Row, 1962).

21. Chris Mooney, *The Republican War on Science* (New York: Basic Books, 2005); John Gibson, *The War on Christmas: How the Liberal Plot to Ban the Sacred Christian Holiday Is Worse Than You Thought* (New York: Sentinel, 2005).

22. Critiquing the war metaphor is a familiar practice in rhetorical studies circles. Robert Scott and Wayne Brockriede's rhetorical criticism of key moments in the Cold War was an influential project that heavily inspired Martin Medhurst's *Cold War Rhetoric: Strategy, Metaphor, and Ideology*, which he dedicated to Brockriede. David Zarefsky wrote extensively about war as it was metaphorically applied to President Johnson's antipoverty effort. William Elwood critiqued mass media framing of American drug wars and its influence on policy decisions. Robert Ivie criticized the vilification process in President Bush's "war" on terror. And Marie Ahearn examined the language and attitudes of war in colonial New England. See J. Michael Hogan and L. Glen Williams, "Defining 'the Enemy' in Revolutionary America: From the Rhetoric of Protest to the Rhetoric of War," *Southern Journal of Communication* 61.4 (1996): 277–288; Robert Scott and Wayne Brockriede, *Moments in the Rhetoric of the Cold War* (New York: Random House, 1970).

23. Lawrence Grossberg, *Cultural Studies in the Future Tense* (Durham, NC: Duke University Press, 2010), 13.

24. For instance, Hugo Liu explored "taste statements," or the way taste is performed through friendship networks and Facebook profiles, in "Social Network Profiles as Taste Performances," *Journal of Computer-Mediated Communication* 13.1 (2007): 252–275.

25. As of January 2013, Facebook boasts over one billion monthly active members and over six hundred million daily users. See Emil Protalinski, "Facebook Passes 1.06 Billion Monthly Active Users, 680 Million Mobile Users, and 618 Million Daily Users," *Next Web*, January 30, 2010, accessed October 13, 2013, http://thenextweb.com/facebook/2013/01/30/facebook-passes-1–06-billion-monthly-active-users-680-million-mobile-users-and-618-million-daily-users/.

26. Vered Amit, "Introduction: Constructing the Field," in *Constructing the Field: Ethnographic Fieldwork in the Contemporary World*, ed. Vered Amit (London: Routledge, 2000), 6.

27. The auditorium was double booked that day. Following the social media class, the Marines had to stay in their seats for a course on sexual harassment. The context of these back-to-back presentations suggests that the military imagines social media, like sexual harassment, to be a public relations issue.

28. Josh Wiseman, "Facebook Chat: Now We're Talking," *Facebook Blog*, April 6, 2008, accessed October 7, 2012, https://blog.facebook.com/blog.php?post=12811122130.

29. "The Marine Corps, a Young and Vigorous Force, Demographics Update," June 2012, accessed December 21, 2012, http://www.usmc mccs.org/display_files/DemographicsBookletJune2012.pdf.

30. The University of Iowa's Institutional Review Board (IRB) approved the use of on-base interviews for the purposes of this research. IRB ID # 201101755.

I've changed the names and identifying details of the participants whose stories I tell. I did not fact-check the stories people told me, but I believe them to be true.

31. John M. Sloop, "Disciplining the Transgendered: Brandon Teena, Public Representation, and Normativity," *Western Journal of Communication* 64.2 (2000): 165–189.

32. The University of Iowa's Institutional Review Board (IRB) approved the use of Facebook screen capture for the purposes of this research. IRB ID # 201109764. The consent process involved a personal message to existing Marine "friends," explaining the purpose and goals for the study and stated: "Taking part in this research study is completely voluntary. If you decide not to be in this study, or if you stop participating at any time, you won't be penalized or lose any benefits for which you otherwise qualify. If you do not wish to participate in this study or if you decide to leave the study early, we will ask you to send the principal investigator a message indicating your decision to withdraw. You may also 'de-friend' the PI through the Facebook option." As expected, I lost a handful of "friends," but a majority agreed to participate. Three years later, however, upon my announcing this book's publication, one participant requested I not include the screen-captured content from his page.

33. Christine Hine, "How Can Qualitative Internet Researchers Define the Boundaries of Their Projects?," in *Internet Inquiry: Conversations about Method*, ed. Annette N. Markham and Nancy K. Baym (Los Angeles: Sage, 2009), 12. See also Howard Becker, *Tricks of the Trade: How to Think about Your Research While You're Doing It* (Chicago: University of Chicago Press, 1998).

34. New digital media change the traditional broadcast model of author and audience by decentralizing production and distribution. The network changes the broadcast model even further. See Yochai Benkler, *The Wealth of Networks* (New Haven, CT: Yale University Press, 2006); Alice Marwick and danah boyd, "I Tweet Honestly, I Tweet Passionately: Twitter Users, Context Collapse and the Imagined Audience," *New Media and Society* 13 (2010): 114–133.

35. Judith Donath and danah boyd playfully call this a "public display of connection" in "Public Displays of Connection," *BT Technology Journal* 22 (2004): 71–82. For more on the unique characteristics of social network sites, see danah boyd and Nicole Ellison, "Social Network Sites: Definition, History, and Scholarship," *Journal of Computer-Mediated Communication* 13 (2007): article 11, accessed October 10, 2013, http://jcmc.indiana.edu/vol13/issue1/boyd.ellison.html.

36. Some social network site research makes a distinction between "network" and "networking." In "Social Network Sites: Definition, History, and Scholarship," boyd and Ellison argue that networking is possible on SNSs, but networking is not the primary practice. Rather SNSs enable users to connect with, articulate, and make visible their existing networks or those who are already part of their extended social network. Similarly Ellison, Steinfield, and Lampe suggest that Facebook is used to solidify off-line connections, not make new ones, arguing that people "search" for friends rather than "browse" for new ones. See Nicole Ellison, Charles Steinfield, and Cliff Lampe, "The Benefits of Facebook

'Friends': Exploring the Relationship between College Students' Use of Online Social Networks and Social Capital," *Journal of Computer-Mediated Communication* 12 (2007): 1143–1168.

37. In her dissertation research boyd argues that MySpace and Facebook enable US youth to socialize with their friends even when they are unable to gather in unmediated situations. In other words, SNSs are networked publics that support sociability just as unmediated public spaces do. See danah boyd, "Taken Out of Context: American Teen Sociality in Networked Publics" (PhD diss., University of California Berkeley, 2008), accessed October 15, 2011, http://www.danah.org /papers/.

38. Zygmunt Bauman, *Liquid Modernity* (Cambridge, MA: Polity, 2000), 81.

39. Naomi Baron, *Always On: Language in an Online and Mobile World* (New York: Oxford University Press, 2008); Naomi Baron and Rich Ling, "Emerging Patterns of American Mobile Phone Use: Electronically-Mediated Communication in Transition," in *Mobile Media 2007: Proceedings of an International Conference on Social and Cultural Aspects of Mobile Phones, Media and Wireless Technologies, June 2–4,* ed. Gerard Goggin and Larissa Hjorth (Sydney: University of Sydney, 2007); Jeffrey A. Hall and Nancy K. Baym, "Calling and Texting (Too Much): Mobile Maintenance Expectations, (Over)dependence, Entrapment, and Friendship Satisfaction," *New Media and Society* 14.2 (2011): 316–331.

40. Hall and Baym, "Calling and Texting," 317.

41. This is a phenomenon researchers have identified among many populations as diverse as American college students and poor, urban Philippine spouses. See Baron and Ling, "Emerging Patterns"; Lourdes Portus, "How the Urban Poor Acquire and Give Meaning to the Mobile Phone," in *Handbook of Mobile Communication Studies,* ed. James Katz (Cambridge, MA: MIT Press, 2008), 105–118.

42. In the early 1900s anthropologist Bronislaw Malinowski described "phatic" as stemming from the Greek *phanein*, which means to show oneself, appear. "The Problem of Meaning in Primitive Languages," in *The Meaning of Meaning,* ed. Charles K. Ogden and Ian A. Richards (London: Routledge, 1923), 146–152.

43. I first saw the phrase "digital intimacy" in a title to a *New York Times* article. The article went on to use the alternate phrase "ambient intimacy" to describe the phatic, personal, play-by-play style of communication ushered in by technologies like Facebook and Twitter. See Clive Thompson, "Brave New World of Digital Intimacy," *New York Times,* September 5, 2008, accessed April 1, 2012, http:// www.nytimes.com/2008/09/07/magazine/07awareness-t.html?pagewanted=all. For an article on a similar idea, "connected presence," see Toke Haunstrup Christensen, "'Connected Presence' in Distributed Family Life," *New Media and Society* 11.3 (2009): 433–451.

44. Ralph Berenger, "Introduction: Global Media Go to War," in *Global Media Go to War: Roles of News and Entertainment Media during the 2003 Iraq War,* ed. Ralph Berenger (Washington, DC: Marquette Books, 2004), xxvii.

45. Jorge Lewinski's *The Camera at War* is a good example of this type of research. His study examines the nature of war photography and its influence on

society's view of war. Similarly, Jeffrey Smith's *War and Press Freedom* argues that photographs from war can prompt important questions and ignite public debate. Essays such as Douglas Kellner's "War Correspondents, the Military, and Propaganda: Some Critical Reflections" analyze how the "shock and awe" campaign of the Persian Gulf War influenced audiences to support the war. Susan Jeffords and Lauren Rabinowitz's collection *Seeing through the Media* also takes up the media's presentation of the Persian Gulf War and how it impacted public opinion. And Gil Kaufman's 2006 documentary, *Iraq Uploaded,* argues that war is watered down by the media and that audiences are not getting an accurate depiction of combat. See Jorge Lewinski, *The Camera at War: A History of War Photography from 1848 to the Present Day* (New York: Simon & Schuster, 1978); Jeffery Allan Smith, *War and Press Freedom: The Problem of Prerogative Power* (New York: Oxford University Press, 1999); Douglas Kellner, "War Correspondents, the Military, and Propaganda: Some Critical Reflections," *International Journal of Communication* 2 (2008): 297–330; Susan Jeffords and Lauren Rabinowitz, eds., *Seeing through the Media: The Persian Gulf War* (Piscataway, NJ: Rutgers University Press, 1994); Gil Kaufman, producer, *Iraq Uploaded: The War Network Television Won't Show You, Shot by Soldiers and Posted Online.* Special report. (New York: Music Television, 2006), accessed October 20, 2009, http://www.mtv.com/news/articles /1536780/20060720/index.jhtml.

46. For essays on "soldier videos," see Kari Andén-Papadopoulos, "US Soldiers Imaging the Iraq War on YouTube," *Popular Communication* 7 (2009): 17–27; Kari Andén-Papadopoulos, "Body Horror on the Internet: U.S. Soldiers Recording the War in Iraq and Afghanistan," *Media, Culture and Society* 31.6 (2009): 921–938; Jessica Ritchie, "Instant Histories of War: Online Combat Videos of the Iraq Conflict, 2003–2010" *History Australia* 8 (2011): 89–108. For an essay on military blogging, see Melissa Wall, "In the Battle(field): The US Military, Blogging and the Struggle for Authority," *Media, Culture and Society* 32.5 (2010): 863–872.

47. Andén-Papadopoulos, "US Soldiers Imaging the Iraq War on YouTube," 26. For articles that criticize traditional news media coverage, see Danny Schechter, *Embedded: Weapons of Mass Deception; How the Media Failed to Cover the War in Iraq* (Amherst, MA: Prometheus Books, 2003); Howard Tumber and Jerry Palmer, *Media at War: The Iraq Crisis* (London: Sage, 2004).

48. Christian Christensen, "Uploading Dissonance: YouTube and the US Occupation of Iraq," *Media, War and Conflict* 1 (2008): 173.

49. I use "social network" here in the sense of new media scholar Patricia Lange's definition of social networks as those "relations among people who deem other network members to be important or relevant to them in some way" (361). Lange's definition of social network can apply to both online and off-line social networks and therefore works best in the fluid spectrum of contemporary online and off-line living. See "Publicly Private and Privately Public: Social Networking on YouTube," *Journal of Computer-Mediated Communication* 13 (2007): 361–380. To arrive at her definition of social networks, Lange draws on Barry Wellman's

work in "Are Personal Communities Local? A Dumptarian Reconsideration," *Social Networks* 18.4 (1996): 347–354.

Chapter 1: Incongruities across Social Media and Military Cultures

1. As quoted in Marisa Taylor, "Marine Faces 'Other Than Honorable' Discharge over Anti-Obama Facebook Comment." *ABC News*, April 15, 2012, accessed September 18, 2012, http://abcnews.go.com/US/federal-judge-rejects-Marine-injunction-stop-discharge/story?id=16139979#.UbXonCvr174.

2. Under Secretary of Defense (Personnel and Readiness), *Political Activities by Members of the Armed Forces* (DOD Directive 1344.10). Washington, DC: DOD, February 19, 2008, http://www.dtic.mil/whs/directives/corres/pdf/134410p.pdf.

3. For a more eloquently worded expression of this idea, see Shirky, *Here Comes Everybody*, 87.

4. Malin Sveningsson Elm, "How Do Various Notions of Privacy Influence Decisions in Qualitative Internet Research?," in *Internet Inquiry: Conversations about Method*, ed. Annette N. Markham and Nancy K. Baym (Los Angeles: Sage, 2009), 84.

5. Sonia Livingstone, "Taking Risky Opportunities in Youthful Content Creation: Teenagers' Use of Social Networking Sites for Intimacy, Privacy and Self-Expression," *New Media and Society* 10 (2008): 339–411. Danah boyd and Nicole Ellison observed a similar phenomenon in their research. According to their interview data, a sense of privacy is related to feelings of being in control of the information you disseminate (when, where, how, and to whom). They found that Facebook's introduction of the "News Feed" feature greatly disrupted a sense of control—and with it a sense of privacy. See boyd and Ellison, "Social Network Sites."

6. In other words, social media promote a particular form of self-expression, which encourages users to differentiate themselves and act as individuals. Lee Raine and Barry Wellman refer to it as "networked individualism," a new communication "operating system" hinging on three primary characteristics—the individual is the autonomous center, people are interacting with multiple others, and people are engaging in several tasks simultaneously. See *Networked: The New Social Operating System* (Cambridge, MA: MIT Press, 2012). See also Elliot T. Panek, Yioryos Nardis, and Sara Konrath, "Mirror or Megaphone? How Relationships between Narcissism and Social Networking Site Use Differ on Facebook and Twitter," *Computers in Human Behavior* 29.5 (2013): 2004–2012.

7. Social media should be conceived as "a continuation of preexisting cultural forces rather than as deterministically transformative." See Alice E. Marwick, *Status Update: Celebrity, Publicity, and Branding in the Social Media Age* (New Haven, CT: Yale University Press, 2013), 27.

8. As one response, the Pentagon's Defense Advanced Research Projects Agency (DARPA) advertised a $42 million grant in 2011 to solicit innovative proposals to build an internet meme tracker. "Internet meme" refers to tags, catchphrases,

or concepts that proliferate through internet-based media such as e-mail, blogs, forums, social networking sites, and the like. A "meme tracker" is an automatically operating tool to comb the internet for the most popular memes and links. See David Streitfeld, "Pentagon Seeks a Few Good Social Networks," *Bits*, August 2, 2011, accessed October 5, 2011, http://bits.blogs.nytimes.com/2011/08/02/pentagon-seeks-social-networking-experts/.

9. Media sociologist Thomas Streeter was one the first to connect policy studies (usually approached through the lens of political economy) and cultural studies (usually approached through textual analysis). See Thomas Streeter, *Selling the Air: A Critique of the Policy of Commercial Broadcasting in the United States* (Chicago: University of Chicago Press, 1996); Pierre Bourdieu, *The Logic of Practice* (Stanford, CA: Stanford University Press, 1980).

10. Detlev F. Vagts, "Free Speech in the Armed Forces," *Columbia Law Review* 57 (1957): 187, 189.

11. Associated Press, "Marine Takes Aim at Military's Free Speech Limit," *CBS News*, April 5, 2012, http://www.cbsnews.com/news/marine-takes-aim-at-militarys-free-speech-limit/.

12. Moving forward it might be worthwhile to meditate on the definition of "crisis" in an era of *unclear* and present danger.

13. Katherine C. Den Bleyker, "The First Amendment versus Operational Security: Where Should the Milblogging Balance Lie?," *Fordham Intellectual Property, Media and Entertainment Law Journal* 17.2 (2006): article 3, http://ir.lawnet.fordham.edu/cgi/viewcontent.cgi?article=1395&context=iplj.

14. Article 117 of the UCMJ 64 Stat 139 (1950), 50 USC.

15. As cited in Vagts, "Free Speech," 191. See also Manual for Courts-Martial, United States para. 168 (1951), http://www.loc.gov/rr/frd/Military_Law/pdf/manual-1951.pdf.

16. Vagts, "Free Speech," 217.

17. DOD directive 1344.10 provision 4.1.2.6, http://www.dod.mil/dodgc/defense_ethics/ethics_regulation/1344-10.html.

18. John Hockenberry, "The Blogs of War," *Wired* 13.8 (2005), http://www.wired.com/wired/archive/13.08/milblogs_pr.html; Christopher Michel, "Let Slip the Blogs of War," *United States Naval Institute Proceeding* 131.3 (March 2005), 112.

19. US Secretary of Defense to All Department of Defense Activities, message 090426Z August 6, 2006, http://www.defense.gov/webmasters/policy/infosec2006 0806.aspx.

20. The most widely publicized user-generated indiscretions involved Marines. Recall Corporal Joshua Belile's "Hadji Girl" song, where Belile performed a song on YouTube in 2006 about a hypothetical encounter with an Iraqi family. Or the more recent 2012 YouTube video of four Marines urinating on the bodies of Taliban fighters in Afghanistan.

21. As quoted in Noah Schachtman, "Marines Ban Twitter, Facebook, Other Sites," *CNN Tech*, August 4, 2009, accessed September 20, 2012, http://articles

/cnn.com/2009-08-04/tech/Marines.social.media.ban_1_social-media-Marines -ban-facebook?_s=PM:TECH.

22. "DOD Releases Policy for Responsible and Effective Use of Internet-Based Capabilities," *U.S. Department of Defense News Release*, February 26, 2010, accessed September 20, 2012, http://www.defense.gov/releases/release.aspx ?releaseid=13338; Amy McCullough, "Corps Lifts Ban on Social Networking Sites," *Marine Corps Times*, March 29, 2010, accessed September 20, 2012, http://www .Marinecorpstimes.com/news/2010/03/Marine_socialnetworking_032910w/.

23. Amber Corrin, "DOD's New Policy 'Likes' Social Media, but with Caveats." *Federal Computer*, August 14, 2012, http://few.com/Articles/2012/08/15/ FEAT-Inside-DOD-social-media-policy.

24. Steffen Albrecht, "Whose Voice Is Heard in Online Deliberation? A Study of Participation and Representation in Political Debates on the Internet," *Information, Communication and Society* 9.1 (2006): 62–82; Daniel Brouwer and Robert Asen, eds., *Public Modalities: Rhetoric, Culture, Media and the Shape of Public Life* (Tuscaloosa: University of Alabama Press, 2010); Craig Calhoun, "Information Technology and the International Public Sphere," in *Shaping the Network Society: The New Role of Civil Society in Cyberspace*, ed. Douglas Schuler and Peter Day (Cambridge: MIT Press, 2004), 229–251; Diana Carlin, Dan Schill, David G. Levasseur, and Anothony S. King, "The Post-9/11 Public Sphere: Citizen Talk about the 2004 Presidential Debates," *Rhetoric and Public Affairs*, 8.4 (2005): 617–638; Victor Pickard, "Assessing the Radical Democracy of Indymedia: Discursive, Technical, and Institutional Constructions," *Critical Studies in Media Communication* 23.1 (2006): 19–38.

25. Zizi Papacharissi, *A Private Sphere: Democracy in a Digital Age* (Malden, MA: Polity, 2010).

26. Mark Poster, "The New as Public Sphere?," *Wired*, March 2011, accessed September 20, 2012, http://www.wired.com/wired/archive/3.11/poster.if _pr.html.

27. Nancy Sherman, *The Untold War: Inside the Hearts, Minds and Souls of Our Soldiers* (New York: W. W. Norton, 2010), 71.

28. Joshua Kastenberg, "Changing the Paradigm of Internet Access from Government Information Systems: A Solution to the Need for the DOD to Take Time-Sensitive Action on the NIPRNET," *Air Force Law Review* 64 (2009): 175, accessed March 15, 2013, http://connection.ebscohost.com/c/articles/45162335 /changing-paradigm-internet-access-from-government-information-systems -solution-need-DOD-take-time-sensitive-action-niprnet.

29. Anthony Giddens, *The Constitution of Society* (Berkeley: University of California Press, 1984), xxv, 89.

30. Alice Marwick, *Status Update: Celebrity, Publicity, and Branding in the Social Media Age* (New Haven, CT: Yale University Press, 2013), 191.

31. General Krulak was writing in the 1990s, yet it is easy to see how strategic consequences, like those resulting from service members burning the Quran, abusing prisoners at Abu Ghraib, or urinating on corpses, have strategic reverber-

ations that make military missions more difficult and more dangerous. See Charles Krulak, "The Strategic Corporal: Leadership in the Three Block War," *Marines Magazine*, January 1999, accessed November 11, 2014, http://www.au.af.mil/au /awc/awcgate/usmc/strategic_corporal.htm.

32. Marwick, *Status Update*, 191.

33. In other words, as Marwick points out, it is possible for the neoliberal subject to "come into being through individual self-regulation rather than through top-down governance." See Marwick, *Status Update*, 13.

34. "Joint Task Force Global Network Operations Report," *National Communications System*, September 7, 2010, accessed September 20, 2012, http://www.ncs .gov/nstac/reports/2009/NSTAC%20CCTF%20Report.pdf.

35. Vagts, "Free Speech," 207.

36. In an upcoming chapter on internet memes, I discuss the ephemeral nature of online social and attention economies.

37. Paul Adams, *Grouped: How Small Groups of Friends Are the Key to Influence on the Social Web* (Berkeley, CA: New Riders, 2012), 136.

38. Marwick, *Status Update*, 196.

39. Ulrich Beck, *Risk Society: Towards a New Modernity* (New Delhi: Sage, 1992).

40. Anthony Giddens, *Modernity and Self-Identity: Self and Society in the Late Modern Age* (Stanford, CA: Stanford University Press, 1991), 133–134.

41. Ulrich Beck, "The Terrorist Threat: World Risk Society Revisited," *Theory, Culture and Society* 19.4 (2002): 39–55; Anthony Giddens, *Runaway World: How Globalization Is Reshaping Our Lives* (London: Profile, 1999), 34.

42. Vagts, "Free Speech," 204.

43. Giddens, *Runaway World*, xiii.

44. Mikkel Vedby Rasmussen, *The Risk Society at War: Terror, Technology, and Strategy in the Twenty-First Century* (Cambridge: Cambridge University Press, 2006), 194.

45. "MCO P1020.34.G Marine Corps Uniform Regulations," March 31, 2003, accessed September 20, 2012, http://www.marines.mil/Portals/59/Publications /MCO%20P1020.34G%20W%20CH%201–5.pdf.

46. Vagts, "Free Speech," 210.

47. Nancy Baym, *Personal Connections in the Digital Age* (Malden, MA: Polity, 2010); Eszter Hargittai and Gina Walejko, "The Participation Divide," *Information, Communication and Society* 11.2 (2008): 239–256; Jessica Vitak and Nicole Ellison, "'There's a Network Out There You Might as Well Tap': Exploring the Benefits of and Barriers to Exchanging Informational and Support-Based Resources on Facebook," *New Media and Society* 15 (2013): 243–259.

48. PFC Zaku, June 2, 2004 (5:35 p.m.), comment on "Rumsfeld Bans Camera Phones in Iraq," *Joi Ito's Web*, May 23, 2004, accessed September 20, 2012, http:// joi.ito.com/weblog/2004/05/23/rumsfeld-bans-c.html.

49. PFC Zaku, comment on "Rumsfeld Bans Camera Phones in Iraq."

50. As quoted in "It's Not the Cell Phone Stupid," *Stop Photo Talk*, June 4, 2004, accessed September 20, 2012, http://talks.blogs.com/phototalk/2004/06/its_not_the_celhtml.

51. Giddens, *Modernity and Self-Identity*, 19.

52. Malin Sveningsson Elm, "How Do Various Notions of Privacy Influence Decisions in Qualitative Internet Research?," 77.

53. Geolocation lets you identify users' location by returning their latitude and longitude. Applications can use this to offer localized experiences such as driving directions, nearby points of interest, local deals, etc. In the past few years, smartphones with dedicated GPS chips have exploded in popularity. Web apps like Facebook use geolocation.

54. Marc Prensky, "Digital Natives, Digital Immigrants," *On the Horizon* 9.5 (2001): 1–6.

55. Ilana Gershon, *The Breakup 2.0: Disconnecting over New Media* (Ithaca, NY: Cornell University Press, 2010).

56. Gershon, *The Breakup*, 10.

57. Thomas Ricks, *The Generals* (New York: Penguin, 2012).

58. Dan Ackman, "Sherron Watkins Had Whistle, but Blew It," *Forbes*, February 14, 2002, accessed December 9, 2011, http://www.forbes.com/2002/02/14/0214watkins.html.

59. Stefana Broadbent, "Approaches to Personal Communication," in *Digital Anthropology*, ed. Heather Horst and Daniel Miller (London: Berg, 2012), 132.

60. As cited in Erik Voeten, "Kansas Board of Regents Restricts Free Speech for Academics," *Washington Post*, December 19, 2013, http://www.washingtonpost.com/blogs/monkey-cage/wp/2013/12/19/kansas-board-of-regents-restricts-free-speech-for-academics/.

Chapter 2: From Posting Mail to Posting Status

1. The wire is the defensive perimeter surrounding the forward operating base. A reference to going outside the wire means you are exposed and open to direct contact with the enemy.

2. For an essay on obligatory communication in a digital culture, see Evan Selinger, "We're Turning Digital Natives into Etiquette Sociopaths," *Wired*, March 26, 2013, accessed September 19, 2013, http://www.wired.com/opinion/2013/03/digital-natives-etiquette-be-damned/.

3. Sherry Turkle, "Can You Hear Me Now?," *Forbes Magazine Online*, May 7, 2007, accessed December 9, 2012, http://www.forbes.com/forbes/2007/0507/176.html.

4. Sarah Green, "The Responsiveness Trap," *Harvard Business Review*, June 6, 2012, accessed December 13, 2012, http://blogs.hbr.org/hbr/hbreditors/2012/06/the_responsiveness_trap.html.

5. Turkle, "Can You Hear Me Now?," n.p.

6. Richard A. Lanham, *The Economics of {Attention}: Style and Substance in the Age of Information* (Chicago: University of Chicago Press, 2006).

7. Judy Wajcman and Emily Rose, "Constant Connectivity: Rethinking Interruptions at Work," *Organization Studies* 32 (2011): 941–961.

8. Kenneth J. Gergen, "Cell Phone Technology and the Realm of Absent Presence," in *Perpetual Contact*, ed. David Katz and Mark Aakhus (New York: Cambridge University Press, 2002), 62–81; Sherry Turkle, *Alone Together: Why We Expect More from Technology and Less from Each Other* (New York: Basic Books, 2011).

9. Tom Simonite, "What Facebook Knows," *MIT Technology Review*, June 13, 2012, accessed September 19, 2013, http://www.technologyreview.com/featured story/428150/what-facebook-knows/.

10. I use the term differently from Jay David Bolter and Richard Grusin, who use "immediacy" to describe transparency in *Remediation: Understanding New Media* (Cambridge, MA: MIT Press, 1999).

11. "The Marine Corps, A Young and Vigorous Force, Demographics Update."

12. Kathleen Richardson and Sue Hessey, "Archiving the Self? Facebook as Biography of Relational Memory," *Journal of Information Communication and Ethics in Society* 7 (2009): 25–38.

13. "Top Sites: The Top 500 Sites on the Web," *Alexa: The Web Information Company*, 2011, accessed December 20, 2012, http://www.alexa.com/topsites.

14. Adams, *Grouped*, 125.

15. Gershon, *The Breakup*, 6, 39.

16. Winner, *The Whale and the Reactor*. This also resonates with Martin Heidegger's observation that we don't notice our tools (a hammer, in his example) until they break or malfunction. For communications media users, this means being disconnected. See Heidegger, *Being and Time*, trans. John Macquarrie and Edward Robinson (New York: Harper & Row, 1962).

17. Winner, *The Whale and the Reactor*, 5, 9.

18. If troops and their loved ones aren't writing letters, then who is? Will the medium persist? Maybe it should be of little wonder that US post offices are going extinct. Mark Memmott, "Post Offices Join List of Nation's Most Endangered Historic Places," *NPR.org*, June 6, 2012, accessed December 6, 2012, http://www.npr.org/blogs/thetwo-way/2012/06/06/154440261/post-offices-join-list-of-nations-most-endangered-historic-places.

19. I use the male pronoun for a few reasons. First, in this immediate context, the male pronoun resonates with the mythology surrounding letters from war. Second, the majority of personnel I spoke with and interviewed were men. And, finally, I use the male pronoun to reflect the exclusion of women from the infantry. For reading on gender representation in the Corps, see James Scott Frampton, *The Influence of Attitudes and Morale on the Performance of Active-Duty United States Marine Corps Female Security Guards* (PhD diss., Walden University, 2011).

20. Of course letter writing in previous conflicts encountered its own constraints with cutouts, censorship stamps, and black bars.

21. Nigel Hall, "The Materiality of Letter Writing: A Nineteenth Century Perspective," *Letter Writing as a Social Practice*, ed. David Barton and Nigel Hall (Philadelphia: John Benjamins, 2000), 83–108.

22. Janet Maybin, "Death Row Penfriends: Some Effects of Letter Writing on Identity and Relationships," *Letter Writing as a Social Practice*, ed. David Barton and Nigel Hall (Philadelphia: John Benjamins, 2000), 151–178.

23. Anita Wilson, "'Absolute Truly Brill to See from You': Visuality and Prisoners' Letters," *Letter Writing as a Social Practice*, ed. David Barton and Nigel Hall (Philadelphia: John Benjamins, 2000), 179–198.

24. Simeon J. Yates, "Computer-Mediated Communication: The Future of the Letter?," in *Letter Writing as a Social Practice*, ed. David Barton and Nigel Hall (Philadelphia: John Benjamins, 2000), 233–252.

25. Andrew Carroll, ed., *War Letters: Extraordinary Correspondence from American Wars* (New York: Scribner, 2001).

26. Victoria Wang, John V. Turner, and Kevin Haines, "Phatic Technologies in Modern Society," *Technology in Society* 34.1 (2012): 84–93.

27. Raine and Wellman, *Networked*.

28. Christine Knopf, "'Language Will Not Convey': Rhetorical Formation of Interpersonal Civil-Military Relations," paper presented at Rhetoric Society of America Conference, Minneapolis, MN, May 2010.

29. David Barton and Nigel Hall, eds., *Letter Writing as a Social Practice*, vol. 9 (Philadelphia: John Benjamins, 2000).

30. Nigel Hall, Anne Robinson, and Leslie Crawford, "Young Children's Explorations of Letter Writing," *Letter Writing as a Social Practice*, ed. David Barton and Nigel Hall (Philadelphia: John Benjamins, 2000), 146.

31. William Merrill Decker, *Epistolary Practices: Letter Writing in America before Telecommunications* (Chapel Hill: University of North Carolina Press, 1998), 19.

32. Personal letters from the author's private collection.

33. Seoyeon Hong, Edson Tandoc Jr., Eunjin Anna Kim, Bokyung Kim, and Kevin Wise, "The Real You? The Role of Visual Cues and Comment Congruence in Perceptions of Social Attractiveness from Facebook Profiles," *Cyberpsychology, Behavior, and Social Networking* 15.7 (2012): 339–344.

34. Chris Gerben notes the user interfaces center on the new and the immediate even at the cost of other modes of organization such as relevance or importance (think Facebook's "news feed"). Gerben writes, "Digital texts not only privilege newness as a default design principle, but also rely on user-produced newness in order to maintain popularity." See "Privileging the 'New' in New Media Literacies: The Future of Democracy, Economy, and Identity in 21st Century Texts," *Media in Transition*, April 2009, accessed September 19, 2013, http://web.mit.edu/comm-forum/mit6/papers/Gerben.pdf.

35. Alan R. Dennis and Susan T. Kinney, "Testing Media Richness Theory in the New Media: The Effects of Cues, Feedback, and Task Equivocality," *Information Systems Research* 9 (1998): 256–274.

36. Emile Christofides, Amy Muise, and Serge Desmarais, "Information Disclosure and Control on Facebook: Are They Two Sides of the Same Coin or Two Different Processes?," *Cyberpsychology and Behavior* 12.3 (2009): 341. For an article on the "network effect," see Abigail Maravalli, "The Network Effect: How Online Organizing Just Got a Little Easier," Center for Social Media, October 5, 2012, accessed September 3, 2013, http://www.centerforsocialmedia.org/blog/network-effect-how-online-organizing-just-got-little-easier.

37. Susan Barnes, "A Privacy Paradox: Social Networking in the United States," *First Monday* 11.9 (2006), accessed August 8, 2008, http://firstmonday.org/htbin/cgiwrap/bin/ojs.

38. As quoted in Robert Gehl, "Ladders, Samurai, and Blue Collars: Personal Branding in Web 2.0," *First Monday* 16.9 (2011), accessed April 4, 2012, http://firstmonday.org/ojs/index.php/fm/article/view/3579/3041. For the full version of Williams's quote see: Robert W. Williams, "Politics and Self in the Age of Digital Re(pro)ducibility," *Fast Capitalism* 1.1 (2005), accessed September 3, 2013, http://www.uta.edu/huma/agger/fastcapitalism/1_1/williams.html.

39. Marwick and boyd, "I Tweet Honestly," 122, 126.

40. The Insanity Workout series is a product of Beachbody LLC, creators of the popular P90X series.

41. See also Andrew Mendelson and Zizi Papacharissi's chapter "'Look at Us': Collective Narcissism in College Student Facebook Photo Galleries," in their volume *The Networked Self: Identity, Community and Culture on Social Network Sites* (New York: Routledge, 2010), 251–274.

42. Glenn Gray, *The Warriors: Reflections on Men in Battle* (Lincoln: University of Nebraska Press, 1998), 90.

43. Chris Hedges, *War Is a Force That Gives Us Meaning* (New York: Anchor Books, 2002), 116.

44. As quoted in Thompson, "Brave New World," n.p.

45. Stefana Broadbent, "Transforming the Home," *Observing the Evolution of Technology Usage Blog*, March 23, 2012, accessed December 9, 2012, http://stefanabroadbent.com/2012/03/23/transforming-the-home/.

46. Turkle, "Can You Hear Me Now?," n.p.

47. Stefana Broadbent, "The Democratisation of Intimacy," *Observing the Evolution of Technology Usage Blog*, March 23, 2012, accessed December 9, 2012, http://stefanabroadbent.com/2012/03/23/the-democratisation-of-intimacy/.

48. David Morely, *Media, Modernity and Technology: The Geography of the New* (Florence, KY: Routledge, 2006), 223.

49. Wiseman, "Facebook Chat: Now We're Talking."

50. Turkle, "Can You Hear Me Now?," n.p.

51. "Digital Nation: Life on the Virtual Frontier," *Frontline* (PBS TV/Web report), February 2, 2010, accessed December 1, 2012, http://www.pbs.org/wgbh/pages/frontline/digitalnation/interviews/turkle.html.

52. As quoted in "Digital Nation," n.p.

53. As a Marine sergeant described, "The more love and attention he [the war-

rior] gives back home, the less able he is to make decisions with the violence of action that is needed. He becomes weaker, he will hesitate and then men will die."

54. Facebook chat introduced a "seen" feature in June 2012. Beneath a sent message, a gray notification reads, "Seen 00:00 pm." Within group posts it tells you who saw it and when.

55. As quoted in "Digital Nation," n.p.

56. Karl Marlantes, *What It Is Like to Go to War* (New York: Grove, 2011), 19.

57. danah boyd, "Streams of Content, Limited Attention: The Flow of Information through Social Media," *Web2.0 Expo*, November 17, 2009, accessed December 9, 2012, http://www.danah.org/papers/talks/Web2Expo.html.

58. Turkle, "Can You Hear Me Now?," n.p.

59. Marlantes, *What It Is Like*, 64, 77.

60. Jed R. Brubaker, Gillian R. Hayes, and Paul Dourish, "Beyond the Grave: Facebook as a Site for the Expansion of Death and Mourning," *Information Society: An International Journal* 29.3 (2013): 152–163.

61. Major Elizabeth Robins, "Muddy Boots 10: The Rise of Soldier Blogs," *Military Review*, September–October 2007, 116.

Chapter 3: Photos from the Field

1. Figures 7 and 8 are screen grabs from Lance Corporal Pine's Facebook page. He wrote the following disclaimer above the series of photos documenting his deployment: "Photos of the Marines of 1st Battalion 2nd Marine Regiment (1/2), documenting their tour in Afghanistan in support of International Security Assistance Force (ISAF) and Operation Enduring Freedom (OEF). 1/2 operated in Musa Qal'eh AO in the Nowzad and Musa Qala District Center. None where [*sic*] taken on government equipment."

2. Mary Madden and Kathryn Zickuhr, "65% of Online Adults Use Social Media Networking Sites," *Pew Internet and American Life Project* (Washington, DC: Pew Research Center), August 26, 2011, http://pewinternet.org/Reports/2011/Social-Newworking-Sites.aspx.

3. Dong-Hoo Lee, "Digital Cameras, Personal Photography and the Reconfiguration of Spatial Experiences," *Information Society* 26.4 (2010): 266–275; Elizabeth Shove, Matt Watson, Martin Hand, and Jack Ingram, *The Design of Everyday Life* (Oxford, UK: Berg, 2007), 81.

4. Richard Chalfen, *Snapshot Versions of Life* (Bowling Green, OH: Bowling Green State University Press, 1987); Susan Murray, "Digital Images, Photo-Sharing, and Our Shifting Notions of Everyday Aesthetics," *Journal of Visual Culture* 7.2 (2008): 147.

5. The significance of the grenade pouch is even more thought provoking. Are cameras and explosive devices equally valuable and/or destructive?

6. This exercise should be familiar to rhetorical critics who read the second- and third-persona essays of the 1970s and 1980s: Edwin Black, "The Second Persona," *Quarterly Journal of Speech* 56.2 (1970): 109–119; Phillip Wander, "The

Third Persona: An Ideological Turn in Rhetorical Theory," *Central States Speech Journal* 35 (1984): 197–216.

7. Daniel Rubinstein and Katrina Sluis, "A Life More Photographic," *Photographies* 1.1 (2008): 13.

8. Theo Van Leeuwen defines discourses as "socially constructed ways of knowing some aspect of reality when that aspect of reality has to be represented" in *Discourse and Practice* (Oxford: Oxford University Press, 2008), 1.

9. Mirca Madianou and Daniel Miller, "Mobile Phone Parenting: Reconfiguring Relationships between Filipina Migrant Mothers and Their Left-Behind Children," *New Media and Society* 13 (2011): 457–470.

10. Caitlin McLaughlin and Jessica Vitak, "Norm Evolution and Violation on Facebook," *New Media and Society* 14.2 (2012): 306.

11. José van Dijck, "Digital Photography: Communication, Identity, Memory," *Visual Communication* 7 (2008): 60.

12. Risto Sarvas and David Frohlich, *From Snapshots to Social Media: The Changing Picture of Domestic Photography* (London: Springer, 2011).

13. Chalfen, *Snapshot*, 10.

14. Nancy West, *Kodak and the Lens of Nostalgia* (Charlottesville: University Press of Virginia, 2000), 1.

15. Patricia Holland, "Introduction: History, Memory and the Family Album," in *Family Snaps: The Meanings of Domestic Photography*, ed. Jo Spence and Patricia Holland (London: Virago, 1991): 1–14.

16. Turkle, "Can You Hear Me Now?," n.p.

17. Daniel Miller, "Social Networking Sites," in *Digital Anthropology*, ed. Heather Horst and Daniel Miller (London: Berg, 2012), 158.

18. Peggy Ornstein, "I Tweet Therefore I Am," *New York Times*, July 30, 2010, http://www.nytimes.com/2010/08/01/magazine/01wwln-lede-t.html?_r=0.

19. Zizi Papacharissi, "Without You, I'm Nothing: Performances of the Self on Twitter," *International Journal of Communication* 6 (2012), 2003; Kenneth Gergen, *Relational Being: Beyond Self and Community* (New York: Oxford University Press, 2009), 152; Barry Wellman, "Physical Place and Cyberplace: The Rise of Personalized Networking," *International Journal of Urban and Regional Research* 25.2 (2001): 227–252.

20. Turkle as quoted in Ornstein, "I Tweet, Therefore I Am," n.p.

21. S. Murray, "Digital Images," 147.

22. S. Murray, "Digital Images," 151.

23. For a visual example, see "Girls-on-Toilet," *College Humor*, March 15, 2014, http://www.collegehumor.com/tag/girl-on-toilet.

24. Christopher Mussello, "Studying the Home Mode: An Exploration of Family Photographs and Visual Communication," *Studies in Visual Communication* 6.1 (1980): 37, 36.

25. Henrik Örnebring, "The Consumer as Producer—Of What?," *Journalism Studies* 9.5 (2008): 771–785; Steve Paulussen and Pieter Ugille, "User Generated Content in the Newsroom: Professional and Organizational Constraints on

Participatory Journalism," *Westminster Papers in Communication and Culture* 5.2 (2008): 16, accessed April 4, 2014, http://www.suebamforddesign.co.uk/ba_cult crit_lewes/week9/ugc%20in%20the%20newsroom.pdf.

26. Wendy Kozol, Life*'s America: Family and Nation in Postwar Photojournalism* (Philadelphia: Temple University Press, 1994), 22.

27. Sarvas and Frohlich, *From Snapshots to Social Media*, 154.

28. Michael Stefanone and Derek Lackoff, "Reality Television as Model for Online Behavior: Blogging, Photo, and Video Sharing," *Computer-Mediated Communication* 14 (2009): 964–987.

29. Van Dijck, "Digital Photography," 58, 59.

30. Nicholas John, "Sharing and Web 2.0: The Emergence of a Keyword," *New Media and Society* 15.2 (2012): 167–183.

31. Tim Kindberg, Mirjana Spasojevic, Rowanne Fleck, and Abigail Sellen, "I Saw This and Thought of You: Some Social Uses of Camera Phones," in *Extended Abstracts of the Conference on Human Factors in Computing Systems* (Portland, OR: ACM, 2005): 1545–1548.

32. McLaughlin and Vitak said their focus group participants acknowledged that their Facebook photos offer a skewed self-presentation of their social lives in "Norm Evolution and Violation on Facebook," 307.

33. Mussello, "Studying the Home Mode," 37, 36; Graham King, *Say "Cheese!": The Snapshot as Art and Social History* (London: William Collins, 1986).

34. Richard Chalfen, "Redundant Imagery: Some Observations on the Use of Snapshots in American Culture," *Journal of American Culture* 4.1 (1981): 106–113; Chalfen, *Snapshot Versions of Life*.

35. Van Dijck, "Digital Photography," 71.

36. Sarvas and Frohlich, *From Snapshots to Social Media*.

37. Amanda Lenhart and Mary Madden, "Teens, Privacy and Online Social Networks: How Teens Manage Their Online Identities and Personal Information in the Age of MySpace," *Pew Internet and American Life Project*, April 18, 2007, http://www.pewinternet.org/PPF/r/211/report_display.asp; Mendelson and Papacharissi, "Look at Us," in *The Networked Self*.

38. Andrew D. Miller and W. Keith Edwards, "Give and Take: A Study of Consumer Photo-Sharing Culture and Practice," *CHI 2007 Proceedings of the SIGCHI Conference on Human Factors in Computing Systems*, San Jose, CA: ACM, April 29, 2007, http://dl.acm.org/citation.cfm?id=1240682.

39. Patricia Lange, "Publicly Private and Privately Public: Social Networking on YouTube," *Journal of Computer-Mediated Communication* 13 (2007): 361–380.

40. Facebook's album feature is distinct from other photo-sharing media such as camera phone picture messaging, or even other Facebook photo-sharing capabilities such as profile pictures or large photo galleries. Whereas the galleries are a dynamic archive where other network members can add and remove photos by tagging, sharing, and so on, Facebook albums are a more fixed, formal mode of presentation. Only profile owners have total control over their albums.

41. For their essay on context collapse, see Alice Marwick and danah boyd, "I Tweet Honestly," 122. In another essay, boyd argues that social media "users" need to "take cues from the social media environment to imagine the community"; see danah boyd, "Why Youth <3 Social Network Sites: The Role of Networked Publics in Teenage Social Life," in *Youth Identity and Digital Media*, ed. David Buckingham (Cambridge MA: MIT Press, 2007), 131.

42. Marwick and boyd, "I Tweet Honestly," 126.

43. Chalfen, *Snapshot*, 142.

44. David Halle, *Inside Culture: Art and Class in the American Home* (Chicago: University of Chicago Press, 1994).

45. Chalfen, *Snapshot*, 98; Karin Becker Orhn, "The Photo Flow of Family Life: A Family Photograph Collection," *Folklore Forum* 13 (1975): 27–36.

46. This is a classic strategy of interpretive, ethnographic research. Clifford Geertz described it as a "continuous dialectical tacking between the most local of local detail and the most global of global structure in such a way as to bring them into simultaneous view" in *Local Knowledge: Further Essays in Interpretive Anthropology* (New York: Basic, 1983), 68.

47. Mendelson and Papacharissi, "Look at Us," in *The Networked Self*.

48. David Perlmutter, *Visions of War: Picturing Warfare from the Stone Age to the Cyberage* (New York: St. Martin's, 1999), 109.

49. S. Murray, "Digital Images"; Mendelson and Papacharissi, "Look at Us," in *The Networked Self*.

50. Erving Goffman, *The Presentation of Self in Everyday Life* (New York: Anchor, 1959), 109.

51. Joseph R. Dominick, "Who Do You Think You Are? Personal Home Pages and Self-Presentation on the World Wide Web," *Mass Communication Quarterly* 76.4 (1999): 646–658; David L. Jacobs, "Domestic Snapshots: Toward a Grammar of Motives," *Journal of American Culture* 7.1 (1981): 93–105; Don Slater "Domestic Photography and Digital Culture," in *The Photographic Image in Digital Culture*, ed. Martin Lister (London: Routledge, 1995), 129–146.

52. Mendelson and Papacharissi, "Look at Us," in *The Networked Self*, n.p.; see also Hugo Liu, "Social Network Profiles as Taster Performances."

53. Penny Tinkler, "A Fragmented Picture: Reflections on the Photographic Practices of Young People," *Visual Studies* 23 (2008): 255–266.

54. Madeline Jenks, "Sneaking into the Frame: Photographers Inverting the Lens," *Curate Africa*, May 20 2013, accessed May 31, 2013, http://www.curate africa.org/wp-content/uploads/2013/05/catalog_compressed.pdf.

55. Barbara Harrison, "Photographic Visions and Narrative Inquiry," *Narrative Inquiry* 12.1 (2002): 87–111.

56. "Ka-Bar" is the contemporary popular name for the USMC combat knife.

57. "Demographics of Active Duty US Military," *Defense Manpower Data Center*, November 23, 2013, accessed May 31, 2001, http://www.statisticbrain.com /demographics-of-active-duty-u-s-military/.

58. On January 23, 2013, Defense Secretary Leon Panetta lifted the ban on women serving in combat. The services will have until 2016 to implement the new legislation. See Lolita C. Baldor, "Women in Combat: Leon Panetta Removes Military Ban, Opening Front-Line Positions," *Associated Press*, January 23, 2013, http://www.huffingtonpost.com/2013/01/23/women-in-combat_n_2535954 .html.

59. Melissa T. Brown, *Enlisting Masculinity: The Construction of Gender in US Military Recruiting Advertising during the All-Volunteer Force* (New York: Oxford University Press, 2012); Ray Bourgeois Zimmerman, "Gruntspeak: Masculinity, Monstrosity and Discourse in Hasford's *The Short-Timers*," *American Studies* 40.1 (1999): 65–93.

60. Nathaniel Fick, *One Bullet Away: The Making of a Marine Officer* (New York: Houghton Mifflin, 2005).

61. Nick Couldry argues performativity becomes an essential step in "presencing," the practice of maintaining a continual online existence for others to encounter in *Media, Society, World: Social Theory and Digital Media Practice* (Cambridge, UK: Polity, 2012); Marwick and boyd's research on identity expression on Twitter suggests a variety of performative approaches that resemble personal branding, microcelebrity, and strategic self-commodification in "I Tweet Honestly."

62. danah boyd, "Why Youth <3 Social Network Sites"; Lynn Miller and Jacqueline Taylor, "The Constructed Self: Strategic and Aesthetic Choices in Autobiographical Performance," in *The Sage Handbook of Performance Studies*, ed. D. Soyini Madison and Judith Hamera (Thousand Oaks, CA: Sage, 2006), 169–187; Zizi Papacharissi, "Conclusion: A Networked Self," in *A Networked Self: Identity, Community, and Culture on Social Network Sites*, ed. Zizi Papacharissi (New York: Routledge, 2011), 304–318.

63. Richard Schechner, *Performance Theory* (New York: Routledge, 1977), 265.

64. Mendelson and Papacharissi, "Look at Us," in *The Networked Self.*

65. Participant 09, August 2011, interview with author.

66. Michael Griffin, "Media Images of War," *Media, War and Conflict* 3.1 (2010): 7–41.

67. Sarvas and Frohlich, *From Snapshots to Social Media.*

68. Gunther Kress and Theo Van Leeuwen, *Reading Images: The Grammar of Visual Design* (London: Routledge, 2006).

69. David Held and Kristian Coates Ulrichsen, "Wars of Decline: Afghanistan, Iraq, and Libya," *OpenDemocracy*, December 12, 2011, http://www.opendemocracy .net/david-held-kristian-coates-ulrichsen/wars-of-decline-afghanistan-iraq-and -libya; Audrey Kurth Cronin, "Behind the Curve: Globalization and International Terrorism," in *New Global Dangers: Changing Dimensions of International Security*, ed. Michael E. Brown, Owen R. Cote, Sean M. Lynn-Jones, and Steven E. Miller (Cambridge, MA: MIT Press, 2004), 448–476; Andrew J. Bacevich, *The New American Militarism: How Americans Are Seduced by War* (Oxford: Oxford

University Press, 2005); Olivier Roy, *The Politics of Chaos in the Middle East* (London: Hurst, 2007).

70. Roger Stahl, "Have You Played the War on Terror?," *Critical Studies in Media Communication* 23.2 (2009): 112–130.

71. Marcus Schulzke, "Rethinking Military Gaming: *America's Army* and Its Critics," *Games and Culture* 8.2 (2013): 59–76.

72. The third Call of Duty game in the series, "Modern Warfare 3," earned $400 million in sales within the first twenty-four hours of being released.

73. Evan Wright, *Generation Kill: Devil Dogs, Iceman, Captain America, and the New Face of American War* (New York: Berkley Caliber / Penguin, 2004); Christina M. Smith and Kelly M. McDonald, "The Mundane to the Memorial: Circulating and Deliberating the War in Iraq through Vernacular Soldier-Produced Videos," *Critical Studies in Media Communication* 28.4 (2011): 298.

74. The sergeant in this interview began his second tour in Iraq in 2007. At the time, President Bush's call for Iraqis to take over more of the responsibility for securing their country reminded the American public of the way President Nixon began to phase out US troops and turn over more of the offensive operations to the South Vietnamese Army during the Vietnam War. The similarities between what became known as "Iraqification" and "Vietnamization" caused the American public to draw parallels between the wars. It could be the case that this Marine is trying to anticipate the way his war, that is, the Iraq War, would be written in the history books. See Robert Brigham, *Iraq, Vietnam, and the Limits of American Power* (New York: Public Affairs, 2008).

75. Miller and Edwards, "Give and Take."

76. Chalfen, *Snapshot*, 70.

77. The title is meant to be ironic because the authors do, in fact, believe captions and context are important. See Robert Hariman and John Louis Lucaites, *No Caption Needed: Iconic Photographs, Public Culture, and Liberal Democracy* (Chicago: University of Chicago Press, 2007).

78. Sarvas and Frohlich, *From Snapshots to Social Media*, 94, 146.

79. West, *Kodak and the Lens*, 143. Publication of these "happy moments" is evidently taking a toll on the mental health of some Facebook users. New research cites a phenomenon known as "Facebook envy," where witnessing people's social lives play out online leads to feelings envy, misery, and loneliness. See Hui-Tzu Grace Chou and Nicholas Edge, "'They Are Happier and Having Better Lives Than I Am': The Impact of Using Facebook on Perceptions of Others' Lives," *Cyberpsychology, Behavior, and Social Networking* 15.2 (2012): 117–121; Rosa Golijan, "It's Not Just You: Facebook Envy Makes People Miserable, Studies Show," *Digital Life on Today*, January 25, 2013, accessed May 31, 2013, http://digital life.today.com/_news/2013/01/25/16698935-its-not-just-you-facebook-envy -makes-people-miserable-studies-show?lite.

80. Witnessing allows us to view ourselves as moral beings whose actions are always subject to adjudication. Following Barbie Zelizer, Susan Tait argues that bearing witness refers to practices of assuming responsibility for contemporary

events. See Barbie Zelizer, "Finding Aids to the Past: Bearing Personal Witness to Traumatic Public Events," *Media, Culture and Society* 24 (2002): 697–714; Susan Tait, "Bearing Witness, Journalism and Moral Responsibility," *Media, Culture, and Society* 33.8 (2011): 1220–1235.

81. Peggy Phelan interrogates the "ideology of visibility," a common misguided logic of representation. She argues that the idea of greater visibility leading to enhanced political power stems from a mistaken judgment about "the relation between the real and the representational." She makes this point with sarcasm: "If representational visibility equals power, then almost-naked young white women should be running Western culture." See *Unmarked: The Politics of Performance* (London: Routledge, 1993), 1, 2, 10.

82. Sadly, Eastman Kodak Company declared bankruptcy and closed its doors for good in January 2012. Facebook, on the other hand, has become the biggest photo storage site, ahead of its contemporaries: Flickr, Photobucket, etc. Facebook currently holds upward of 140 billion photos, ten thousand times more than the collection at the Library of Congress. Chalfen, "Redundant Imagery"; Chalfen, *Snapshot Versions of Life*; Mussello, "Studying the Home Mode," 23–42.

83. Pierre Bourdieu, *Photography: A Middle Brow Art*, trans. S. Whiteside (Stanford, CA: Stanford University Press, 1996), 87.

84. Lange, "Publicly Private."

85. Ellison, Steinfield, and Lampe, "The Benefits of Facebook 'Friends,'" 243.

86. Thomas Larson, *The Memoir and the Memoirist: Reading and Writing Personal Narrative* (Columbus: Ohio University Press / Swallow), 16.

87. Marita Sturken, "The Image as Memorial: Personal Photographs in Cultural Memory" in *The Familial Gaze*, ed. Marianne Hirsch (Hanover, NH: New England Press, 1999), 178.

88. As a civilian researcher interviewing active-duty service members about their personal media habits, I faced considerable curiosity and trepidation from almost everyone I encountered. One of the only things I had in my favor was that I was "not the media."

89. Thomas Rid and Marc Hecker, *War 2.0: Irregular Warfare in the Information Age* (Westport, CT: Praeger Security International, 2009), 4.

Chapter 4: Marine Corps Video Memes

1. Limor Shifman, *Memes in Digital Culture* (Cambridge, MA: MIT Press, 2013).

2. Nicholas John, "The Social Logics of Sharing," *Communication Review* 16.3 (2013): 113–131.

3. Shifman, *Memes in Digital Culture*, 19.

4. Richard Dawkins, *The Selfish Gene* (Oxford: Oxford University Press, 1976), 206.

5. "Top Trending Videos of 2013," *YouTube Rewind*, July 1, 2014, accessed January 10, 2014, https://www.youtube.com/playlist?list=PLSTz8jpJdr5pn9LFw-pX bgoIOFy2Z_td_.

6. Lisa Silvestri, "Surprise Homecomings and Vicarious Sacrifices," *Media, War & Conflict* 6.2 (2013): 101–115.

7. Social presence can be linked to the concept of immediacy that I highlighted in chapter 2. Interpersonally, immediacy, or a sense of social presence, is understood as the psychological distance a communicator puts between himself and the object of his communication. See Liam Rourke, Terry Anderson, D. Randy Garrison, and Walter Archer, "Assessing Social Presence in Asynchronous, Text-Based Computer Conferencing," *Journal of Distance Education* 14.3 (1999): 51–70; Charlotte Gunawardena and Frank Zittle, "Social Presence as a Predictor of Satisfaction within a Computer-Mediated Conferencing Environment," *American Journal of Distance Education* 11.3 (1997): 9. The need for us to be psychologically aware or attuned to the presence of others is especially important since we are becoming more and more socially interdependent. Following Lauren Berlant, I believe that the hyphen separating nation-state has collapsed, and following Zizi Papacharissi, that notions of public and private have disintegrated into a private sphere of affectivity. Lauren Berlant, *The Queen of America Goes to Washington City* (Durham, NC: Duke University Press, 1997); Zizi Papacharissi, *A Private Sphere.*

8. Frank Biocca, Chad Harms, and Judee K. Burgoon, "Toward a More Robust Theory and Measure of Social Presence: Review and Suggested Criteria," *Presence* 12.5 (2003): 465.

9. Cohen Research Group, "The Public Awareness Poll: Needs and Support for our OIF/OEF Military and Veteran Community," April 2–6, 2010, accessed October 25, 2011, www.cohenresearchgroup.com/media/ciav_201006.pdf.

10. James Fallows, "The Tragedy of the American Military," *Atlantic*, January 2015, http://www.theatlantic.com/features/archive/2014/12/the-tragedy-of-the-american-military/383516/.

11. Remember those "Support the Troops" magnets for the back of our cars? When's the last time you saw one of those?

12. Susan L. Carruthers, "No One's Looking: The Disappearing Audience for War," *Media, War and Conflict* 1.1 (2008): 72.

13. Gabrielle Murray, "Fact and Fiction: The Iraq War Film in Absence," *Screening the Past*, November 7, 2010, accessed May 31, 2013, http://tlweb.latrobe.edu.au/humanities/screeningthepast/29/fact-and-fiction-iraq-war-film-in-absence.html.

14. As quoted in Adi Robertson "YouTube to Advertisers: We're the New TV, Because We're Nothing Like TV," *Verge*, May 6, 2013, http://www.theverge.com/2013/5/6/4305640/youtube-to-advertisers-were-the-new-tv-because-were-nothing-like-tv?utm_source=feedly.

15. I refer to "popular culture," "public discourse," and "domestic" or "civilian" culture almost interchangeably. Popular culture offers easy access to a symbolic collective. As Peter Dahlgren argues, "In the contemporary media world, popular culture and politics cannot be fully separated. They are discursively structured in many similar ways, and they inform each other, feed off each other." *Media and Political Engagement: Citizens, Communication, and Democracy* (Cambridge:

Cambridge University Press, 2009), 141. Similarly Liesbet van Zooen detaches "popular culture" from its common synonymous connection with "entertainment," to say that pop culture should be thought of as the discourse of everyday life, standing in "opposition to elite affairs and politics." In this way, van Zooen argues that "popular genres and means" allow for fuller participation in public discourse, in *Entertaining the Citizen: When Politics and Popular Culture Converge* (Lanham, MD: Rowman & Littlefield, 2005), 10.

16. For a good example of how complicated and ephemeral social media norms are, see Andrew Fischer, "21 Really Annoying Facebook Friends We All Have," *General Forum*, September 20, 2013, http://www.generalforum.com/general-discussion/21-really-annoying-facebook-friends-we-all-have-106532.html.

17. Jeff Blagdon, "YouTube Hits a Billion Monthly Viewers," *Verge*, March 20, 2013, accessed May 31, 2013, http://www.theverge.com/2013/3/20/4129808/youtube-hits-a-billion-monthly-viewers; "YouTube Stats: Site Has 1 Billion Active Users Each Month," *Reuters*, March 20, 2012, accessed March 31, 2013, http://www.huffingtonpost.com/2013/03/21/youtube-stats_n_2922543.html. Helping spread the popularity of YouTube is its unofficial affiliate, Facebook, Inc., which reached one billion active users in September 2012, a level of global penetration that has made its quest for sustained growth more challenging. See Liana Baker and Gerry Shih, "Facebook Crosses Billion Threshold, on Quest for Growth," *Reuters*, October 4, 2012, accessed October 16, 2012, http://www.reuters.com/article/2012/10/04/us-facebook-idUSBRE8930N320121004; Dawn C. Chmielewski, "'Gangnam Style' Is YouTube's All-Time Most-Viewed Video," *Los Angeles Times*, December 17, 2012, accessed December 25, 2012, http://www.latimes.com/entertainment/envelope/cotown/la-fi-ct-viral-video-top-ten-20121218,0,674675.story. For a Marine Corps version of Gangnam Style, see Ryan Pomicter, "US Navy and Marines in Afghanistan Gangnam Style Parody," YouTube video, February 1, 2013, http://www.youtube.com/watch?v=Wt7pevIvCbQ.

18. New media scholars refer to the transgression of the broadcast, producer-consumer model as a network or "prosumer" model, where every user has the ability to produce and consume content on the web. See Mark Poster, *What's the Matter with the Internet?* (Minneapolis: University of Minnesota Press, 2001); Shirky, *Here Comes Everybody*.

19. Steve Fore, "America, America, This Is You: The Curious Case of 'America's Funniest Home Videos,'" *Journal of Popular Film and Television* 21.1 (1993): 37.

20. Fore, "America, America," 38.

21. Robert W. Sweeny, "'This Performance Art Is for the Birds': Jackass, 'Extreme' Sports, and the De(con)struction of Gender," *Studies in Art Education* 49.2 (2009): 136–146.

22. Sean Brayton, "MTV's Jackass: Transgression, Abjection and the Economy of White Masculinity," *Journal of Gender Studies* 16.1 (2007): 57–72.

23. Jawed Karim, "Me at the Zoo," YouTube video, April 23, 2005, accessed April 10, 2012, http://www.youtube.com/watch?v=jNQXAC9IVRw.

24. Terry O'Reilly and Mike Tennant, "The YouTube Revolution," in *The Age*

of Persuasion: How Marketing Ate Our Culture, ed. Terry O'Reilly and Mike Tennant (Berkeley, CA: Counterpoint, 2009), 97–118.

25. Desiree Adib, "Pop Star Justin Bieber Is on the Brink of Superstardom," *ABC News*, November 14, 2009, http://abcnews.go.com/GMA/Weekend/teen -pop-star-justin-bieber-discovered-youtube/story?id=9068403#.UU3PgFsjpUs.

26. Lei Guo and Lorin Lee, "The Critique of YouTube-Based Vernacular Discourse: A Case Study of YouTube's Asian Community," *Critical Studies in Media Communication* 30.5 (2013): 391–406; Aaron Hess, "Resistance Up in Smoke: Analyzing the Limitations of Deliberation on YouTube," *Critical Studies in Media Communication* 26.5 (2009): 411–434; Aaron Hess, "Democracy through the Polarized Lens of the Camcorders: Argumentation and Vernacular Spectacle on YouTube in the 2008 Election," *Argumentation and Advocacy* 47 (2010): 106–122.

27. Limor Shifman, "An Anatomy of a YouTube Meme," *New Media and Society* 14 (2012): 188.

28. Judsonlaipply, "Evolution of Dance—By Judson Laipply," YouTube video, April 6, 2006, accessed May 31, 2013, http://www.youtube.com/watch?v=dMHob HeiRNg.

29. Jim Loves, "Star Wars Kid," YouTube video, January 15, 2006, accessed May 31, 2013, http://www.youtube.com/watch?v=HPPj6viIBmU.

30. Shifman undertakes an analysis of thirty "mega-memetic" videos, which yielded six common features: a focus on ordinary people, flawed masculinity, humor, simplicity, repetitiveness, and whimsical content. Each of these attributes marks the video as incomplete or flawed, thereby invoking further creative dialogue. In Shifman's words, it seems that "bad" videos make "good" memes in contemporary participatory culture. See Shifman, "An Anatomy of a YouTube Meme."

31. William Babcock and Virginia Whitehouse, "Celebrity as a Postmodern Phenomenon, Ethical Crisis for Democracy, and Media Nightmare," *Journal of Mass Media Ethics* 20.2 (2005): 176–191; John Corner and Dick Pels, *Media and the Restyling of Politics* (London: Sage, 2003); Timothy Weiskel, "From Sidekick to Sideshow—Celebrity, Entertainment, and the Politics of Distraction," *American Behavioral Scientist* 49.3 (2005): 393–409.

32. Clay Johnson, *The Information Diet: A Case for Conscious Consumption* (Sebastopol, CA: O'Reilly Media, 2012); Olga Goriunova, "New Media Idiocy," *Convergence: The International Journal of Research into New Media Technologies* 19.2 (2013): 223–235.

33. Richard Bauman and Charles Briggs, "Poetics and Performance as Critical Perspectives on Language and Social Life," *Annual Review of Anthropology* 19.1 (1990): 59–88.

34. Shifman, *Memes in Digital Culture*, 4.

35. Shifman, *Memes in Digital Culture*, 150.

36. Scott Galupo, "Internet a Battlefield Press Pass: Can Public Opinion Stomach War Video?," *Washington Times*, August 4, 2006, http://washington-times .vlex.com/vid/internet-battlefield-pass-stomach-video-194577859.

37. Pentagon spokesperson Colonel Gary Keck, as cited in "Military Pulls Plug on Popular Sites," *Virginian Pilot*, May 15, 2007, accessed May 31, 2013, http://www.highbeam.com/doc/1G1-163398074.html.

38. Anna Badkhen, "Popular Web Sites Now Off Limits to Troops," *San Francisco Chronicle*, May 15, 2007, http://www.sfgate.com/news/article/Popular-Web-sites-now-off-limits-to-troops-2560359.php.

39. Wright, *Generation Kill*; David Sax, "Combat Rock," *Rolling Stone*, June 15, 2006, http://www.bujrum.ba/showthread.php?p=39232.

40. Wright, *Generation Kill*, 5.

41. Kari Andén-Papadopoulos, "US Soldiers Imaging the Iraq War on YouTube," 20.

42. James Poniewozik and Karen Tumulty, "The Beast with a Billion Eyes," *Time International* 168.26 (2006): 63–64.

43. Cara A. Finnegan, "Doing Rhetorical History of the Visual: The Photograph and the Archive," *Defining Visual Rhetorics*, ed. Charles Hill and Marguerite Helmers (Mahwah, NJ: Lawrence Erlbaum, 2004): 195–214.

44. Douglas Rushkoff, *Present Shock: When Everything Happens Now* (New York: Penguin Group, 2013).

45. As quoted in R. U. Sirius, "Living in the Present Is a Disorder," *Wired*, April 8, 2013, http://www.wired.com/opinion/2013/04/present-shock-rushkoff-r-u-sirius/.

46. Mike Nizza, "Pentagon Blocks MySpace and YouTube," *Lede*, March 14, 2007, http://thelede.blogs.nytimes.com/2007/05/14/pentagon-blocks-myspace-and-youtube/.

47. Christensen, "Uploading Dissonance," 171.

48. Smith and McDonald, "The Mundane to the Memorial."

49. The United Service Organization, Inc., founded in 1941, is a nonprofit organization to provide programs and services including live entertainment to US troops and their families. See Lisa Gilman "An American Soldier's iPod: Layers of Identity and Situated Listening in Iraq," *Music and Politics* 4.2 (2010), http://quod.lib.umich.edu/m/mp/9460447.0004.201/—american-soldiers-ipod-layers-of-identity-and-situated?rgn=main;view=fulltext#N35-ptr1.

50. Jean Burgess and Joshua Green, *YouTube: Online Video and Participatory Culture* (Cambridge, UK: Polity, 2009), 81.

51. Mirca Madianou and Daniel Miller, "Polymedia: Towards a New Theory of Digital Media in Interpersonal Communication," *International Journal of Cultural Studies* 16.2 (March 2013): 169–187.

52. James Gleick, "What Defines a Meme?," *Smithsonian*, May 2011, accessed May 31, 2013, http://www.smithsonianmag.com/arts-culture/What-Defines-a-Meme.html?c=y&story=fullstory.

53. Jeff Huang, Katherine M. Thornton, and Efthimis N. Efthimiadis, "Conversational Tagging in Twitter," paper presented at the twenty-first ACM Conference on Hypertext and Hypermedia, 2010, http://jeffhuang.com/Final_TwitterTagging_HT10.pdf.

54. Patricia Lange and Ito Mizuko, "Creative Production," in *Hanging Out, Messing Around, Geeking Out: Kids Living and Learning with New Media*, eds. Ito et al. (Cambridge, MA: MIT Press, 2010), 243–293.

55. Amanda Lenhart and Mary Madden, "Teens, Privacy and Online Social Networks."

56. Military-Civilian Group, "War and Sacrifice in the Post-9/11 Era," *Pew Research Social and Demographic Trends*, October 5, 2011, http://www.pewsocial trends.org/2011/10/05/war-and-sacrifice-in-the-post-911-era/.

57. The website "Know Your Meme" documents internet phenomena, accessed May 31, 2013, http://knowyourmeme.com/. For a montage of military ghost riding clips, see CatzDaLegit, "Military Ghost Ride Montage," YouTube video, April 4, 2008, accessed April 10, 2013, http://www.youtube.com/watch?v=X6tdUHi5o3o; Passtheammo, "Marines Ghost Ride the MRAP," YouTube video, March 14, 2008, http://www.youtube.com/watch?v=BX13Pdxrn-k.

58. As cited in "Harlem Shake," *Know Your Meme*, March 15, 2013, accessed March 31, 2013, http://knowyourmeme.com/memes/harlem-shake.

59. Nancy Baym, *Personal Connections in the Digital Age* (Malden, MA: Polity Press, 2010), 90.

60. There is a good deal of scholarly debate as to whether YouTube is an archive or a mode of dissemination. For example, Frank Kessler and Mirko Tobias Schafer argue that YouTube is for dissemination, whereas Rick Prelinger argues that You-Tube is not only an archive but also the ideal form of archive because users are the curators, deciding what goes into the archive as well as how to control its metadata, dictating organization of archival documents through voices of titles and keywords that determine what documents are retrieved during searches. See Frank Kessler and Mirko Tobias Schafer, "Navigating YouTube: Constituting a Hybrid Information System," in *The YouTube Reader*, ed. Pelle Snickars and Patrick Vonde-rau (Stockholm: National Library of Sweden, 2009), 276; Rick Prelinger, "The Appearance of Archives," in *The YouTube Reader*, ed. Pelle Snickars and Patrick Vonderau, 268–274 (Stockholm: National Library of Sweden, 2009), 270.

61. David Hill, "Troops Spoof Dolphins Cheerleaders' Call Me Maybe Video," *NMC Miami*, October 24, 2012, accessed March 15, 2013, http://www.nbc miami.com/news/local/Troops-Spoof-Dolphins-Cheerleaders-Call-Me-Maybe -Video-175699431.html.

62. "Top Trending Videos of 2013."

63. Shifman, *Memes in Digital Culture*, 105.

64. Muhammad Lila and Suzan Clarke, "The Making of Marine 'Call Me Maybe' Video in Afghanistan," *ABC News*, July 19, 2012, https://www.google .com/url?sa=f&rct=j&url=http://abcnews.go.com/Entertainment/making-hit -Marine-call-video-afghanistan/story%3Fid%3D16809981&q=&esrc=s&ei =ShWRUZuDPdKCoQHZoYCgCw&usg=AFQjCNGUMQZbSilmXzrObmbd vPhgS2d3GQ.

65. ABC News, "'Call Me Maybe' Spoofed by U.S. Marines: Carly Rae Jep-

sen's Hit Song Parodied Again," YouTube video, July 18, 2012, http://www.you tube.com/watch?v=R2ySHSTEzjQ.

66. For the single-screen version, please see: Andrew Stupfel, "Miami Dolphins Cheerleaders 'Call Me Maybe' by Carly Rae Jepson Military Tribute," YouTube video, September 30, 2012, https://www.youtube.com/watch?v=B_zhaji 9e0s. "Out of regs" facial hair suggests these men may be part of a special operations unit, or MARSOC.

67. For the split-screen version, please see Haider Alwash, "Miami Dolphins Cheerleaders 'Call Me Maybe' vs US Troops 'Call Me Maybe'," YouTube video, February 19, 2013, https://www.youtube.com/watch?v=KOffsOHOCXo.

68. Cultural studies scholar Jeff Lewis refers to the contemporary "public sphere" as a "mediasphere" or a critical "culturescape" in which meanings flow through various channels of human and technologically enhanced modes of communication in *Cultural Studies: The Basics* (London: Sage, 2008).

69. Christensen, "Uploading Dissonance"; Ralph D. Berenger, "Introduction: War in Cyberspace," special section, *Journal of Computer-Mediated Communication* 12.1 (2006), http://jcmc.indiana.edu/vol12/issue1/berenger.html; Michael A. Cohen and Maria Figueroa Kupcu, "Congress and the 'YouTube War,'" *World Policy Journal* 23.4 (2007): 49–54.

70. Kevin McSorley, "Helmetcams, Militarized Sensation and 'Somatic War,'" *Journal of War and Culture Studies* 5.1 (2012): 47–58.

71. "Jumping the shark" is an idiom used to describe the moment in the evolution of a television program when it has outlived its freshness. It references a scene from the fifth season of *Happy Days* when Fonzie demonstrates his bravery and water-skiing skills by jumping over a shark.

72. Lilie Chouliaraki, "Spectacular Ethics," *Journal of Language and Politics* 4.2 (2005): 143–159; Susan Moeller, *Compassion Fatigue: How the Media Sell Disease, Famine, War and Death* (New York: Routledge, 1999); Martha Nussbaum, *Hiding from Humanity: Shame, Disgust, and the Law* (Princeton, NJ: Princeton University Press, 2004); Carrie Rentschler, "Witnessing: US Citizenship and the Vicarious Experience of Suffering," *Media, Culture and Society* 26 (2004): 296–304; Susan Sontag, *Regarding the Pain of Others* (New York: Picador/Farrar, Straus & Giroux, 2003).

73. Kari Andén-Papadopoulos, "US Soldiers Imaging the Iraq War on You Tube"; Christian Christensen, "'Hey Man, Nice Shot': Setting the Iraq War to Music on YouTube." In *The YouTube Reader*, edited by Pelle Snickars and Patrick Vonderau, 204–217 (Stockholm: National Library of Sweden, 2009); Christensen "Uploading Dissonance," 173; McSorely, "Helmetcams"; Jonathan Pieslak, *Sound Targets: American Soldiers and Music in the Iraq War* (Bloomington: Indiana University Press, 2009); Jessica Ritchie, "Instant Histories of War"; Smith and McDonald, "The Mundane to the Memorial."

74. Susan Moeller, *Shooting War: Photography and the American Experience of Combat* (New York: Basic Books, 1989).

75. McSorely argues we need to study visual representations beyond their representational logic, and more for their emotional resonance, in "Helmetcams," 55.

76. Carruthers, "No One's Looking," 71.

77. Brian Castner, *The Long Walk* (New York: Anchor Books, 2012), 179–180.

78. Since ancient Greek theater, comedy and tragedy have been the dialectic poles animating life's drama. See Matthew M. Hurley, Daniel C. Dennett, and Reginald B. Adams Jr., *Inside Jokes: Using Humor to Reverse-Engineer the Mind* (Cambridge, MA: MIT Press, 2011).

79. Linda Weiser Friedman and Hershey H. Friedman, "I-Get-It as a Type of Bonding Humor: The Secret Handshake," SSRN 913622 (2003), accessed April 4, 2013, http://ssrn.com/abstract=913622 or http://dx.doi.org/10.2139/ssrn.913622.

80. Slyvestri, "MEU xmas," YouTube video, January 26, 2008, accessed March 30, 2015, http://www.youtube.com/watch?v=5-yE1QC8tHE.

81. This exchange typically occurs on large air bases or company FOBs before the units move to their COPs.

82. irice80, "Ar Ramadi Iraq. Fox Co 2/5 2004," YouTube video, November 9, 2009, http://www.youtube.com/watch?v=_lNqb3WCtTE.

83. Nancy Thumim, *Self-Representation and Digital Culture* (Palgrave Macmillan, 2012).

84. Letters from author's personal collection dated November 30, 2005, January 3, 2006, and January 26, 2006, respectively.

85. Amy Belasco, "The Cost of Iraq, Afghanistan, and Other Global War on Terror Operations since 9/11," *Congressional Research Service*, March 29, 2011, accessed May 31, 2013, http://www.fas.org/sgp/crs/natsec/RL33110.pdf.

86. A marginally reported "symbolic" end to combat operations was reported to have occurred on December 8, 2014. Anna Muirine, "Symbolic 'End' to Afghanistan War Overshadowed by New Obama Plans," *Christian Science Monitor*, December 8, 2014, http://www.csmonitor.com/USA/Military/2014/1208/Symbolic-end-to-Afghanistan-war-overshadowed-by-new-Obama-plans-video.

87. In a podcast analyzing the Authorization to Use Military Force, Jad Abumrad and Robert Krulwich argue that the lines between war and peace have blurred to such an extent that the usual business of declaring (and subsequently ending) war no longer exists. War today is "one long improvisation." In podcast by Radiolab, "60 Words," podcast audio 12.7, accessed April 20, 2014, http://www.stitcher.com/podcast/wnycs-radiolab/episode/33467725?refid=asi_eml&autoplay=true.

88. Lisa Silvestri, "Together We Stand, Divided We Fall: Building Alliances with Combat Veterans," *Soundings* 95.3 (2012): 287.

89. Cass Sunstein and Reid Hastie recently wrote about the dynamics of groupthink, arguing that we need diverse perspectives to get at the heart of an issue. When like-minded people talk to one another they become more calcified, and even radical, in their views. See *Wiser: Getting beyond Groupthink to Make Groups Smarter* (Cambridge, MA: Harvard Business Review Press, 2014).

Conclusion: This Means War

1. Henrik Örnebring argues that content typically includes images of cats, dogs, babies, weddings, personal life, and pop culture in "The Consumer as Producer—of What?"

2. Todd Gitlin, "How Journalism Misses the Big Stories and Why We Still Need It," paper presented at the M. Holly McGranahan Lecture, University of Iowa, Iowa City, April 4, 2013. Gitlin was channeling the work of Ethan Zuckerman's Cute Cat Theory. See Ethan Zuckerman, "The Cute Cat Theory Talk at ETech," *My Heart's in Accra*, March 2008, accessed May 31, 2013, http://www.ethanzuckerman.com/blog/2008/03/08/the-cute-cat-theory-talk-at-etech/; Shirky, "The Political Power of Social Media"; Samantha M. Shapiro, "Revolution, Facebook-Style," *New York Times Magazine*, January 22, 2009, accessed May 31, 2013, http://www.nytimes.com/2009/01/25/magazine/25bloggers-t.html?_r= 2&pagewanted=all&.

3. Malcolm Gladwell, "Small Change: Why the Revolution Will Not Be Tweeted," *New Yorker*, October 4, 2010, http://www.newyorker.com/reporting /2010/10/04/101004fa_fact_gladwell; Ashley Mentzer, "Kony 2012: Fake Advocacy?," *Huffington Post*, March 12, 2012, http://www.huffingtonpost.com/the -state-press/kony-2012_b_1339081.html; Elise Danielle Thorburn "Social Media, Subjectivity, and Surveillance: Moving On from Occupy, the Rise of Live Streaming Video," *Communication and Critical/Cultural Studies* 11.1 (2014): 52–63.

4. Lisa Silvestri, "Shiny Happy People Holding Guns: 21st-Century Images of War," *Visual Communication Quarterly* 21.2 (2014): 106–118.

5. Marwick, *Status Update*, 25.

6. Kari Andén-Papadopoulos and Mervi Pantti argue that discursive authority rests on eyewitness accounts. Similarly, Samuel Hynes describes "the authority of the ordinary man's witness." See Kari Andén-Papadopoulos and Mervi Pantti, "Re-imagining Crisis Reporting: Professional Ideology of Journalists and Citizen Eyewitness Images," *Journalism* 14.7 (2013): 960–977; Samuel Hynes, *The Soldier's Tale: Bearing Witness to Modern War* (New York: Allen Lane, 1997), 1.

7. My selection of the term "everyday" is not haphazard, nor is it a direct nod to Michel de Certeau or other everyday life theorists. The reason I selected the term "everyday" is because that is the term the Marines in this study used to describe their experiences in Iraq and Afghanistan.

8. Mike Fritz, "The Civil War: Between Battles," *Rundown*, April 12, 2011, http://www.pbs.org/newshour/rundown/2011/04/the-civil-war-between-the -battles.html.

9. Chris Hables Gray, *Postmodern War: The New Politics of Conflict* (New York: Guilford, 1997).

10. David Kilcullen, *The Accidental Guerrilla: Fighting Small Wars in the Midst of a Big One* (New York: Oxford University Press, 2009), 279.

11. David Axe, "How to Prevent Drone Pilot PTSD: Blame the 'Bot," *Wired*, June 7, 2012, accessed June 26, 2013, http://www.wired.com/dangerroom/2012/06

/drone-pilot-ptsd/; Elisabeth Bumiller, "A Day Job Waiting for a Kill Shot a World Away," *New York Times*, July 29, 2012, accessed July 31, 2012, http://www .nytimes.com/2012/07/30/us/drone-pilots-waiting-for-a-kill-shot-7000-miles -away.html?pagewanted=all&_r=2&.

12. Michelle Tan, "2 Million Troops Have Deployed since 9/11," *Marine Corps Times*, December 18, 2009, http://www.marinecorpstimes.com/article/20091218 /NEWS/912180312/2-million-troops-deployed-since-9-11.

13. As quoted in Sabrina Tabernise, "Civilian-Military Gap Grows as Fewer Americans Serve," *New York Times*, November 24, 2011, accessed November 11, 2012, http://www.nytimes.com/2011/11/25/us/civilian-military-gap-grows-as -fewer-americans-serve.html?_r=1.

14. Rushkoff, *Present Shock*.

15. John Lucaites, "The Classic Game of World Domination," *No Caption Needed*, September 6, 2011, http://www.nocaptionneeded.com/2011/09/9248/.

16. Forward operating bases (FOBs) are small bases located forward or away from the main base accessible by helicopter and vehicle. The FOB is where most of the mobile assets used by the units in the AOR (area of responsibility) will be based. It is smaller than the air bases but larger than a patrol base.

17. Richard White notes the "importance of the tourist model in giving shape to the war experience" in "The Soldier as Tourist: The Australian Experience of the Great War," *War and Society* 5 (1987): 69.

18. Amanda Cedrone, "An Emotional Surprise," *Boston Globe*, September 15, 2011, http://www.bostonglobe.com/metro/2011/09/15/girl-birthday-surprise -her-father-leave-from-afghanistan/YWUI6Ec597y4IenRyEo9xM/picture.html.

19. Daniel Tosh, *Completely Serious*, DVD, Image Entertainment, 2007.

20. Barack Obama, "Remarks by the President at the National Defense University," speech, Washington, DC, May 23, 2013, White House Office of the Press Secretary, http://www.whitehouse.gov/the-press-office/2013/05/23/remarks -president-national-defense-university.

21. Greg Myre, "The U.S. Bombing Campaign: Is It War or Counterterrorism?," *NPR.org*, September 24, 2014, http://www.npr.org/blogs/parallels/2014 /09/24/350579005/the-u-s-bombing-campaign-is-it-war-or-counterterrorism.

22. As quoted in Helen Regan, "John Kerry: ISIS Action Is Not a War, It's Counter-terrorism," *Time*, September 12, 2014, http://time.com/3334712/john -kerry-isis-war-counterterrorism-syria/.

23. For more about the distinction between two types of realities in wartime— myth and sensory—read Lawrence LeShan, *The Psychology of War* (New York: Helios, 1992).

24. Alan Zarembo, "Cost of Iraq, Afghanistan Wars Will Keep Mounting," *Los Angeles Times*, March 29, 2013, http://articles.latimes.com/2013/mar/29/nation /la-na-0329-war-costs-20130329.

25. The end is symbolic in the sense that eleven thousand troops will remain and policy will not shift dramatically.

26. Ted Remington, "Ceci N'est Pas Une Guerre: The Misuse of War as Metaphor in Iraq," *KB Journal* 7.2 (2011), http://www.kbjournal.org/Remington.

27. Protest movements against social and economic inequality have also appropriated the term "occupation" as in "Occupy Wall Street."

28. M. Elizabeth Weiser, "Burke and War: Rhetoricizing the Theory of Dramatism," *Rhetoric Review* 26.3 (2007): 286–302.

29. Johan Galtung, "Violence, Peace, and Peace Research," *Journal of Peace Research* 6.3 (1969): 167–191; Kenneth E. Boulding, "Future Directions in Conflict and Peace Studies," *Journal of Conflict Resolution* 22.2 (1978): 342–354; David P. Barash and Charles P. Webel, *Peace and Conflict Studies*, 2nd ed. (Thousand Oaks, CA: Sage, 2009).

30. Hedges, *War Is a Force*, 81.

31. Kenneth Burke, *Permanence and Change: An Anatomy of Purpose* (Berkeley: University of California Press, 1984), 69.

32. I borrow the phrase "moral imagination" from John Paul Lederbach, *The Moral Imagination: The Art and Soul of Building Peace* (New York: Oxford University Press, 2005).

33. Eli Pariser, "When the Internet Thinks It Knows You," *New York Times*, May 22, 2011, http://www.nytimes.com/2011/05/23/opinion/23pariser.html.

References

ABC News. "'Call Me Maybe' Spoofed by U.S. Marines: Carly Rae Jepsen's Hit Song Parodied Again." YouTube video, July 18, 2012. http://www.youtube.com/watch?v=R2ySHSTEzjQ.

Ackman, Dan. "Sherron Watkins Had Whistle, but Blew It." *Forbes*, February 14, 2002. Accessed December 9, 2011. http://www.forbes.com/2002/02/14/0214watkins.html.

Adams, Paul. *Grouped: How Small Groups of Friends Are the Key to Influence on the Social Web*. Berkeley, CA: New Riders, 2012.

Adib, Desiree. "Pop Star Justin Bieber Is on the Brink of Superstardom." *ABC News*, November 14, 2009. http://abcnews.go.com/GMA/Weekend/teen-pop-star-justin-bieber-discovered-youtube/story?id=9068403#.UU3PgFsjpUs.

Ahern, Marie L. *The Rhetoric of War: Training Day, the Militia, and the Military Sermon*. Westport, CT: Greenwood Press, 1989.

Albrecht, Steffen. "Whose Voice Is Heard in Online Deliberation? A Study of Participation and Representation in Political Debates on the Internet." *Information, Communication and Society* 9.1 (2006): 62–82.

Alwash, Haider. "Miami Dolphins Cheerleaders 'Call Me Maybe' vs US Troops 'Call Me Maybe.'" YouTube video, February 19, 2013. https://www.youtube.com/watch?v=KOffsOHOCXo.

Amit, Vered. "Introduction: Constructing the Field." In *Constructing the Field: Ethnographic Fieldwork in the Contemporary World*, edited by Vered Amit, 1–18. London: Routledge, 2000.

Andén-Papadopoulos, Kari. "Body Horror on the Internet: U.S. Soldiers Recording the War in Iraq and Afghanistan." *Media, Culture and Society* 31.6 (2009): 921–938.

———. "US Soldiers Imaging the Iraq War on YouTube." *Popular Communication* 7 (2009): 17–27.

Andén-Papadopoulos, Kari, and Mervi Pantti. "Re-imagining Crisis Reporting: Professional Ideology of Journalists and Citizen Eyewitness Images." *Journalism* 14.7 (2013): 960–977.

Andersen, Robin. *A Century of Media, a Century of War*. New York: Peter Lang, 2006.

Arnold, M. "On the Phenomenology of Technology: The 'Janus' Faces of Mobile Phones." *Information and Organization* 13 (2003): 231–256.

Associated Press. "Marine Takes Aim at Military's Free Speech Limit." *CBS News*, April 5, 2012. http://www.cbsnews.com/news/marine-takes-aim-at-militarys-free-speech-limit/.

Axe, David. "How to Prevent Drone Pilot PTSD: Blame the 'Bot." *Wired*, June 7, 2012. Accessed June 26, 2013. http://www.wired.com/dangerroom/2012/06/drone-pilot-ptsd/.

Babcock, William, and Virginia Whitehouse. "Celebrity as a Postmodern Phenomenon, Ethical Crisis for Democracy, and Media Nightmare." *Journal of Mass Media Ethics* 20.2 (2005): 176–191.

Bacevich, Andrew J. *The New American Militarism: How Americans Are Seduced by War.* Oxford: Oxford University Press, 2005.

Badkhen, Anna. "Popular Web Sites Now Off Limits to Troops." *San Francisco Chronicle*, May 15, 2007. http://www.sfgate.com/news/article/Popular-Web-sites-now-off-limits-to-troops-2560359.php.

Baker, Liana, and Gerry Shih. "Facebook Crosses Billion Threshold, on Quest for Growth." *Reuters*, October 4, 2012. Accessed October 16, 2012. http://www.reuters.com/article/2012/10/04/us-facebook-idUSBRE8930N320121004.

Baldor, Lolita C. "Women in Combat: Leon Panetta Removes Military Ban, Opening Front-Line Positions." *Associated Press*, January 23, 2013. http://www.huffingtonpost.com/2013/01/23/women-in-combat_n_2535954.html.

Barash, David P., and Charles P. Webel. *Peace and Conflict Studies.* 2nd ed. Thousand Oaks, CA: Sage, 2009.

Barnes, Susan. "A Privacy Paradox: Social Networking in the United States." *First Monday* 11.9. Accessed August 8, 2008. http://firstmonday.org/htbin/cgiwrap/bin/ojs.

Baron, Naomi. *Always On: Language in an Online and Mobile World.* New York: Oxford University Press, 2008.

Baron, Naomi, and Rich Ling. "Emerging Patterns of American Mobile Phone Use: Electronically-Mediated Communication in Transition." In *Mobile Media 2007: Proceedings of an International Conference on Social and Cultural Aspects of Mobile Phones, Media and Wireless Technologies, June 2–4*, edited by Gerard Goggin and Larissa Hjorth. Sydney: University of Sydney, 2007.

Barton, David, and Nigel Hall, eds. *Letter Writing as a Social Practice.* Vol. 9. Philadelphia: John Benjamins, 2000.

Bauman, Richard, and Charles Briggs. "Poetics and Performance as Critical Perspectives on Language and Social Life." *Annual Review of Anthropology* 19.1 (1990): 59–88.

Bauman, Zygmunt. *Liquid Modernity.* Cambridge, MA: Polity, 2000.

Baym, Nancy. *Personal Connections in the Digital Age.* Malden, MA: Polity, 2010.

Beck, Ulrich. *Risk Society: Towards a New Modernity.* New Delhi: Sage, 1992.

———. "The Terrorist Threat: World Risk Society Revisited." *Theory, Culture and Society* 19.4 (2002): 39–55.

Becker, Howard. *Tricks of the Trade: How to Think about Your Research While You're Doing It*. Chicago: University of Chicago Press, 1998.

Belasco, Amy. "The Cost of Iraq, Afghanistan, and Other Global War on Terror Operations since 9/11." *Congressional Research Service*, March 29, 2011. Accessed May 31, 2013. http://www.fas.org/sgp/crs/natsec/RL33110.pdf.

Benkler, Yochai. *The Wealth of Networks*. New Haven, CT: Yale University Press, 2006.

Berenger, Ralph. "Introduction: Global Media Go to War." In *Global Media Go to War: Roles of News and Entertainment Media during the 2003 Iraq War*, edited by Ralph Berenger, xxvii-1. Washington, DC: Marquette Books, 2004.

Berenger, Ralph D. "Introduction: War in Cyberspace." Special section. *Journal of Computer-Mediated Communication* 12.1 (2006). http://jcmc.indiana.edu/vol12/issue1/berenger.html.

Berlant, Lauren. *The Queen of America Goes to Washington City*. Durham, NC: Duke University Press, 1997.

Biocca, Frank, Chad Harms, and Judee K. Burgoon. "Toward a More Robust Theory and Measure of Social Presence: Review and Suggested Criteria." *Presence* 12.5 (2003): 456–480.

Black, Edwin. "The Second Persona." *Quarterly Journal of Speech* 56.2 (1970): 109–119.

Blagdon, Jeff. "YouTube Hits a Billion Monthly Viewers." *Verge*, March 20, 2013. Accessed May 31, 2013. http://www.theverge.com/2013/3/20/4129808/youtube-hits-a-billion-monthly-viewers.

Bolter, Jay David, and Richard A. Grusin. "Remediation." *Configurations* 4 (1996): 311–358.

———. *Remediation: Understanding New Media*. Cambridge, MA: MIT Press, 1999.

Boulding, Kenneth E. "Future Directions in Conflict and Peace Studies." *Journal of Conflict Resolution* 22.2 (1978): 342–354.

Bourdieu, Pierre. *Distinction: A Social Critique of the Judgment of Taste*. Translated by Richard Nice. Cambridge, MA: Harvard University Press, 1984.

———. *The Logic of Practice*. Stanford, CA: Stanford University Press, 1980.

———. *Photography: A Middle Brow Art*. Translated by S. Whiteside. Stanford, CA: Stanford University Press, 1996.

boyd, danah. "Friends, Friendsters, and MySpace: Top 8; Writing Community into Being on Social Network Sites." *First Monday* 11 (2006). Accessed December 9, 2012. http://firstmonday.org/htbin/cgiwrap/bin/ojs/index.php/fm/article/view/1418/1336.

———. "Friendster and Publicly Articulated Social Networks." Conference on Human Factors and Computing Systems (CHI 2004). Vienna: ACM, April 24–29, 2004.

———. "None of This Is Real." In *Structures* of Participation in Digital Culture, edited by Joe Karaganis, 132–157. New York: Social Science Research Council, 2008.

————. "Streams of Content, Limited Attention: The Flow of Information through Social Media." *Web 2.0 Expo*, November 17, 2009. Accessed December 9, 2012. http://www.danah.org/papers/talks/Web2Expo.html.

————. "Taken Out of Context: American Teen Sociality in Networked Publics." PhD diss., University of California Berkeley, 2008. Accessed October 15, 2011. http://www.danah.org/papers/.

————. "White Flight in Networked Publics? How Race and Class Shaped American Teen Engagement with MySpace and Facebook." In *Race after the Internet*, edited by Lisa Nakamura and Peter Chow-White, 203–222. New York: Routledge, 2011.

————. "Why Youth <3 Social Network Sites: The Role of Networked Publics in Teenage Social Life." In *Youth Identity and Digital Media*, edited by David Buckingham, 119–142. Cambridge, MA: MIT Press, 2007.

boyd, danah, and Nicole Ellison. "Social Network Sites: Definition, History, and Scholarship." *Journal of Computer-Mediated Communication* 13 (2007): article 11. Accessed October 10, 2013. http://jcmc.indiana.edu/vo113/issue1/boyd .ellison.html.

boyd, danah, and Jeffrey Heer. "Profiles as Conversation: Networked Identity Performance on Friendster." Paper presented at the Hawaii International Conference on System Sciences, Kauai, HI, January 4–7, 2006. Accessed February 5, 2012. http://www.danah.org/papers/.

Brayton, Sean. "MTV's Jackass: Transgression, Abjection and the Economy of White Masculinity." *Journal of Gender Studies* 16.1 (2007): 57–72.

Brigham, Robert. *Iraq, Vietnam, and the Limits of American Power.* New York: Public Affairs, 2008.

Broadbent, Stefana. "Approaches to Personal Communication." In *Digital Anthropology*, edited by Heather Horst and Daniel Miller, 127–139. London: Berg, 2012.

————. "The Democratisation of Intimacy." *Observing the Evolution of Technology Usage Blog*, March 23, 2012. http://stefanabroadbent.com/2012/03/23/the -democratisation-of-intimacy/.

————. "Transforming the Home." *Observing the Evolution of Technology Usage Blog*. March 23, 2012. Accessed December 9, 2012. http://stefanabroadbent .com/2012/03/23/transforming-the-home/.

Brockriede, Wayne, and Robert Scott. *Moments in the Rhetoric of the Cold War.* New York: Random House, 1970.

Brodie, Richard. *Virus of the Mind: The New Science of the Meme.* Seattle, WA: Integral, 1996.

Brouwer, Daniel, and Robert Asen, eds. *Public Modalities: Rhetoric, Culture, Media and the Shape of Public Life.* Tuscaloosa: University of Alabama Press, 2010.

Brown, Melissa T. *Enlisting Masculinity: The Construction of Gender in US Military Recruiting Advertising during the All-Volunteer Force.* New York: Oxford University Press, 2012.

Brubaker, Jed R., Gillian R. Hayes, and Paul Dourish. "Beyond the Grave: Facebook as a Site for the Expansion of Death and Mourning." *Information Society: An International Journal* 29.3 (2013): 152–163.

Bumiller, Elisabeth. "A Day Job Waiting for a Kill Shot a World Away." *New York Times*, July 29, 2012. Accessed July 31, 2012. http://www.nytimes.com /2012/07/30/us/drone-pilots-waiting-for-a-kill-shot-7000-miles-away.html ?pagewanted=all&_r=2&.

Burgess, Jean, and Joshua Green. *YouTube: Online Video and Participatory Culture.* Cambridge, UK: Polity, 2009.

Burke, Kenneth. *Language as Symbolic Action.* Berkeley: University of California Press, 1966.

———. *Permanence and Change: An Anatomy of Purpose.* Berkeley: University of California Press, 1984.

Calhoun, Craig. "Information Technology and the International Public Sphere." In *Shaping the Network Society: The New Role of Civil Society in Cyberspace,* edited by Douglas Schuler and Peter Day, 229–251. Cambridge, MA: MIT Press, 2004.

———. "Social Theory and the Politics of Identity." In *Social Theory and the Politics of Identity,* edited by Craig Calhoun, 9–36. Oxford, UK: Blackwell, 1994.

Carlin, Diana, Dan Schill, David G. Levasseur, and Anthony S. King. "The Post-9/11 Public Sphere: Citizen Talk about the 2004 Presidential Debates." *Rhetoric and Public Affairs* 8.4 (2005): 617–638.

Carroll, Andrew, ed. *War Letters: Extraordinary Correspondence from American Wars.* New York: Scribner, 2001.

Carruthers, Susan L. "No One's Looking: The Disappearing Audience for War." *Media, War and Conflict* 1.1 (2008): 70–76.

Castner, Brian. *The Long Walk.* New York: Anchor Books, 2012.

CatzDaLegit. "Military Ghost Ride Montage." YouTube video, April 4, 2008. Accessed April 10, 2013. http://www.youtube.com/watch?v=X6tdUHi5030.

Cedrone, Amanda. "An Emotional Surprise." *Boston Globe*, September 15, 2011. http://www.bostonglobe.com/metro/2011/09/15/girl-birthday-surprise-her -father-leave-from-afghanistan/YWUI6Ec597y4IenRyEo9xM/picture.html.

Chalfen, Richard. "Redundant Imagery: Some Observations on the Use of Snapshots in American Culture." *Journal of American Culture* 4.1 (1981): 106–113.

———. *Snapshot Versions of Life.* Bowling Green, OH: Bowling Green State University Press, 1987.

Chmielewski, Dawn C. "'Gangnam Style' Is YouTube's All-Time Most-Viewed Video." *Los Angeles Times*, December 17, 2012. http://www.latimes .com/entertainment/envelope/cotown/la-fi-ct-viral-video-top-ten-20121218,0 ,674675.story.

Chou, Hui-Tzu Grace, and Nicholas Edge. "'They Are Happier and Having Better Lives Than I Am': The Impact of Using Facebook on Perceptions of Others' Lives." *Cyberpsychology, Behavior, and Social Networking* 15.2 (2012): 117–121.

Chouliaraki, Lilie. "Spectacular Ethics." *Journal of Language and Politics* 4.2 (2005): 143–159.

Christensen, Christian. "'Hey Man, Nice Shot': Setting the Iraq War to Music on YouTube." In *The YouTube Reader*, edited by Pelle Snickars and Patrick Vondereau, 204–217. Stockholm: National Library of Sweden, 2009.

———. "Uploading Dissonance: YouTube and the US Occupation of Iraq." *Media, War and Conflict* 1 (2008): 155–175.

Christensen, Toke Haunstrup. "'Connected Presence' in Distributed Family Life." *New Media and Society* 11.3 (2009): 433–451.

Christofides, Emile, Amy Muise, and Serge Desmarais. "Information Disclosure and Control on Facebook: Are They Two Sides of the Same Coin or Two Different Processes?" *Cyberpsychology and Behavior* 12.3 (2009): 341–345.

Clausewitz, Carl von. *On War*. Translated by J. J. Graham. Middlesex, England: Penguin Books, 1968.

Cohen, Michael A., and Maria Figueroa Kupcu. "Congress and the 'YouTube War.'" *World Policy Journal* 23.4 (2007): 49–54.

Cohen Research Group. "The Public Awareness Poll: Needs and Support for our OIF/OEF Military and Veteran Community," April 2–6, 2010. www.cohen researchgroup.com/media/ciav_201006.pdf.

Condit, Celeste. "Diverse Bodies Learning New Languages." *Rhetoric Review* 25 (2006): 370–381.

Corner, John, and Dick Pels. *Media and the Restyling of Politics*. London: Sage, 2003.

Corrin, Amber. "DOD's New Policy 'Likes' Social Media, but with Caveats." *Federal Computer*, August 14, 2012. http://few.com/Articles/2012/08/15/FEAT -Inside-DOD-social-media-policy.

Couldry, Nick. *Media, Society, World: Social Theory and Digital Media Practice*. Cambridge, UK: Polity, 2012.

Cox, Adam. "The YouTube War." *Time*, July 19, 2006. Accessed July 31, 2012. http://www.time.com/time/nation/article/0,8599,1216501,00.html.

Crawford, Kate. "Following You: Disciplines of Listening in Social Media." *Continuum: Journal of Media and Cultural Studies* 23.4 (2009): 525–535.

Cronin, Audrey Kurth. "Behind the Curve: Globalization and International Terrorism." In *New Global Dangers: Changing Dimensions of International Security*, edited by Michael E. Brown, Owen R. Cote, Sean M. Lynn-Jones, and Steven E. Miller, 448–476. Cambridge, MA: MIT Press, 2004.

Dahlgren, Peter. *Media and Political Engagement: Citizens, Communication, and Democracy*. Cambridge: Cambridge University Press, 2009.

Dawkins, Richard. *The Selfish Gene*. Oxford: Oxford University Press, 1976.

de Certeau, Michel. *The Practice of Everyday Life*. Berkeley: University of California Press, 1984.

Decker, William Merrill. *Epistolary Practices: Letter Writing in America before Telecommunications*. Chapel Hill: University of North Carolina Press, 1998.

"Demographics of Active Duty US Military." *Defense Manpower Data Center*,

November 23, 2013. Accessed May 31, 2014. http://www.statisticbrain.com/demographics-of-active-duty-u-s-military/.

Den Bleyker, Katherine C. "The First Amendment versus Operational Security: Where Should the Milblogging Balance Lie?" *Fordham Intellectual Property, Media and Entertainment Law Journal* 17.2 (2006): article 3. http://ir.lawnet.fordham.edu/cgi/viewcontent.cgi?article=1395&context=iplj.

Dennis, Alan R., and Susan T. Kinney. "Testing Media Richness Theory in the New Media: The Effects of Cues, Feedback, and Task Equivocality." *Information Systems Research* 9 (1998): 256–274.

"Digital Nation: Life on the Virtual Frontier." *Frontline* (PBS TV/Web report), February 2, 2010. Accessed December 1, 2012. http://www.pbs.org/wgbh/pages/frontline/digitalnation/interviews/turkle.html.

DOD directive 1344.10 provision 4.1.2.6. http://www.dod.mil/dodgc/defense_ethics/ethics_regulation/1344-10.html.

"DOD Releases Policy for Responsible and Effective Use of Internet-Based Capabilities." *U.S. Department of Defense News Release*, February 26, 2010. Accessed September 20, 2012. http://www.defense.gov/releases/release.aspx?releaseid=13338.

Dominick, Joseph R. "Who Do You Think You Are? Personal Home Pages and Self-Presentation on the World Wide Web." *Mass Communication Quarterly* 76.4 (1999): 646–658.

Donath, Judith, and danah boyd. "Public Displays of Connection." *BT Technology Journal* 22 (2004): 71–82.

Ellison, Nicole, Charles Steinfield, and Cliff Lampe. "The Benefits of Facebook 'Friends': Exploring the Relationship between College Students' Use of Online Social Networks and Social Capital." *Journal of Computer-Mediated Communication* 12 (2007): 1143–1168.

Fairclough, Norman. *Language and Power*. London: Longman, 2011.

Fallows, James. "The Tragedy of the American Military." *Atlantic*, January 2015. http://www.theatlantic.com/features/archive/2014/12/the-tragedy-of-the-american-military/383516/.

Fick, Nathaniel. *One Bullet Away: The Making of a Marine Officer*. New York: Houghton Mifflin, 2005.

Finnegan, Cara A. "Doing Rhetorical History of the Visual: The Photograph and the Archive." *Defining Visual Rhetorics*, edited by Charles Hill and Marguerite Helmers, 195–214. Mahwah, NJ: Lawrence Erlbaum, 2004.

Fischer, Andrew. "21 Really Annoying Facebook Friends We All Have." *General Forum*, September 20, 2013. http://www.generalforum.com/general-discussion/21-really-annoying-facebook-friends-we-all-have-106532.html.

Fiske, John. "Popular Forces and the Culture of Everyday Life." *Southern Review* 21.3 (1988): 288–306.

Fore, Steve. "America, America, This Is You: The Curious Case of 'America's Funniest Home Videos.'" *Journal of Popular Film and Television* 21.1 (1993): 37–46.

Foucault, Michel. *The Archaeology of Knowledge and the Discourse on Language.* New York: Pantheon, 1972.

———. *Power/Knowledge: Selected Interviews and Other Writings, 1972–1977.* London: Harvester, 1980.

———. "Two Lectures." In *Power/Knowledge: Selected Interviews and Other Writings, 1972–1977,* edited by Colin Gordon. Brighton, UK: Harvester, 1980.

Frampton, James Scott. *The Influence of Attitudes and Morale on the Performance of Active-Duty United States Marine Corps Female Security Guards.* PhD diss., Walden University, 2011.

Friedman, Devon, ed. *This Is Our War: Servicemen's Photographs of Life in Iraq.* New York: Artisan, 2006.

Friedman, Linda Weiser, and Hershey H. Friedman. "I-Get-It as a Type of Bonding Humor: The Secret Handshake." SSRN 913622 (2003). Accessed April 4, 2013. http://papers.ssrn.com/so13/papers.cfm?abstract_id=913622.

Fritz, Mike. "The Civil War: Between Battles." *Rundown,* April 12, 2011. http://www.pbs.org/newshour/rundown/2011/04/the-civil-war-between-the-battles.html.

Galtung, Johan. "Violence, Peace, and Peace Research." *Journal of Peace Research* 6.3 (1969): 167–191.

Galupo, Scott. "Internet a Battlefield Press Pass: Can Public Opinion Stomach War Video?" *Washington Times,* August 4, 2006. http://washington-times.vlex.com/vid/internet-battlefield-pass-stomach-video-194577859.

Geertz, Clifford. *Local Knowledge: Further Essays in Interpretive Anthropology.* New York: Basic, 1983.

Gehl, Robert. "Ladders, Samurai, and Blue Collars: Personal Branding in Web 2.0." *First Monday* 16.9 (2011). Accessed April 4, 2012. http://firstmonday.org/ojs/index.php/fm/article/view/3579/3041.

Geisler, Cheryl. "How Ought We to Understand the Concept of Rhetorical Agency? Report from the ARS." *Rhetoric Society Quarterly* 34.3 (2004): 9–17.

Gerben, Chris. "Privileging the 'New' in New Media Literacies: The Future of Democracy, Economy, and Identity in 21st Century Texts." *Media in Transition,* April 2009. Accessed April 19, 2013. http://web.mit.edu/comm-forum/mit6/papers/Gerben.pdf.

Gergen, Kenneth J. "Cell Phone Technology and the Realm of Absent Presence." In *Perpetual Contact,* edited by David Katz and Mark Aakhus, 62–81. New York: Cambridge University Press, 2002.

———. *Relational Being: Beyond Self and Community.* New York: Oxford University Press, 2009.

Gershon, Ilana. *The Breakup 2.0: Disconnecting over New Media.* Ithaca, NY: Cornell University Press, 2010.

Gibson, John. *The War on Christmas: How the Liberal Plot to Ban the Sacred Christian Holiday Is Worse Than You Thought.* New York: Sentinel, 2005.

Giddens, Anthony. *The Constitution of Society.* Berkeley: University of California Press, 1984.

————. *Modernity and Self-Identity: Self and Society in the Late Modern Age.* Stanford, CA: Stanford University Press, 1991.

————. *Runaway World: How Globalization Is Reshaping Our Lives.* London: Profile, 1999.

Gilman, Lisa. "An American Soldier's iPod: Layers of Identity and Situated Listening in Iraq." *Music and Politics* 4.2 (2010). http://quod.lib.umich.edu/m/mp/9460447.0004.201/-american-soldiers-ipod-layers-of-identity-and-situated?rgn=main;view=fulltext#N35-ptr1.

"Girls-on-Toilet," *College Humor*, March 15, 2014. http://www.collegehumor.com/tag/girl-on-toilet.

Gitlin, Todd. "How Journalism Misses the Big Stories and Why We Still Need It." Paper presented at the M. Holly McGranahan Lecture, University of Iowa, Iowa City, April 4, 2013.

Gladwell, Malcolm. "Small Change: Why the Revolution Will Not Be Tweeted." *New Yorker*, October 4, 2010. http://www.newyorker.com/reporting/2010/10/04/101004fa_fact_gladwell.

Gleick, James. "What Defines a Meme?" *Smithsonian*, May 1, 2011. Accessed May 31, 2013. http://www.smithsonianmag.com/arts-culture/what-defines-a-meme-1904778/.

Goffman, Erving. *The Presentation of Self in Everyday Life.* New York: Anchor, 1959.

Golijan, Rosa. "It's Not Just You: Facebook Envy Makes People Miserable, Studies Show." *Digital Life on Today*, January 25, 2013. Accessed May 31, 2013. http://digitallife.today.com/_news/2013/01/25/16698935-its-not-just-you-facebook-envy-makes-people-miserable-studies-show?lite.

Goriunova, Olga. "New Media Idiocy." *Convergence: The International Journal of Research into New Media Technologies* 19.2 (2013): 223–235.

Gray, Chris Hables. *Postmodern War: The New Politics of Conflict.* New York: Guilford, 1997.

Gray, Glenn. *The Warriors: Reflections on Men in Battle.* Lincoln: University of Nebraska Press, 1998.

Green, Sarah. "The Responsiveness Trap." *Harvard Business Review*, June 6, 2012. Accessed December 13, 2012. http://blogs.hbr.org/hbr/hbreditors/2012/06/the_responsiveness_trap.html.

Griffin, Michael. "Media Images of War." *Media, War and Conflict* 3.1 (2010): 7–41.

Grossberg, Lawrence. *Cultural Studies in the Future Tense.* Durham, NC: Duke University Press, 2010.

Gunawardena, C., and F. Zittle. "Social Presence as a Predictor of Satisfaction within a Computer-Mediated Conferencing Environment." *American Journal of Distance Education* 11.3 (1997): 8–26.

Guo, Lei, and Lorin Lee. "The Critique of YouTube-Based Vernacular Discourse: A Case Study of YouTube's Asian Community." *Critical Studies in Media Communication* 30.5 (2013): 391–406.

Haeri, Safa. "Concocting a 'Greater Middle East' Brew." *Asia Times*, March 4, 2004. http://www.atimes.com/atimes/Middle_East/FC04Ak06.html.

Hall, Jeffrey A., and Nancy K. Baym. "Calling and Texting (Too Much): Mobile Maintenance Expectations, (Over)dependence, Entrapment, and Friendship Satisfaction." *New Media and Society* 14.2 (2011): 316–331.

Hall, Nigel. "The Materiality of Letter Writing: A Nineteenth Century Perspective." In *Letter Writing as a Social Practice*, edited by David Barton and Nigel Hall, 83–108. Philadelphia: John Benjamins, 2000.

Hall, Nigel, Anne Robinson, and Leslie Crawford. "Young Children's Explorations of Letter Writing." In *Letter Writing as a Social Practice*, edited by David Barton and Nigel Hall, 145–160. Philadelphia: John Benjamins, 2000.

Hall, Stuart, ed. *Representation: Cultural Representations and Signifying Practices.* London: Sage, 1997.

Halle, David. *Inside Culture: Art and Class in the American Home.* Chicago: University of Chicago Press, 1994.

Hargittai, Eszter, and Gina Walejko. "The Participation Divide." *Information, Communication and Society* 11.2 (2008): 239–256.

Hariman, Robert, and John Louis Lucaites. *No Caption Needed: Iconic Photographs, Public Culture, and Liberal Democracy.* Chicago: University of Chicago Press, 2007.

"Harlem Shake." *Know Your Meme*, March 15, 2013. Accessed March 31, 2013. http://knowyourmeme.com/memes/harlem-shake.

Harrison, Barbara. "Photographic Visions and Narrative Inquiry." *Narrative Inquiry* 12.1 (2002): 87–111.

Hedges, Chris. *War Is a Force That Gives Us Meaning.* New York: Anchor Books, 2002.

Heidegger, Martin. *Being and Time.* Translated by John Macquarrie and Edward Robinson. New York: Harper & Row, 1962.

Held, David, and Kristian Coates Ulrichsen. "Wars of Decline: Afghanistan, Iraq, and Libya." *Open Democracy*, December 12, 2011. Accessed December 9, 2012. http://www.opendemocracy.net/david-held-kristian-coates-ulrichsen/wars-of-decline-afghanistan-iraq-and-libya.

Hess, Aaron. "Democracy through the Polarized Lens of the Camcorders: Argumentation and Vernacular Spectacle on YouTube in the 2008 Election." *Argumentation and Advocacy* 47 (2010): 106–122.

———. "Resistance Up in Smoke: Analyzing the Limitations of Deliberation on YouTube." *Critical Studies in Media Communication* 26.5 (2009): 411–434.

Hill, David. "Troops Spoof Dolphins Cheerleaders' Call Me Maybe Video." *NBC Miami*, October 24, 2012. Accessed March 15, 2013. http://www.nbcmiami.com/news/local/Troops-Spoof-Dolphins-Cheerleaders-Call-Me-Maybe-Video-175699431.html.

Hine, Christine. "How Can Qualitative Internet Researchers Define the Boundaries of Their Projects?" In *Internet Inquiry: Conversations about Method*, edited by Annette N. Markham and Nancy K. Baym, 12–25. Los Angeles: Sage, 2009.

Hockenberry, John. "The Blogs of War." *Wired* 9.08. http://www.wired.com/wired/archive/13.08/milblogs_pr.html.

Hogan, J. Michael, and L. Glen Williams. "Defining 'the Enemy' in Revolutionary America: From the Rhetoric of Protest to the Rhetoric of War." *Southern Journal of Communication* 61.4 (1996): 277–288.

Holland, Patricia. "Introduction: History, Memory and the Family Album." In *Family Snaps: The Meanings of Domestic Photography*, edited by Jo Spence and Patricia Holland, 1–14. London: Virago, 1991.

Hong, Seoyeon, Edson Tandoc, Anna Eunjin, Kim Bokyung, and Kevin Wise. "The Real You? The Role of Visual Cues and Comment Congruence in Perceptions of Social Attractiveness from Facebook Profiles." *Cyberpsychology, Behavior, and Social Networking* 15.7 (2012): 339–344.

Hoskins, Andrew. "Ghosts in the Machine: Television and Wars' Past(s)." In *Communicating War: Memory, Media and Military*, edited by Sarah Maltby and Richard Keeble, 18–28. Suffolk, UK: Arima, 2007.

Huang, Jeff, Katherine M. Thornton, and Efthimis N. Efthimiadis. "Conversational Tagging in Twitter." Paper presented at the Twenty-First ACM Conference on Hypertext and Hypermedia, Toronto, ON, Canada, June 13–16, 2010. http://jeffhuang.com/Final_TwitterTagging_HT10.pdf.

Hurley, Matthew M., Daniel C. Dennett, and Reginald B. Adams Jr. *Inside Jokes: Using Humor to Reverse-Engineer the Mind*. Cambridge, MA: MIT Press, 2011.

Hynes, Samuel. *The Soldier's Tale: Bearing Witness to Modern War*. New York: Allen Lane, 1997.

"Immediate Ban of Internet Social Networking Sites (SNS) on Marine Corps Enterprise Network (MCEN) NIPRNET, 0458." *Marine Corps Administration*, August 3, 2009. Accessed September 18, 2012. http://www.marines.mil/News/Messages/MessagesDisplay/tabid/13286/Article/112458/immediate-ban-of-internet-social-networking-sites-sns-on-marine-corps-enterpris.aspx.

irice80. "Ar Ramadi Iraq. Fox Co 2/5 2004." YouTube video, November 9, 2009. http://www.youtube.com/watch?v=_lNqb3WCtTE.

"It's Not the Cell Phone Stupid." *Stop Photo Talk*, June 4, 2004. Accessed September 20, 2012. http://talks.blogs.com/phototalk/2004/06/its_not_the_celhtml.

Ivie, Robert K. "The Rhetoric of Bush's War on Evil." *K.B. Journal*, 2004. Accessed March 27, 2015. http://kbjournal.org/ivie_Bush.

Jacobs, David L. "Domestic Snapshots: Toward a Grammar of Motives." *Journal of American Culture* 7.1 (1981): 93–105.

James, David. "The Vietnam War and American Music." *Social Text* 23 (1989): 122–143.

Jeffords, Susan, and Lauren Rabinowitz, eds. *Seeing through the Media: The Persian Gulf War*. Piscataway, NJ: Rutgers University Press, 1994.

Jenkins, Henry. *Convergence Culture: Where Old and New Media Collide*. New York: New York University Press, 2006.

———. *Textual Poachers: Television Fans and Participatory Culture*. New York: Routledge, 1992.

Jenks, Madeline. "Sneaking into the Frame: Photographers Inverting the Lens." *Curate Africa*, May 20, 2013. Accessed May 31, 2013. http://www.curateafrica.org/wp-content/uploads/2013/05/catalog_compressed.pdf.

John, Nicholas. "Sharing and Web 2.0: The Emergence of a Keyword." *New Media and Society* 15.2 (2012): 167–183.

———. "The Social Logics of Sharing." *Communication Review* 16.3 (2013): 113–131.

Johnson, Clay. *The Information Diet: A Case for Conscious Consumption.* Sebastpol, CA: O'Reilly Media, 2012.

Joi Ito's Web. Accessed September 20, 2012. http://joi.ito.com/weblog/2004/05/23/rumsfeld-bans-c.html.

"Joint Task Force Global Network Operations Report." *National Communications System.* Accessed September 20, 2012. http://www.ncs.gov/nstac/reports/2009/NSTAC%20CCTF%20Report.pdf.

Judsonlaipply. "Evolution of Dance—By Judson Laipply." YouTube video, April 6, 2006. Accessed May 31, 2013. http://www.youtube.com/watch?v=dMHobHeiRNg.

Karim, Jawed. "Me at the Zoo." YouTube video, April 23, 2005. Accessed April 10, 2012. http://www.youtube.com/watch?v=jNQXAC9IVRw.

Kastenberg, Joshua. "Changing the Paradigm of Internet Access from Government Information Systems: A Solution to the Need for the DOD to Take Time-Sensitive Action on the NIPRNET." *Air Force Law Review* 64 (2009): 175–285. Accessed March 15, 2013. http://connection.ebscohost.com/c/articles/45162335/changing-paradigm-internet-access-from-government-information-systems-solution-need-DoD-take-time-sensitive-action-niprnet.

Katz, James, and Mark Aakhus. *Perpetual Contact: Mobile Communication, Private Talk, Public Performance.* Cambridge, UK: Cambridge University Press, 2001.

Kaufman, Gil, producer. *Iraq Uploaded: The War Network Television Won't Show You, Shot by Soldiers and Posted Online.* Special report. New York: Music Television, 2006. Accessed October 20, 2009. http://www.mtv.com/news/articles/1536780/20060720/index.jhtml.

Kellner, Douglas. "War Correspondents, the Military, and Propaganda: Some Critical Reflections." *International Journal of Communication* 2 (2008): 297–330.

Kennedy, Liam. "Soldier Photography: Visualizing the War in Iraq." *Review of International Studies* 35 (2009): 817–833.

Kessler, Frank, and Mirko Tobias Schafer. "Navigating YouTube: Constituting a Hybrid Information System." In *The YouTube Reader*, edited by Pelle Snickars and Patrick Vonderau, 275–291. Stockholm: National Library of Sweden, 2009.

Kilcullen, David. *The Accidental Guerrilla: Fighting Small Wars in the Midst of a Big One.* New York: Oxford University Press, 2009.

Kindberg, Tim, Mirjana Spasojevic, Rowanne Fleck, and Abigail Sellen. "I Saw This and Thought of You: Some Social Uses of Camera Phones." In *Extended*

Abstracts of the Conference on Human Factors in Computing Systems, CHI 1545–1548. Portland, OR: ACM, 2005.

King, Graham. *Say "Cheese!": The Snapshot as Art and Social History*. London: William Collins, 1986.

Knopf, Christine. "'Language Will Not Convey': Rhetorical Formation of Interpersonal Civil-Military Relations." Paper presented at Rhetoric Society of America Conference, Minneapolis, MN, May 2010.

Know Your Meme. Accessed May 31, 2013. http://knowyourmeme.com/.

Kozol, Wendy. *Life's America: Family and Nation in Postwar Photojournalism*. Philadelphia: Temple University Press, 1994.

Krakaya Polat, Rabia. "The Internet and Political Participation." *European Journal of Communication* 20.4 (2005): 436–459.

Kress, Gunther, and Theo Van Leeuwen. *Reading Images: The Grammar of Visual Design*. London: Routledge, 2006.

Krulak, Charles. "The Strategic Corporal: Leadership in the Three Block War." *Marines Magazine*, January 1999. Accessed November 11, 2014. http://www.au.af.mil/au/awc/awcgate/usmc/strategic_corporal.htm.

Lakoff, George, and Mark Johnson. *Metaphors We Live By*. Chicago: University of Chicago Press, 1980.

Lange, Patricia. "Publicly Private and Privately Public: Social Networking on YouTube." *Journal of Computer-Mediated Communication* 13 (2007): 361–380.

Lange, Patricia, and Mizuko Ito. "Creative Production." In *Hanging Out, Messing Around, Geeking Out: Kids Living and Learning with New Media*, edited by Ito et al., 243–293. Cambridge, MA: MIT Press, 2010.

Lanham, Richard A. *The Economics of {Attention}: Style and Substance in the Age of Information*. Chicago: University of Chicago Press, 2006.

Larson, Thomas. *The Memoir and the Memoirist: Reading and Writing Personal Narrative*. Columbus: Ohio University Press / Swallow, 2007.

Lederbach, John Paul. *The Moral Imagination: The Art and Soul of Building Peace*. New York: Oxford University Press, 2005.

Lee, Dong-Hoo. "Digital Cameras, Personal Photography and the Reconfiguration of Spatial Experiences." *Information Society* 26.4 (2010): 266–275.

Lenhart, Amanda, and Mary Madden. "Teens, Privacy and Online Social Networks: How Teens Manage Their Online Identities and Personal Information in the Age of MySpace." *Pew Internet and American Life Project*, April 18, 2007. http://www.pewinternet.org/PPF/r/211/report_display.asp.

LeShan, Lawrence. *The Psychology of War*. New York: Helios, 1992.

Lewinski, Jorge. *The Camera at War: A History of War Photography from 1848 to the Present Day*. New York: Simon & Schuster, 1978.

Lewis, Jeff. *Cultural Studies: The Basics*. London: Sage, 2008.

Licoppe, Christian. "Connected Presence: The Emergence of a New Repertoire for Managing Social Relationships in a Changing Communication Technoscape." *Society and Space* 22 (2004): 135–156.

Lila, Muhammad, and Suzan Clarke. "The Making of Marine 'Call Me Maybe'

Video in Afghanistan." *ABC News*, July 19, 2012. https://www.google.com /url?sa=f&rct=j&url=http://abcnews.go.com/Entertainment/making-hit -Marine-call-video-afghanistan/story%3Fid%3D16809981&q=&esrc=s&ei= ShWRUZuDPdKCoQHZoYCgCw&usg=AFQjCNGUMQZbSilmXzrObmb dvPhgS2d3GQ.

Ling, Rich, and B. Ytrri. "Hyper-coordination Via Mobile Phones in Norway." In *Perpetual Contact: Mobile Communication, Private Talk, Public Performance*, edited by James Katz and Mark Aakhus, 139–169. Cambridge: Cambridge University Press, 2002.

Liu, Hugo. "Social Network Profiles as Taste Performances." *Journal of Computer-Mediated Communication* 13.1 (2007): 252–275.

Livingstone, Sonia. "Taking Risky Opportunities in Youthful Content Creation: Teenagers' Use of Social Networking Sites for Intimacy, Privacy and Self-Expression." *New Media and Society* 10 (2008): 339–411.

Loves, Jim. "Star Wars Kid." YouTube video, January 15, 2006. Accessed May 31, 2013. http://www.youtube.com/watch?v=HPPj6viIBmU.

Lucaites, John. "The Classic Game of World Domination." *No Caption Needed*, September 6, 2011. http://www.nocaptionneeded.com/2011/09/9248/.

Lundberg, Christian, and Joshua Gunn. "'Ouija Board, Are There Any Communications?': Agency, Ontotheology, and the Death of the Humanist Subject, or, Continuing the ARS Conversation." *Rhetoric Society Quarterly* 35.4 (2005): 83–105.

Madden, Mary, and Kathryn Zickuhr. "65% of Online Adults Use Social Media Networking Sites." *Pew Internet and American Life Project*. Washington, DC: Pew Research Center, August 26, 2011. http://pewinternet.org/Reports/2011 /Social-Newworking-Sites.aspx.

Madianou, Mirca, and Daniel Miller. "Mobile Phone Parenting: Reconfiguring Relationships between Filipina Migrant Mothers and Their Left-Behind Children." *New Media and Society* 13 (2011): 457–470.

———. "Polymedia: Towards a New Theory of Digital Media in Interpersonal Communication." *International Journal of Cultural Studies* 16.2 (March 2013): 169–187.

Malinowski, Bronislaw. "The Problem of Meaning in Primitive Languages." In *The Meaning of Meaning*, edited by Charles K. Ogden and Ian A. Richards, 146–152. London: Routledge, 1923.

Manual for Courts-Martial, United States para. 168 (1951). http://www.loc.gov /rr/frd/Military_Law/pdf/manual-1951.pdf.

Maravalli, Abigail. "The Network Effect: How Online Organizing Just Got a Little Easier." *Center for Social Media*, October 5, 2012. Accessed September 3, 2013. http://www.centerforsocialmedia.org/blog/network-effect-how-online-or ganizing-just-got-little-easier.

"The Marine Corps, a Young and Vigorous Force, Demographics Update." *The Marine Corps Demographic Booklet*, June 1, 2012. Accessed December 21, 2012. http://www.usmcmccs.org/display_files/DemographicsBookletJune2012.pdf.

Marlantes, Karl. *What It Is Like to Go to War*. New York: Grove, 2011.

Marvin, Carolyn. *When Old Technologies Were New: Thinking about Electric Communication in the Late Nineteenth Century*. New York: Oxford University Press, 1988.

Marwick, Alice. *Status Update: Celebrity, Publicity, and Branding in the Social Media Age*. New Haven, CT: Yale University Press, 2013.

Marwick, Alice, and danah boyd. "I Tweet Honestly, I Tweet Passionately: Twitter Users, Context Collapse and the Imagined Audience." *New Media and Society* 13 (2010): 114–133.

Maybin, Janet. "Death Row Penfriends: Some Effects of Letter Writing on Identity and Relationships." *Letter Writing as a Social Practice*, edited by David Barton and Nigel Hall, 151–178. Philadelphia: John Benjamins, 2000.

McCullough, Amy. "Corps Lifts Ban on Social Networking Sites." *Marine Corps Times*, March 29, 2010. Accessed September 20, 2012. http://www.Marinecorps times.com/news/2010/03/Marine_socialnetworking_032910w/.

McLaughlin, Caitlin, and Jessica Vitak. "Norm Evolution and Violation on Facebook." *New Media and Society* 14.2 (2012): 299–315.

"MCO P1020.34.G Marine Corps Uniform Regulations." Marine Corps Order P1020.34G, March 31, 2003. Accessed September 20, 2012. http://www.marines .mil/Portals/59/Publications/MCO%20P1020.34G%20W%20CH%201-5 .pdf.

McSorley, Kevin. "Helmetcams, Militarized Sensation and 'Somatic War.'" *Journal of War and Culture Studies* 5.1 (2012): 47–58.

Medhurst, Martin J., ed. *Cold War Rhetoric: Strategy, Metaphor, and Ideology*. East Lansing: Michigan State University Press, 1997.

Memmott, Mark. "Post Offices Join List of Nation's Most Endangered Historic Places." *NPR.org*, June 6, 2012. Accessed December 6, 2012. http://www.npr .org/blogs/thetwo-way/2012/06/06/154440261/post-offices-join-list-of -nations-most-endangered-historic-places.

Mentzer, Ashley. "Kony 2012: Fake Advocacy?" *Huffington Post*, March 12, 2012. http://www.huffingtonpost.com/the-state-press/kony-2012_b_1339081.html.

Michel, Christopher. "Let Slip the Blogs of War." *United States Naval Institute Proceeding* 131.3 (March 2005).

Middleton, Catherine, and Wendy Cukier. "Is Mobile Email Functional or Dysfunctional: Two Perspectives on Mobile Email Usage." *European Journal of Information Systems* 15.3 (2006): 252–260.

Military-Civilian Group. "War and Sacrifice in the Post-9/11 Era." *Pew Research Social and Demographic Trends*, October 5, 2011. http://www.pewsocialtrends .org/2011/10/05/war-and-sacrifice-in-the-post-911-era/.

"Military Pulls Plug on Popular Sites." *Virginian Pilot*, May 15, 2007. Accessed May 31, 2013. http://www.highbeam.com/doc/1G1-163398074.html.

Miller, Andrew D., and W. Keith Edwards. "Give and Take: A Study of Consumer Photo-Sharing Culture and Practice." *CHI 2007 Proceedings*, San Jose, CA: ACM. April 29, 2007. 347–356. http://dl.acm.org/citation.cfm?id=1240682.

Miller, Daniel. "Social Networking Sites." In *Digital Anthropology*, edited by Heather Horst and Daniel Miller, 146–160. London: Berg, 2012.

Miller, Lynn, and Jacqueline Taylor. "The Constructed Self: Strategic and Aesthetic Choices in Autobiographical Performance." In *The Sage Handbook of Performance Studies*, edited by D. Soyini Madison and Judith Hamera, 169–187. Thousand Oaks, CA: Sage, 2006.

Mitchell, William J. T. *Picture Theory: Essays on Verbal and Visual Representation*. Chicago: University of Chicago Press, 1995.

Moeller, Susan. *Compassion Fatigue: How the Media Sell Disease, Famine, War and Death*. New York: Routledge, 1999.

———. *Shooting War: Photography and the American Experience of Combat*. New York: Basic Books, 1989.

Mooney, Chris. *The Republican War on Science*. New York: Basic Books, 2005.

Morely, David. *Media, Modernity and Technology: The Geography of the New*. Florence, KY: Routledge, 2006.

"MotoMail." Last modified January 1, 2012. https://www.motomail.us/login.cfm?CFID=4067925&CFTOKEN=89b5e9e3598333f6-4668547B-9625-466B-A040E991E7694AAB.

Muirine, Anna. "Symbolic 'End' to Afghanistan War Overshadowed by New Obama Plans." *Christian Science Monitor*, December 8, 2014. http://www.csmonitor.com/USA/Military/2014/1208/Symbolic-end-to-Afghanistan-war-overshadowed-by-new-Obama-plans-video.

Murray, Gabrielle. "Fact and Fiction: The Iraq War Film in Absence." *Screening the Past*, November 7, 2010. Accessed May 31, 2013. http://tlweb.latrobe.edu.au/humanities/screeningthepast/29/fact-and-fiction-iraq-war-film-in-absence.html.

Murray, Susan. "Digital Images, Photo-Sharing, and Our Shifting Notions of Everyday Aesthetics." *Journal of Visual Culture* 7.2 (2008): 147–163.

Mussello, Christopher. "Studying the Home Mode: An Exploration of Family Photographs and Visual Communication." *Studies in Visual Communication* 6.1 (1980): 23–42.

Myre, Greg. "The U.S. Bombing Campaign: Is It War or Counterterrorism?" *NPR.org*, September 24, 2014. http://www.npr.org/blogs/parallels/2014/09/24/350579005/the-u-s-bombing-campaign-is-it-war-or-counterterrorism.

Nizza, Mike. "Pentagon Blocks MySpace and YouTube." *Lede*, March 14, 2007. http://thelede.blogs.nytimes.com/2007/05/14/pentagon-blocks-myspace-and-youtube/.

Norton, Bonny. "Language, Identity, and the Ownership of English." *TESOL Quarterly* 31.3 (1997): 409–429.

Nussbaum, Martha. *Hiding from Humanity: Shame, Disgust, and the Law*. Princeton, NJ: Princeton University Press, 2004.

Obama, Barack. "Remarks by the President at the National Defense University." Speech, Washington, DC, May 23, 2013. White House Office of the Press

Secretary. http://www.whitehouse.gov/the-press-office/2013/05/23/remarks -president-national-defense-university.

Office of the Press Secretary. "Statement by the President on Afghanistan." May 27, 2014. http://www.whitehouse.gov/the-press-office/2014/05/27/statement -president-afghanistan.

O'Reilly, Terry, and Mike Tennant. "The YouTube Revolution." In *The Age of Persuasion: How Marketing Ate Our Culture*, edited by Terry O'Reilly and Mike Tennant, 97–118. Berkeley, CA: Counterpoint, 2009.

Orhn, Karin Becker. "The Photo Flow of Family Life: A Family Photograph Collection." *Folklore Forum* 13 (1975): 27–36.

Örnebring, Henrik. "The Consumer as Producer—Of What?" *Journalism Studies* 9.5 (2008): 771–785.

Ornstein, Peggy. "I Tweet Therefore I Am." *New York Times*, July 30, 2010. http://www.nytimes.com/2010/08/01/magazine/01wwln-lede-t.html?_r=0.

Ostman, Johan. "Information, Expression, Participation: How Involvement in User-Generated Content Relates to Democratic Engagement among Young People." *New Media and Society* 14.6 (2012): 1004–1021.

Panek, Elliot, Yioryos Nardis, and Sara Konrath. "Mirror or Megaphone? How Relationships between Narcissism and Social Networking Site Use Differ on Facebook and Twitter." *Computers in Human Behavior* 29.5 (2013): 2004–2012.

Papacharissi, Zizi. *A Private Sphere: Democracy in a Digital Age.* Malden, MA: Polity, 2010.

———. "Without You, I'm Nothing: Performances of the Self on Twitter." *International Journal of Communication* 6 (2012): 1989–2006.

———, ed. *The Networked Self: Identity, Community and Culture on Social Network Sites.* New York: Routledge, 2011.

Pariser, Eli. "When the Internet Thinks It Knows You." *New York Times*, May 22, 2011. http://www.nytimes.com/2011/05/23/opinion/23pariser.html.

Passtheammo. "Marines Ghost Ride the MRAP." YouTube video, March 14, 2008. http://www.youtube.com/watch?v=BX13Pdxrn-k.

Paulussen, Steve, and Pieter Ugille. "User Generated Content in the Newsroom: Professional and Organizational Constraints on Participatory Journalism." *Westminster Papers in Communication and Culture* 5. 2 (2008). Accessed April 4, 2014. http://www.suebamforddesign.co.uk/ba_cultcrit_lewes/week9 /ugc%20in%20the%20newsroom.pdf.

Peirce, Bonny Norton. "Social Identity, Investment, and Language Learning." *TESOL Quarterly* 29.1 (1995): 9–31.

Perlmutter, David. *Visions of War: Picturing Warfare from the Stone Age to the Cyberage.* New York: St. Martin's, 1999.

Peters, John Durham. *Speaking into the Air: A History of the Idea of Communication.* Chicago: University of Chicago Press, 1999.

Phelan, Peggy. *Unmarked: The Politics of Performance.* London: Routledge, 1993.

Phillips, Kendall. "Spaces of Invention: Dissension, Freedom, and Thought in Foucault." *Philosophy and Rhetoric* 35.4 (2002): 328–344.

Phillips, Nelson, and Cynthia Hardy. *Discourse Analysis—Investigating Processes of Social Construction.* London: Sage, 2002.

Pickard, Victor. "Assessing the Radical Democracy of Indymedia: Discursive, Technical, and Institutional Constructions." *Critical Studies in Media Communication* 23.1 (2006): 19–38.

Pieslak, Jonathan. *Sound Targets: American Soldiers and Music in the Iraq War.* Bloomington: Indiana University Press, 2009.

Pomicter, Ryan. "US Navy and Marines in Afghanistan Gangnam Style Parody." YouTube video, February 1, 2013. http://www.youtube.com/watch?v=Wt7pevIvCbQ.

Poniewozik, James, and Karen Tumulty. "The Beast with a Billion Eyes." *Time International* 168.26 (2006): 63–64.

Portus, Lourdes. "How the Urban Poor Acquire and Give Meaning to the Mobile Phone." In *Handbook of Mobile Communication Studies,* edited by James Katz, 105–118. Cambridge, MA: MIT Press, 2008.

Poster, Mark. "The Net as Public Sphere?" *Wired* 3.11. Accessed September 20, 2012. http://www.wired.com/wired/archive/3.11/poster.if_pr.html.

———. *What's the Matter with the Internet?* Minneapolis: University of Minnesota Press, 2001.

Prelinger, Rick. "The Appearance of Archives." In *The YouTube Reader,* edited by Pelle Snickars and Patrick Vonderau, 268–274. Stockholm: National Library of Sweden, 2009.

Prensky, Marc. "Digital Natives, Digital Immigrants." *On the Horizon* 9.5 (2001): 1–6.

Protalinski, Emil. "Facebook Passes 1.06 Billion Monthly Active Users, 680 Million Mobile Users, and 618 Million Daily Users." *Next Web,* January 30, 2010. Accessed October 13, 2013. http://thenextweb.com/facebook/2013/01/30/facebook-passes-1-06-billion-monthly-active-users-680-million-mobile-users-and-618-million-daily-users/.

Rabinow, Paul, and Nikolas Rose, eds. *The Essential Foucault: Selections from Essential Works of Foucault, 1954–1984.* New York: New Press, 2003.

Radiolab. "60 Words." Podcast audio 12.7. Accessed April 20, 2014. http://www.stitcher.com/podcast/wnycs-radiolab/episode/33467725?refid=asi_eml&autoplay=true.

Raine, Lee, and Barry Wellman. *Networked: The New Social Operating System.* Cambridge, MA: MIT Press, 2012.

Rasmussen, Mikkel Vedby. *The Risk Society at War: Terror, Technology, and Strategy in the Twenty-First Century.* Cambridge: Cambridge University Press, 2006.

Regan, Helen. "John Kerry: ISIS Action Is Not a War, It's Counter-terrorism." *Time,* September 12, 2014. http://time.com/3334712/john-kerry-isis-war-counterterrorism-syria/.

Remington, Ted. "Ceci N'est Pas Une Guerre: The Misuse of War as Metaphor in Iraq." *KB Journal* 7.2 (2011). http://www.kbjournal.org/Remington.

Rentschler, Carrie. "Witnessing: US Citizenship and the Vicarious Experience of Suffering." *Media, Culture and Society* 26 (2004): 296–304.

Richardson, Kathleen, and Sue Hessey. "Archiving the Self? Facebook as Biography of Social and Relational Memory." *Journal of Information Communication and Ethics in Society* 7 (2009): 25–38.

Ricks, Thomas. *The Generals.* New York: Penguin, 2012.

Rid, Thomas, and Marc Hecker. *War 2.0: Irregular Warfare in the Information Age.* Westport, CT: Praeger Security International, 2009.

Ritchie, Jessica. "Instant Histories of War: Online Combat Videos of the Iraq Conflict, 2003–2010." *History Australia* 8 (2011): 89–108.

Robertson, Adi. "YouTube to Advertisers: We're the New TV, Because We're Nothing Like TV." *Verge,* May 6, 2013. http://www.theverge.com/2013/5/6/4305640/youtube-to-advertisers-were-the-new-tv-because-were-nothing-like-tv?utm_source=feedly.

Robins, Major Elizabeth. "Muddy Boots 10: The Rise of Soldier Blogs." *Military Review,* September–October 2007, 116–119.

Rourke, Liam, Terry Anderson, D. Randy Garrison, and Walter Archer. "Assessing Social Presence in Asynchronous, Text-Based Computer Conferencing." *Journal of Distance Education* 14.3 (1999): 51–70.

Roy, Olivier. *The Politics of Chaos in the Middle East.* London: Hurst, 2007.

Rubinstein, Daniel, and Katrina Sluis. "A Life More Photographic." *Photographies* 1.1 (2008): 9–28.

Rushkoff, Douglas. *Present Shock: When Everything Happens Now.* New York: Penguin Group, 2013.

Sarvas, Risto, and David M. Frohlich. *From Snapshots to Social Media: The Changing Picture of Domestic Photography.* London: Springer, 2011.

Sax, David. "Combat Rock." *Rolling Stone,* June 15, 2006. http://www.bujrum.ba/showthread.php?p=39232.

Schachtman, Noah. "Marines Ban Twitter, Facebook, Other Sites." *CNN Tech,* August 4, 2009. http://articles/cnn.com/2009-08-04/tech/Marines.social.media.ban_1_social-media-Marines-ban-facebook?_s=PM:TECH.

Schechner, Richard. *Performance Theory.* New York: Routledge, 1977.

Schechter, Danny. *Embedded: Weapons of Mass Deception; How the Media Failed to Cover the War in Iraq.* Amherst, NY: Prometheus Books, 2003.

Schulzke, Marcus. "Rethinking Military Gaming: *America's Army* and Its Critics." *Games and Culture* 8.2 (2013): 59–76.

Selinger, Evan. "We're Turning Digital Natives into Etiquette Sociopaths." *Wired,* March 26, 2013. Accessed September 19, 2013. http://www.wired.com/opinion/2013/03/digital-natives-etiquette-be-damned/.

Shapiro, Samantha M. "Revolution, Facebook-Style." *New York Times Magazine,* January 22, 2009. Accessed May 31, 2013. http://www.nytimes.com/2009/01/25/magazine/25bloggers-t.html?_r=2&pagewanted=all&.

Sherman, Nancy. *The Untold War: Inside the Hearts, Minds and Souls of Our Soldiers*. New York: W. W. Norton, 2010.

Shifman, Limor. "An Anatomy of a YouTube Meme." *New Media and Society* 14 (2012): 187–203.

———. *Memes in Digital Culture*. Cambridge, MA: MIT Press, 2013.

Shirky, Clay. *Here Comes Everybody: The Power of Organizing without Organizations*. New York: Penguin, 2008.

———. "The Political Power of Social Media." *Foreign Affairs*, January/February 2011. Accessed May 10, 2013. http://www.foreignaffairs.com/articles/67038/clay-shirky/the-political-power-of-social-media.

Shove, Elizabeth, Matt Watson, Martin Hand, and Jack Ingram. *The Design of Everyday Life*. Oxford, UK: Berg, 2007.

Silverstone, Roger. "What's New about New Media?" *New Media and Society* 1.1 (1999): 10–82.

Silvestri, Lisa. "Shiny Happy People Holding Guns: 21st-Century Images of War." *Visual Communication Quarterly* 21.2 (2014): 106–118.

———. "Surprise Homecomings and Vicarious Sacrifices." *Media, War & Conflict* 6.2 (2013): 101–115.

———. "Together We Stand, Divided We Fall: Building Alliances with Combat Veterans." *Soundings* 95.3 (2012): 284–308.

Simonite, Tom. "What Facebook Knows." *MIT Technology Review*, June 13, 2012. Accessed September 19, 2013. http://www.technologyreview.com/featured story/428150/what-facebook-knows/.

Sirius, R. U. "Living in the Present Is a Disorder," *Wired*, April 8, 2013. http://www.wired.com/opinion/2013/04/present-shock-rushkoff-r-u-sirius/.

Slater, Don. "Domestic Photography and Digital Culture." In *The Photographic Image in Digital Culture*, edited by Martin Lister, 129–146. London: Routledge, 1995.

Sloop, John M. "Disciplining the Transgendered: Brandon Teena, Public Representation, and Normativity." *Western Journal of Communication* 64.2 (2000): 165–189.

Slyvestri. "MEU xmas." YouTube video, January 26, 2008. Accessed March 30, 2015. http://www.youtube.com/watch?v=5-yE1QC8tHE.

Smith, Christina M., and Kelly M. McDonald. "The Mundane to the Memorial: Circulating and Deliberating the War in Iraq through Vernacular Soldier-Produced Videos." *Critical Studies in Media Communication* 28.4 (2011): 292–313.

Smith, Jeffery Allan. *War and Press Freedom: The Problem of Prerogative Power*. New York: Oxford University Press, 1999.

"Social Media Guidance for Unofficial Posts." *Official U.S. Marine Corps Web Site*, June 30, 2010. Accessed September 18, 2012. http://www.Marines.mil/usmc/Pages/SocialMediaGuidance.aspx.

Sontag, Susan. *Regarding the Pain of Others*. New York: Picador/Farrar, Straus & Giroux, 2003.

Srinivasan, Ramesh, and Adam Fish. "Revolutionary Tactics, Media Ecologies, and Repressive States." *Public Culture* 23.3 (2011): 505–510.

Stahl, Roger. "Have You Played the War on Terror?" *Critical Studies in Media Communication* 23.2 (2009): 112–130.

Stefanone, Michael, and Derek Lackoff. "Reality Television as Model for Online Behavior: Blogging, Photo, and Video Sharing." *Computer-Mediated Communication* 14 (2009): 964–987.

Streeter, Thomas. *Selling the Air: A Critique of the Policy of Commercial Broadcasting in the United States.* Chicago: University of Chicago Press, 1996.

Streitfeld, David. "Pentagon Seeks a Few Good Social Networks." *Bits*, August 2, 2011. Accessed October 5, 2011. http://bits.blogs.nytimes.com/2011/08/02/pentagon-seeks-social-networking-experts/.

Struk, Janine. *Private Pictures: Soldiers' Inside View of War.* London: I. B. Tauris, 2011.

Stupfel, Andrew. "Miami Dolphins Cheerleaders 'Call Me Maybe' by Carly Rae Jepson Military Tribute." YouTube video, September 30, 2012. https://www.youtube.com/watch?v=B_zhaji9eos.

Sturken, Marita. "The Image as Memorial: Personal Photographs in Cultural Memory." In *The Familial Gaze*, edited by Marianne Hirsch, 178–195. Hanover, NH: New England Press, 1999.

Stutzman, Fred. "An Evolution of Identity-Sharing Behavior in Social Network Communities." *Journal of International Digital Media and Arts Association* 3 (2006): 10–18.

Sunstein, Cass, and Reid Hastie. *Wiser: Getting beyond Groupthink to Make Groups Smarter.* Cambridge, MA: Harvard Business Review Press, 2014.

Sveningsson Elm, Malin. "How Do Various Notions of Privacy Influence Decisions in Qualitative Internet Research?" In *Internet Inquiry: Conversations about Method*, edited by Annette N. Markham and Nancy K. Baym, 75–90. Los Angeles: Sage, 2009.

Sweeny, Robert W. "'This Performance Art Is for the Birds': Jackass, 'Extreme' Sports, and the De(con)struction of Gender." *Studies in Art Education* 49.2 (2008): 136–146.

Tabernise, Sabrina. "Civilian-Military Gap Grows as Fewer Americans Serve." *New York Times*, November 24, 2011. Accessed November 11, 2012. http://www.nytimes.com/2011/11/25/us/civilian-military-gap-grows-as-fewer-americans-serve.html?_r=1.

Tait, Susan. "Bearing Witness, Journalism and Moral Responsibility." *Media Culture and Society* 33.8 (2011): 1220–1235.

———. "Pornographies of Violence? Internet Spectatorship on Body Horror." *Critical Studies in Media Communication* 25.1 (2008): 91–111.

Tan, Michelle. "2 Million Troops Have Deployed since 9/11." *Marine Corps Times*, December 18, 2009. http://www.marinecorpstimes.com/article/20091218/NEWS/912180312/2-million-troops-deployed-since-9-11.

Taylor, Marissa. "Marine Faces 'Other Than Honorable' Discharge over Anti-

Obama Facebook Comment." *ABC News*, April 15, 2012. Accessed September 18, 2012. http://abcnews.go.com/US/federal-judge-rejects-Marine-injunction-stop-discharge/story?id=16139979#.UbXonCvr174.

Terry, Jennifer. "Killer Entertainments." *Vectors: Journal of Culture and Technology in a Dynamic Vernacular* 3 (2007). Accessed April 4, 2013. http://www.vectorsjournal.org/projects/index.php?project=86&Thread=ProjectCredits.

Thompson, Clive. "Brave New World of Digital Intimacy." *New York Times*, September 5, 2008. Accessed April 1, 2012. http://www.nytimes.com/2008/09/07/magazine/07awareness-t.html?pagewanted=all.

Thorburn, Elise Danielle. "Social Media, Subjectivity, and Surveillance: Moving On from Occupy, the Rise of Live Streaming Video." *Communication and Critical/Cultural Studies* 11.1 (2014): 52–63.

Thumim, Nancy. *Self-Representation and Digital Culture*. New York: Palgrave Macmillan, 2012.

Tinkler, Penny. "A Fragmented Picture: Reflections on the Photographic Practices of Young People." *Visual Studies* 23 (2008): 255–266.

"Top Sites: The Top 500 Sites on the Web." *Alexa: The Web Information Company*. Accessed December 20, 2012. http://www.alexa.com/topsites.

"Top Trending Videos of 2013." *YouTube Rewind*, July 1, 2014. Accessed January 10, 2014. https://www.youtube.com/playlist?list=PLSTz8jpJdr5pn9LFw-pX bgoIOFy2Z_td_.

Tosh, Daniel. *Completely Serious*. DVD. Image Entertainment, 2007.

Tumber, Howard, and Jerry Palmer. *Media at War: The Iraq Crisis*. London: Sage, 2004.

Turkle, Sherry. *Alone Together: Why We Expect More from Technology and Less from Each Other*. New York: Basic Books, 2011.

———. "Always-on/Always-on-You: The Tethered Self." In *Handbook of Mobile Communication Studies*, edited by James E. Katz, 120–137. Cambridge, MA: MIT Press, 2008.

———. "Can You Hear Me Now?" *Forbes Magazine Online*. Accessed December 9, 2012. http://www.forbes.com/forbes/2007/0507/176.html.

———. "The Tethered Self: Technology Reinvents Intimacy and Solitude." *Continuing Higher Education Review* 75 (2011): 28–31.

UCMJ (Uniform Code of Military Justice). Accessed September 18, 2012. http://www.ucmj.us/.

Under Secretary of Defense (Personnel and Readiness). *Political Activities by Members of the Armed Forces* (DOD Directive 1344.10). Washington, DC: DOD, February 19, 2008. http://www.dtic.mil/whs/directives/corres/pdf/134410p.pdf.

US Secretary of Defense to All Department of Defense Activities, message 090426Z, August 6, 2006. http://www.defense.gov/webmasters/policy/infosec 20060806.aspx.

Vagts, Detlev F. "Free Speech in the Armed Forces." *Columbia Law Review* 57 (1957): 187–211.

van Dijck, José. "Digital Photography: Communication, Identity, Memory." *Visual Communication* 7 (2008): 57–76.

Van Leeuwen, Theo. *Discourse and Practice*. Oxford: Oxford University Press, 2008.

van Zooen, Liesbet. *Entertaining the Citizen: When Politics and Popular Culture Converge*. Lanham, MD: Rowman & Littlefield, 2005.

Vitak, Jessica, and Nicole Ellison. "'There's a Network Out There You Might as Well Tap': Exploring the Benefits of and Barriers to Exchanging Informational and Support-Based Resources on Facebook." *New Media and Society* 15 (2013): 243–259.

Voeten, Erik. "Kansas Board of Regents Restricts Free Speech for Academics." *Washington Post*, December 19, 2013. http://www.washingtonpost.com/blogs/monkey-cage/wp/2013/12/19/kansas-board-of-regents-restricts-free-speech-for-academics/.

Wajcman, Judy, and Emily Rose. "Constant Connectivity: Rethinking Interruptions at Work." *Organization Studies* 32 (2011): 941–961.

Wall, Melissa. "In the Battle(field): The US Military, Blogging and the Struggle for Authority." *Media, Culture and Society* 32.5 (2010): 863–872.

Walther, Joseph B., Brandon Van Der Heide, Sang-Yeon Kim, David Westerman, and Stephanie Tom Tong. "The Role of Friends' Appearance and Behavior on Evaluations of Individuals on Facebook: Are We Known by the Company We Keep?" *Human Communication Research* 34 (2008): 28–49.

Wander, Phillip. "The Third Persona: An Ideological Turn in Rhetorical Theory." *Central States Speech Journal* 35 (1984): 197–216.

Wang, Victoria, John V. Turner, and Kevin Haines. "Phatic Technologies in Modern Society." *Technology in Society* 34.1 (2012): 84–93.

Weiser, M. Elisabeth. "Burke and War: Rhetoricizing the Theory of Dramatism." *Rhetoric Review* 26.3 (2007): 286–302.

Weiskel, Timothy. "From Sidekick to Sideshow—Celebrity, Entertainment, and the Politics of Distraction." *American Behavioral Scientist* 49.3 (2005): 393–409.

Wellman, Barry. "Are Personal Communities Local? A Dumptarian Reconsideration." *Social Networks* 18.4 (1996): 347–354.

———. "Physical Place and Cyberplace: The Rise of Personalized Networking." *International Journal of Urban and Regional Research* 25.2 (2001): 227–252.

West, Nancy. *Kodak and the Lens of Nostalgia*. Charlottesville: University Press of Virginia, 2000.

White, Richard. "The Soldier as Tourist: The Australian Experience of the Great War." *War and Society* 5 (1987): 63–77.

Williams, Robert W. "Politics and Self in the Age of Digital Re(pro)ducibility." *Fast Capitalism* 1.1 (2005). Accessed December 25, 2012. http://www.uta.edu/huma/agger/fastcapitalism/1_1/williams.html.

Wilson, Anita. "'Absolute Truly Brill to See from You': Visuality and Prisoners' Letters." *Letter Writing as a Social Practice*, edited by David Barton and Nigel Hall, 179–198. Philadelphia: John Benjamins, 2000.

Wilson, Elaine. "'Cheetahs' Offer Swift Connection Home for Deployed Troops."

Defense.gov, February 4, 2011. Accessed February 5, 2012. http://www.defense
.gov/news/newsarticle.aspx?id=62707.

Winner, Langdon. *The Whale and the Reactor: A Search for Limits in an Age of High Technology*. Chicago: University of Chicago Press, 1986.

Wiseman, Josh. "Facebook Chat: Now We're Talking." *Facebook Blog*. Accessed October 7, 2012. https://blog.facebook.com/blog.php?post=12811122130.

Wortham, Jenna. "'Puppy Torture' Video Sparks Outrage, Military Investigation." *Wired*. Accessed March 20, 2012. http://www.wired.com/underwire/2008/03 /puppy-torture-v/.brun.

Wright, Evan. *Generation Kill: Devil Dogs, Iceman, Captain America, and the New Face of American War*. New York: G. P. Putnam's Sons, 2004.

Yates, Simeon J. "Computer-Mediated Communication: The Future of the Letter?" *Letter Writing as a Social Practice*, edited by David Barton and Nigel Hall, 233–252. Philadelphia: John Benjamins, 2000.

"YouTube Stats: Site Has 1 Billion Active Users Each Month." *Reuters*, March 20, 2012. Accessed March 31, 2013. http://www.huffingtonpost.com/2013/03/21 /youtube-stats_n_2922543.html.

Zarefsky, David. *President Johnson's War on Poverty: Rhetoric and History*. Tuscaloosa: University of Alabama Press, 1986.

Zarembo, Alan. "Cost of Iraq, Afghanistan Wars Will Keep Mounting." *Los Angeles Times*, March 29, 2013. http://articles.latimes.com/2013/mar/29/nation /la-na-0329-war-costs-20130329.

Zelizer, Barbie. "Finding Aids to the Past: Bearing Personal Witness to Traumatic Public Events." *Media, Culture and Society* 24 (2002): 697–714.

Zimmerman, Ray Bourgeois. "Gruntspeak: Masculinity, Monstrosity and Discourse in Hasford's *The Short-Timers*." *American Studies* 40.1 (1999): 65–93.

Zoroya, Gregg. "Repeated Deployments Weigh Heavily on U.S. Troops." *USA Today*, January 13, 2010. http://usatoday30.usatoday.com/news/military/2010 -01-12-four-army-war-tours_N.htm.

Zuckerman, Ethan. "The Cute Cat Theory Talk at ETech." *My Heart's in Accra*, March 2008. Accessed May 31, 2013. http://www.ethanzuckerman.com/blog /2008/03/08/the-cute-cat-theory-talk-at-etech/.